Computer Software
in Music and
Music Education:

a guide

by

BARTON K. BARTLE

The Scarecrow Press, Inc.
Metuchen, N.J., & London
1987

Library of Congress Cataloging-in-Publication Data

Bartle, Barton K., 1943–
   Computer software in music and music education.

   Bibliography: p.
   Includes indexes.
   1. Music--Software--Catalogs. I. Title.
ML74.35.B33 1987   016.78'028'5536   87-16532
ISBN 0-8108-2056-0

Acknowledgements

I am especially grateful to Stuart Mindlin, Gordon
Rowland, Peter Wright, and my wife, Ann, for their
invaluable help, generously given.

Gratitude is also due the State of New Jersey
Department of Higher Education for a grant which
made possible the establishment of the Computer-
Based Instruction Center on the campus of
Westminster Choir College in Princeton, New
Jersey.

ALF is a trademark of ALF Products, Apple II, II+,
IIe, IIc, and IIGS are trademarks of Apple
Computer, Inc., Atari is a trademark of Atari,
Inc., Commodore 64 and 128 are trademarks of
Commodore Electronics, Ltd., Control Data and
Control Data Corporation are trademarks of Control
Data Corporation, GUIDO is a trademark of the
University of Delaware, IBM-PC, PC JR., IBM XT,
AT, and Personal Systems/2 are trademarks of
International Business Machines, Koala Pad is a
trademark of Koala Technologies Corporation,
Mockingboard is a trademark of Sweet Micro
Systems, Inc., Mountain Computer MusicSystem is a
trademark of Mountain Computer Incorporated, Music
Construction Set is a trademark of Electronic
Arts, Inc., Music Maestro is a trademark of
Springboard Software, MusicPrinter is a trademark
of Temporal Acuity Products, Inc., Passport Design
MIDI Interface Card, Passport Designs Klavier,
FourTrak, Polywriter, and Soundchaser Music System
are trademarks of Passport Designs, Inc., PLATO is
a trademark of Control Data Corporation, Roland
MIDI Interface Card is a trademark of Roland Corp.

TABLE OF CONTENTS

Introduction

Many musicians, whether composers, performers, or music educators, have been taking advantage of the power of computers since the late 1960's, utilizing large, expensive mainframe computers to write music educational programs or to generate and store sounds for music compositional purposes. Located at colleges, universities, and firms concerned with technology, these computing facilities were not available to everyone. By the late 1970's, however, with the introduction of the microcomputer, the computing power that a few years earlier would have required a room full of expensive equipment, could be placed on a desk or table top. These stand-alone or self-contained computers also became available at a fraction of the cost of their larger counterparts and were accessible to many more people. Software for a variety of educational, business, and entertainment uses began to be written for these small, but powerful, computers.

Innovation in the way sound is synthesized has accompanied the advent of the microcomputer. The new technique involves digitizing sounds (representing sounds with computer data--information expressed as numbers), either for live performance or for storage until a later performance. When the music is actually produced, the numbers are converted to analog electrical signals by means of a digital-to-analog converter (DAC). The resulting wave forms are then amplified and sent to speakers to produce the sound. Because they can provide the speed necessary for the transfer and processing of this data, computers are employed to carry out the quantifying aspects of digital sound synthesis.

Microcomputer technology and the development of digital sound synthesis have provided the impetus for the development of music applications software in four main areas: composition (music editing), music printing (transcription), performance (both real time and recorded), and music education. Microcomputer music software uses sounds produced either by synthesizers built into the computer or

v

by the addition of synthesizer circuit boards, sometimes called DAC boards or cards (digital-to-analog converters), plugged into one or more of the expansion slots of some models of Apple and IBM microcomputers.

Some of the software described in this bibliography takes advantage of MIDI, an industry-wide protocol for the interconnection of digital hardware and software built into electronic instruments. MIDI, an acronym for Musical Instrument Digital Interface, was developed by electronic instrument manufacturers to increase the compatibility of musical instruments capable of transmitting and receiving computer data. Instruments such as synthesizers, sampling devices, programmable electronic keyboards, digital drum machines, and sequencers from different manufacturers can be linked together in order to create complete music systems. Prior to the introduction of MIDI, instrument connection was possible only if the equipment was made by the same company or if a custom system was created.

With the assistance of microcomputers connected to sound-producing devices, musicians are transcribing (notating and printing) music, composing, controlling synthesizers, drum machines, and digital instruments, and creating multi-track recordings. Due to microelectronic technology, the portability of microcomputers and electronic instruments allows musicians to carry their equipment from one performance location to another.

Microcomputer and sound synthesis technology has also expanded the scope of computer learning applications in music. While music educational software may provide tutorials and simulations, drill and practice are its most common forms. Its main emphasis is to supplement concepts taught in the classroom, not to instruct. This software, referred to as CAI (Computer-Assisted Instruction), CBI (Computer-Based Instruction), CBMI (Computer-Based Music Instruction), CBE (Computer-Based Education), or MBI (Microcomputer-Based Instruction), uses the computer as a means of providing drill and practice in music theory

fundamentals, ear training, music terms,
composers, and musical instrument fingerings.

Individualizing drill and practice, this software
allows the student to work at his or her own pace,
and at an appropriate level of difficulty.
Students working at a computer receive immediate
feedback regarding the correctness of their
responses. The computer has infinite patience,
and many programs provide motivation in the form
of games, time constraints, and imaginative
graphics. Furthermore, these interactive programs
require the student to be actively involved in the
learning process.

Hardware

Most of the music and music educational software
included in this guide has been produced for
popular microcomputers whose features and
capabilities lend themselves to the creation of
sound and graphics. None of these microcomputers
is compatible with any of the others.

The sound capabilities of the Commodore 64, with
its internal three-voice multi-timbral analog
synthesizer, have made it a popular machine among
music and music educational software producers.
Although it is limited to one expansion device at
a time (it has only one cartridge slot), that
slot can be used for a MIDI interface; there are
additional control ports for game paddles,
joysticks, and a Koala Pad. A more significant
drawback of the Commodore 64 is its slow disk
drive access. The newer Commodore 128 can run in
64-compatible mode, has a larger internal memory,
and provides faster disk access.

The Atari 800XL and the newer 130XE are
inexpensive powerful computers, but not many
software manufacturers have produced music or
music educational software for them.

Although the Apple II, II+, and IIe computers lack
an internal synthesizer, and the sound they can
produce is limited to a monophonic square wave,
they were among the first computers for which

music and music educational software was written.
A number of features and capabilities make them
suitable for music use. The speed of the
operating system and the disk drives is excellent.
A great deal of very good software is available
for the Apple II+ and IIe, both of which can also
be MIDI-equipped. These computers have the
advantage of lots of extra slots which can be used
for peripheral devices such as synthesizer cards
and MIDI interfaces, as well as additional ports
for game paddles, joy sticks, valve simulator, or
mouse. In addition, many of the programs written
for the Apple II, II+, and IIe will run on the
IIGS, the latest addition to the Apple II series.

Like the Apple II+ and IIe, the IBM-PC and
compatibles have good disk drive access speeds and
several expansion slots (the number varies
depending upon the compatible) for connecting
synthesizer cards and MIDI interfaces. The memory
capacity of the IBM-PC and compatibles (up to
640K or more with expanded memory boards) is very
appealing to those interested in more data storage
for MIDI or other music applications. Adding a
peripheral such as a mouse is very easy.

Music educational software has been written for
Control Data Corporation mainframe computers and
microcomputers under PLATO (Programmed Logic for
Automatic Teaching Machines). Control Data's high
resolution monitors provide excellent graphics for
music notation, and the programs written for these
computers, with their touch-sensitive screens,
require very little use of the computer keyboard
on the part of the user.

By and large, the computers mentioned above
represent the first stage in microcomputer
technology. As new, faster, and more powerful
microcomputers come on the market, new software
will be written for them. Computer manufacturers
have thus far assured that the software written
for the "older" machines will run on the new.
Commodore 64 software will run on the Commodore
128, software written for the Apple II series of
computers will run on the Apple IIGS, and software
written for the IBM-PC is supposed to run on the

new Personal System/2 microcomputers, to which the author has not yet had access.

For the reader's information Appendix A provides the addresses of the computer manufacturers included in this bibliography. The "Computer Index" provides listings of software arranged by the computers on which they run.

Peripherals

Much of the software described in the following pages utilizes accessories, or peripheral devices, which must be purchased separately from and in addition to the software itself. These items are often produced by a company other than the manufacturer of the computer to which they are attached.

Rather than relying solely on the computer keyboard for input, some music and music educational programs require special devices through which the user makes choices, enters responses, or moves a cursor to various locations on the monitor screen. The Micro-Brass Series of programs, for instance, written for the Apple II series of computers, requires the use of a valve simulator, a hand-held device with movable valves which resemble the valves of a brass instrument. Other programs require the use of game paddles (a pair of hand-held controls with a dial and a button), a joystick (a single stick control), a touch pad (a flat surface on which input is entered by touching or drawing) or a mouse (a hand-held desk top control). A mouse works on the same principle as a trackball used in a video game. As the mouse is dragged along a smooth table or desk top, the ball on its underside rolls; the ball's motion is then mirrored by the changing position of the cursor on the monitor screen. Other software, such as the Soundchaser software, produced by Passport Designs, employs a piano keyboard, or "klavier," on which the user enters a composition.

The single-voice sound produced by the speaker in the Apple II, II+, IIe, and IIc, as well as the

speaker in the IBM-PC, is not suitable for musical
performance, nor is it satisfactory for music
educational purposes beyond the most elementary
concepts. A DAC board or card not only provides
better sound quality, but also provides the means
for producing multiple voices.

DAC boards are not all alike, nor are they
compatible with one another; software written for
one DAC board will not work on a different board.
Each manufacturer produces a DAC board with
different specifications, including the number of
voices the card or board will produce. ALF's MC1
produces nine voices; the ALF MC16 (the one
employed by the software in the following
descriptions) is a three-voice card; the Mockingboard, produced by Sweet Micro Systems, is a six-
voice card; the Micro Music, Inc. DAC card
produces four voices; the University of Delaware
Sound Card produces six voices; and the double DAC
board included in the Mountain MusicSystem
produces sixteen voices.

The use of a small amplifier and speaker may be a
consideration to improve the sound still further.
The use of headphones should certainly be a
consideration in situations where two or more
microcomputers will be used in the same room.

Appendix B provides a list of manufacturers of
these peripheral devices along with their
addresses.

Software

All of the software described in this bibliography
is copyrighted, making it illegal to duplicate any
of it. Some software publishers provide a back-up
copy for storage purposes, while others allow the
purchaser to duplicate one back-up copy in case
the original is destroyed or damaged. Still other
publishers forbid the copying of programs, even
for back-up purposes. These companies generally
have a replacement policy and will replace damaged
disks at a low cost.

Organized alphabetically by title, the music
software descriptions included in this
bibliography provide information regarding author,
publisher, date of publication, cost, and, where
applicable, a version number. (The version number
is similar to an edition number of a book.)

Each description includes a brief list of the
hardware for which the various programs on the
disk were written. Since microcomputers built by
different manufacturers are not compatible with
one another, software producers must write
programs which will run only on a specific
computer. A program written for one brand of
microcomputer will not run on a computer built by
another manufacturer. Some software publishers
provide two, and sometimes three different
versions of the same program, each version written
for a different computer. In those cases where
the software is available for more than one
computer, the first one listed is the version used
for descriptive purposes. Various programs
require differing amounts of computer internal
memory. These amounts are usually described in
terms of kilobytes or "K" and are included in the
hardware section of each description. A program
requiring 64K will not run on a machine with only
48K, but a program requiring 48K will run on a
machine with 64K.

With few exceptions, the software described in the
following pages is packaged on 5 1/4" diskettes.
The hardware section also mentions how many disk
drives each piece of software requires. In most
instances a single disk drive is all that is needed.
The hardware section also discusses any additional
devices needed to run the software. A particular
program may require a joystick, game paddle,
mouse, or valve simulator, while these accessories
may be optional on others. What sound source, if
any, is required for each program is also listed
in this section.

The publisher's suggested audience for whom the
software was written is included next. It should
be kept in mind, however, that these are only
suggestions. Software titles can be misleading.
A juvenile title may misrepresent the musical

sophistication of the software. The user or
teacher must be familiar with the content, not
just the title, before choosing a piece of
software. There is no editorializing of these
suggestions. Later in the "Evaluation" part of
the description any discrepancies that this author
feels exist between the suggested audience and the
content of the program are mentioned. The
"Audience Index" provides lists of software
arranged by the audiences suggested by the
software publishers. Some items appear in more
than one audience category because the programs
included on the disks provide a wide range of
difficulty levels, adjustable by the user at the
time of the drill session, or by the teacher prior
to student use of the drill.

Some publishers include lengthy, informative,
written documentation with their software, while
others do not. Each description provides some
indication of how extensive the documentation is
and whether it includes a list of objectives,
summary, prerequisite skills and knowledge,
operating instructions, or any guidance for
teachers.

The descriptions themselves not only include
discussions of the subject matter covered by each
piece of software, but also provide a brief account
of the kinds of interactions that occur between the
program and the user. This often involves
discussing details regarding which keys on the
computer keyboard are employed to enter responses.
These keys are set in brackets "< >."

Most of the programs reviewed have replay value
because the items and the musical examples in them
are generated or composed using various methods of
randomization. The descriptions include remarks to
the contrary only when this is not the case.

The evaluation of each piece of software attempts
to address a number of questions. Are the
operating instructions clear, within the program,
and can they be bypassed by those already familiar
with them? Can these instructions be reviewed
during the program, can the user exit from a
program at any time, and does the software provide

a "menu" allowing the user to change the order of
materials or adjust their difficulty?

What is the quality of the graphics of music
notation, and what is the quality of the sound
produced by the program? Is the screen neat and
uncluttered, and are the prompts clear and
consistent so that the user is not at a loss as to
what to do next? Are the methods of response
consistent throughout the program?

Is the program logically organized and factually
correct? Do the reading and typing levels, as
well as the level of the material itself, match the
audience suggested by the publisher? Are the
methods of response consistent? Do errors on the
part of the user lead to hints and/or repeated
tries?

What does the program do in order to provide
motivation? Are the responses timed, is a game
format employed, and is there positive reinforcement through sound effects or remarks displayed on
the screen? Is there any personalization? Many
programs request the user to type his or her name
at the beginning of the program. The name is then
used throughout the program in both positive and
negative comments to the user. Frequently
programs provide long-term record keeping where
user names are stored along with their scores.
Some programs include a "Hall of Fame" for those
users who have achieved high scores.

Finally, the evaluations provide information
regarding any features of the software which are
deemed to be strong points or weaknesses.

The evolution of computer hardware has exceeded
the pace of software development. The advent of
the microcomputer is only about ten years old.
The software written for what might be considered
the first generation of microcomputers is not
perfect. New generations of microcomputers will
be forthcoming, and much more software will be
written for them. Critical appraisal of music and
music educational programs being offered in the
marketplace is essential. Composers, performers,
and teachers will want to be careful in selecting
materials of high quality, suitable to their needs

and to the needs of their students. It is for this purpose that this book has been written.

Appendix C provides the addresses of the software publishers included in this bibliography.

Advanced Ear Training Tutorial Programs by Bruce
Benward with Brian Moore, Wm. C. Brown Educational
and Professional Software, 1986.

Hardware: Apple II, II+, or IIe, single disk
drive, and monitor; also required is a standard 8-
bit digital to analog converter (DAC) such as the
Temporal Acuity Products DAC, amplifier (if not
included on the DAC), and headphones or a speaker.

Cost: $200 for 9 disks.

Publisher's suggested audience: Second year
college level students.

Documentation: A detailed user's manual includes
a complete description of each unit of the series,
whether or not a testing unit is also available,
and computer operating instructions.

Description

Intended as tutorials for extra drill and practice
of the concepts presented in the classroom, this
collection of programs is designed to be used with
Bruce Benward's Advanced Ear Training, Wm. C.
Brown Publishers, 1985. Each of the 67 units
found on the nine disks matches a unit, section,
and page in the book. Most of the units provide
scoring for the user; however, there is no long-
term record keeping utility on any of the disks.

Intervals

The series includes five graduated interval speed
drill programs in which the computer plays sets of
five intervals (ascending in one unit, descending
in the others), and the user is asked to identify
a particular interval among the five heard. Two
of the units involve compound intervals.

Melodic dictation/error detection

The programs include ten graduated melodic
dictation units in which the user selects both the
pitch and the rhythm of each note. Four speed
drills ask the user to find errors in five-note
chromatic melodies. Other units provide drill in
scale and mode recognition.

In two units a subject is heard followed by a
transformation of it; the user identifies the
transformation by selecting among retrograde,
contrary motion, augmentation, diminution, change-
of-mode, tonal answer, real answer, or motivic
excerpts.

Several units deal with twentieth century
melodies. In two of these, the program plays a
melody and the user is asked to identify the scale
on which it is based--whole tone, pentatonic,
dorian, mixolydian, or phrygian. In a third unit,
a scale is played (pentatonic, whole tone, lydian,
or mixolydian) and then the program plays a melody
based upon that scale with one note that does not
belong. The user then names (by order number) the
note which is not part of the scale.

Three units are concerned with finding errors in
twentieth century melodies of six notes. The
program displays the six notes on the screen and
then plays each note, pausing between each one.
The user must identify the wrong note as quickly
after it is played as possible.

Chord recognition/harmonic dictation

The series includes two triad position units in
which the user hears a single chord (in three
voices in one unit, four in the second) and must
determine whether it is in root position, first,
or second inversion.

Two units deal with seventh chord types; the user
hears a seventh chord and must determine the
quality (MM, Mm, mm, dm, or dd). In one unit the
seventh is in the soprano, in the other, it is in
the alto or tenor voice.

Three units are devoted to secondary dominant
drills in which three chords are played. The

first is always the original tonic, the second is
either a secondary dominant or a secondary leading
tone chord, and the third is always tonicized.
Two units use only root position chords, while a
third unit employs inverted chords.

Drill in hearing implied harmonies is provided in
three units; in these units the user must indicate
the implied harmony (by choosing the correct
analysis symbols) underlying four-beat
two-voice eighteenth century excerpts. Two of the
units involve secondary dominants.

The series includes a "suspension types" unit in
which suspensions are played in two-voice
settings; the user identifies the type of
suspension by choosing among 9-8, 7-6, 4-3, and 2-
3 possibilities.

Chromatic harmony is dealt with in six units in
which a series of three chords are heard, the
first being the tonic. The second chord may be a
borrowed chord, a 9th, 11th, or 13th chord, a
Neapolitan 6th, augmented 6th, altered dominant,
or a chromatic mediant chord. Only the analysis
of the second chord is required.

Nine units provide drill in determining the
incorrect pitch in single chords. A chord is
displayed on the screen and played with one
incorrect note. The user must identify which
pitch in the chord is incorrect. Different units
emphasize 9th, 11th, and 13th chords, the
Neapolitan 6th, augmented 6th chords, and altered
dominants, as well as twentieth century chords.

Seven units are devoted to the analysis of
chorales. In these units a seven-chord chorale
phrase is played, beginning with the first and
adding an additional chord until all seven have
been heard, allowing the user to analyze each
chord separately. The first of these units
emphasizes borrowed chords and uses all root
position chords except the supertonic, which is
found in first inversion. Other units emphasize
9th, 11th, and 13th chords, the Neapolitan 6th,
augmented 6th chords, altered dominants, and
chromatic mediants.

Two units provide drill in early twentieth century
chord types. In one unit the user is asked to
identify a chord after it has been played by
selecting among these possibilities: added tone,
chord of omission, quartal chord, whole tone
chord, or 13th chord. In another unit a chord
type is displayed and five chords are played. The
user must identify which one represents the chord
type requested. In this unit speed is a factor.

A "planed" chord unit plays a series of four
planed chords, three of which are of the same type
(MM, Mm, mm, etc.). The user is asked to identify
the chord which has a different quality.

Identifying tetrachords and trichords is drilled
in four units. In one unit the program plays a
tetrachord and asks the user to identify the pitch
relationships using interval class numbers (0
through 6) representing the number of half-steps
above the first note for each of the four notes.
In another unit the program plays a tetrachord and
asks the user to choose its type among four
choices. Two additional units display four
trichords on the screen and then play a single
melodic trichord containing the same pitches as
one of the four displayed. In the first unit,
this trichord has the same pitches as one of the
ones displayed, but in a different order. The
user must mentally reorder them in order to make
the identification. In the other unit, the
identification is made more difficult, because the
program not only reorders the pitches of the
played chord, but also transposes them.

Evaluation

A menu is provided on each disk, allowing the user
to choose the unit on which (s)he wants to work.
Instructions are clear, included within each unit,
and can be bypassed by users already familiar with
them. The user may exit a unit at any time and
pick a different one. The first screen display of
each unit provides users who are using the Benward
book with the unit number, letter of the section,
and the page number of the corresponding unit in
the book. In some units, the user may choose the
order of the exercises as they appear in the
workbook, or may choose to have the exercises

played in random order. Each unit has between 10
and 25 exercises. The exercises themselves are
preset, rather than being constructed randomly by
the program.

Users may hear exercises repeated by pressing <H>.
The programs allow second tries and offer hints
when mistakes are made. Some of the exercises,
however, never provide the correct answer, no
matter how many times the user errs. In some
cases when mistakes are made, the program
automatically plays the user's wrong answer
followed by the correct answer. Some units
provide a short tutorial when mistakes are made.

For the most part the graphics of music notation
and the sounds produced by these programs are
good. However, no beams are used in the notation,
and occasionally one notices some crackling in the
synthesized sounds. In the chorale phrases, some
of the notes sound out-of-tune.

Some errors were discovered in the programs. In
unit 1A, "Ascending Intervals," some strange
characters were displayed for the major 6th in set
#4. In the same unit, set #5, the program played
a minor seventh, but would only accept a major 6th
as the answer.

In some units, the user may also be notating his
or her answers in the workbook while using the
program. However, in some of the melodic
dictation units, due to space limitations, a few
of the melodies are shortened versions of their
counterparts in the book. The user must read the
description of those units in the documentation in
order to find this out.

***

Arnold by J. Timothy Kolosick, Micro Music
Software Library, published by Temporal Acuity
Products, Inc., 1982, version 2.0.

Hardware: Apple II, II+, or IIe computer with a
minimum of 48K memory, 3.2 or 3.3 Disk II drive
with controller, video monitor; MMI DAC music card
and headphones required.

Cost: $150

Publisher's suggested audience: Third grade to adult.

Documentation: A user's guide includes teaching objectives, prerequisite skills and knowledge, as well as details about the program.

Description

This program drills users in scale degree recognition and melodic memory. The melodic fragments do not include rhythm. Arnold plays a scale and displays it on a musical staff. He then plays a "melody" (pitch strings) either one note at a time (in early levels) or two or three notes at a time (in the higher levels). The user responds by choosing the scale degree for each note played. The scale degrees are displayed on the bottom of the screen either as solfeggio syllables (movable Do) or as scale degree numbers, depending upon which the user chooses. Answers are entered by moving the cursor with an arrow key to the appropriate scale degree and then pressing the <SPACE BAR>. As each note is entered it is notated by the program on the staff. No key signatures are used. As Arnold adds more notes to the "melodies," he always starts back at the beginning, and the user must reenter all the notes from the beginning. When a mistake is made, Arnold notates and displays the mistake and then plays the correct pitches again for the user to compare. At the end of each session, the user may choose to see a score card displaying the following: how many exercises were completed, the level of the exercises, how many errors were made and a percentage score.

The user may select among the following levels: "Beginner," in which the "melodies" are seven notes long, with one note added during each playing; "Novice," in which the "melodies" are nine notes long, with one note added during each playing; "Intermediate," in which the "melodies" are twelve notes long, with two notes added each time; "Advanced," in which the "melodies" are fifteen notes long, with three notes added each time; and "Professional," in which the "melodies"

are twenty notes long, entered in groups of four
notes. The "Beginner" and "Novice" levels contain
melodies with a one octave range, while the
melodies in the "Intermediate," "Advanced" and
"Professional" levels have ranges of a twelfth.
The user may jump ahead in the same level to more
difficult material, continue at the pace of the
program, or change levels.

Evaluation

The instructions are clear, within the program,
and can be bypassed by those users who are
familiar with them. The <ESC>ape key allows the
user to quit the program at any time. The
graphics of musical notation are good, as is the
sound. The display is neat and uncluttered, the
prompts are clear and consistent, the methods of
response are consistent, and when mistakes are
made, the program allows repeated tries.

The program is in game format; points are lost
when mistakes are made and when the user requests
additional hearings of the melodies. The program
calls the user by name at various points in the
program.

Both the documentation and the instructions within
the program neglect to warn the Apple IIe user
that the <CAPS LOCK> key must be depressed
throughout the program in order to make any
responses.

***

Aural Fundamentals by John E. Hatmaker, Wenger
Corporation, 1985.

See Music Drills: Ear Training Series Part II:
Aural Fundamentals.

***

Aural Interval Recognition by Virgil Hicks (the University of Akron Series), published by Wenger Corporation, 1981, 1982, 1985, version 2. This program is now included in The Music Class: Ear Training, part of the Music Class Series.

Hardware: Apple II, II+, or IIe, one disk drive, video monitor; ALF synthesizer card, headphones optional (the sound can be routed through the computer's internal speaker).

Cost: $99

Publisher's suggested audience: Intermediate: students who can read music; or advanced: students ready to compose or arrange music.

Documentation: Brief descriptive pamphlet includes summary, operating instructions, and instructions for changing any options.

Description

Aural Interval Recognition provides practice in identifying intervals presented melodically, at random. The program has eleven levels:

1) major/minor seconds; 2) major/minor thirds; 3) major/minor seconds and thirds; 4) perfect fourths and fifths; 5) major/minor seconds, thirds and perfect fourths and fifths; 6) major/minor sixths; 7) major/minor seconds, thirds, perfect fourths and fifths, and major/minor sixths; 8) unisons, augmented fourth, perfect fourths and fifths, and major/minor sixths; 9) unisons, major/minor seconds, thirds, perfect fourths and fifths, and major/minor sixths; 10) perfect octave and major/minor sevenths; 11) all of the above intervals.

During these drills a running score is kept. The user may select the level and the type of intervals to be presented: ascending, descending, or both. The user selects the name of the interval heard from a list of all interval names displayed on the left side of the screen by moving the up and down cursor keys to highlight the appropriate interval. The correct answer may be

requested, but credit towards the score is not
given when this option is selected. The tempo of
the presentation may also be selected by the user.
The user may replay the interval without penalty.
Through the Manager Utility the instructor can
control the number of intervals required in order
for a score to be recorded. The default number is
a minimum of 20. After work is stopped on a
level, the display tells how many and which
intervals were missed, and how many were
attempted. The program provides a Manager Utility
for student record keeping and for setting
standards for student ratings.

Evaluation

The program is logically organized and factually
correct. The prompts are clear and consistent and
the methods of response are also the same
throughout. The program allows repeated tries
when an interval is missed, but offers no hints to
help the user reach the correct answer. The
graphics are good; the sound is good when the ALF
synthesizer card is used, but poor when the sound
is being channeled through the Apple speaker.

The instructions are clear and within the program
and can be called at any time during the program.
However, a single screen of instructions (always
the same) precedes each unit and cannot be
bypassed. An additional annoyance about the
program is the fact that the menu from which the
user selects a level does not include descriptions
of what is covered at each level. An additional
screen has to be requested in order to make an
intelligent selection from the menu.

An error was noted in the program. Displayed at
the top of the screen during each level is a list
of the intervals to be drilled in that lesson.
During level seven the program displays major and
minor seconds, major and minor thirds, and perfect
fourths and fifths. However, in addition to these
intervals, the program also plays major and minor
sixths for the user to identify.

***

Aural Skills Trainer by Vincent Oddo. Electronic
Courseware Systems, Inc., 1984. Aural Skills
Trainer is a three-disk series including
Intervals, Basic Chords amd Seventh Chords.

Hardware: Commodore 64 or 128, one disk drive and
monitor (color monitor optional). Also available
for Apple II+ or IIe with at least 48K, or Apple
IIc with at least 128K, one disk drive, and
monitor; and the IBM-PC or IBM-PC JR. with at
least 128K, one 360K double-sided disk drive,
color graphics card, and monitor.

Cost: $39.95 for each disk, or $99.95 for all
three Aural Skills Trainer disks.

Publisher's suggested audience: None stated.

Documentation: Brief description on back of
diskette box, and a brief pamphlet on instructor
management options.

Description

For a complete description of these three disks
see LISTEN! A Music Skills Program.

Intervals, Basic Chords, and Seventh Chords
contain the same programs as the "Interval Drill,"
"Basic Chords," and "Seventh Chords" programs
found in LISTEN! A Music Skills Program with some
differences. The Aural Skills Trainer disks have
Instructor Management Options allowing student
data to be kept for several different instructors.
The data consists of the category of basic chords
attempted, the number of chords played, the number
correct, the percent score and a letter grade for
each session, as well as a coded listing of which
chords were missed and how many times they were
missed. The instructor may delete names (although
(s)he must delete the entire file) or print the
student data on the screen or on a printer.

The Aural Skills Trainer disks include a card to
be placed over the number keys on the computer
keyboard. For the Intervals disk, the card
reminds the user which keys represent various
sizes of intervals. In Basic Chords and Seventh
Chords this card shows which number indicates
which chord type or inversion. A diagram showing

which computer keyboard keys represent various
intervals, chord types, and inversions is also
displayed on the bottom of each screen during the
programs.

Evaluation

The user cannot quit the programs at any time.
(The user can do this in LISTEN! An Aural Skills
Program, for example, by pressing the <F1> key on
the Commodore.) Aural Skills Trainer programs do
not allow the user to hear an item, interval or
chord, more than once, whereas the programs in
LISTEN! An Aural Skills Program permit additional
hearings. The user cannot get instructions once
the program has been started, nor can (s)he change
a response once (s)he has pressed a number key,
because the program does not use the <RETURN> key
or any other key as an "enter" key.

***

Basic Chords by Vincent Oddo, Electronic
Courseware Systems, Inc., 1984.

See Aural Skills Trainer.

***

Basic Guitar I by Michael Fink, Digital Concept
Systems, Inc., 1982.

Hardware: Apple II, II+, or IIe computer with a
minimum of 48K memory, 3.3 Disk II drive with
controller, video monitor (color monitor
optional); an amplifier and head phones may be
desired.

Cost: $50

Publisher's suggested audience: None listed.

Documentation: Includes a player's manual which
includes instruction on operating the software,
discussion about each of the programs on the disk,
and hints about practicing the guitar.

Description

This two-disk set includes a "chords" disk with
tutorial programs designed to teach chord playing
on the guitar, and a "song" disk which provides
the melodies of eight songs for which the user
provides chordal accompaniment. The programs make
the assumption that the user is sitting at the
computer with a guitar in his or her hands.

The "chord" disk provides a tuning routine, as
well as tutorials and drills in how to finger
certain chords on the guitar. The diagrams in
"How to Read Chord Diagrams" show the guitar
fingerboard in a vertical position with the nut
and the pegs at the top of the screen. Each
string--E, A, D, G, B, and E--is labeled in the
diagram. Large dots placed on the fingerboard
indicate where the fingers of the left hand should
be placed on each string, and numbers indicate
which fingers to use. A chord symbol appears at
the top of each diagram, for example "B7."

"Chord Theory" reviews the theoretical principles
and the primary functions of the tonic,
subdominant, and dominant seventh chords.

"Let's Tune Up" provides a routine for tuning the
strings before playing. It allows the user to
tune each string individually at his or her own
pace. The left and right arrow keys are used to
move from one string to another, and the <SPACE
BAR> is used to hear the pitch of the string being
tuned. The program offers some tuning hints. It
suggests tuning "high" at first and then lowering
the pitch until it is in tune, maintaining that
the string will stay in tune longer if tuned this
way. The program also suggests tuning the lowest
note first.

In "Learn and Practice Chords," the user is taught
the fingering for the three "primary" chords in
the keys of E, A, D, G, and C Major, and of e and
a minor through the use of chord diagrams. In the
"Practice Routine" the user sees diagrams of the
three chords, below which appear the chord symbols
of a song. Each chord symbol or "/" (a repeated
chord) represents a beat. The program sets the
tempo by sounding four clicks on the speaker,

and the user strums a chord once or twice per
measure while a pointer moves across the screen.

The Song Disk contains eight songs, with a "Warmup
Routine" and "Play the Song" for each, and "Let's
Tune Up." The warmup routine is similar to the
"Practice Routine" discussed above. In "Play the
Song," a melody is played by the computer, and
chord diagrams and a key signature followed by
chord names and slashes are displayed. A moving
pointer indicates which chords are to be played in
rhythm as accompaniment. The songs included on
the disk are "Red River Valley" in E Major, "This
Old Man" in A Major, "Jingle Bells" in D Major,
"Molly Malone" in G Major, "When the Saints Go
Marching In" in C Major, "Hatikvah" in e minor,
"Go Down, Moses" in a minor, and "Greensleeves,"
which uses the chords of a minor, E Major, C
Major, and G Major.

Evaluation

The graphics of the guitar fingerboard are good in
the program. However, the sound coming through
the Apple speaker is poor. The documentation
includes a discussion about improving the sound by
interfacing the software with an amplifier and
speaker or headphone. The instructions are clear,
within the program, and can be bypassed by users
already familiar with them. The program is
factually correct and the prompts are clear and
consistent.

One wonders why this software was written at all.
The program does not use the computer to interact
with the user. There are no questions for the
user to answer, nor is the computer used to judge
the user's playing or intonation. There is a lot
of reading about chords and music theory, which
could probably be accomplished as well or better
in book form. The melodies played for the user to
accompany could be placed on a tape or a record
and be just as meaningful.

***

Basic Musicianship Skills I by Allen Winold, John
William Schaffer, Susan Tepping, and Chris Payne.
Indiana University Audio-Visual Center, 1984.

Hardware: Apple II+ or Apple IIe with a minimum
of 48K, DOS 3.3, one disk drive, and monitor.

Cost: $35.00

Publisher's suggested audience: None stated.

Documentation: Brief pamphlet describing the
programs and providing operating instructions.

Description

This disk contains four programs: "Note Reading,"
"Intervals," "Scale and Key Signatures," and
"Musical Terms." Each of these programs includes
its own set of instructions and a reference
section, as well as a number of subprograms from
which the user may choose. The user may also
choose to work with a dark on light or a light on
dark display. None of the exercises includes time
constraints. At the end of each session the
number of correct answers, the number of wrong
answers, the total number of tries, and a
percentage score are displayed on the screen.
None of the programs includes record keeping.

Seven lessons are included in "Note Reading," as
well as a reference section or tutorial which
explains note names and ledger lines. The user
may follow a regular lesson plan designed by the
authors or design his or her own plan. If a
custom plan is desired, the user must choose among
G, C, F clefs or the grand staff, choose the staff
line on which the clef is to be placed, decide
whether the drills will include no accidentals,
single sharps and flats, or double flats and
sharps, decide whether ledger lines are to used,
and finally decide whether to employ the 8va and
15va signs in the exercises.

If the user opts for the regular plan, Lesson 1
drills notes in the treble clef, Lesson 2 employs
the bass clef and the grand staff, Lesson 3
incorporates ledger lines, Lesson 4 is a keyboard
drill without accidentals, Lesson 5 employs single
sharps and flats in the keyboard mode, Lesson 6

uses double sharps and flats in the keyboard mode,
and Lesson 7 uses bass and treble clef with
accidentals and the 8va and 15va signs. The user
responds to lessons 1, 2, 3, and 7 by typing in a
letter name (<A> through <G>), an accidental, if
needed (<+> and <++> for sharps and double sharps
and <-> and <--> for flats and double flats), and
the octave register of the note (<0> through <7>),
with middle C being "C4." There are two modes of
presentation in the keyboard drills. A one-octave
piano keyboard is displayed on the screen. In one
type of drill the program points to a key on the
piano and asks the user to type in the letter name
of the key and an accidental if necessary. In the
other drill, the user must use the cursor keys to
locate a given note on the keyboard. Octave
numbers are not used in the keyboard section of
the program.

Visual recognition of intervals and interval
spelling are drilled in "Intervals." The
reference section of this program provides a
tutorial on the size and the various qualities of
intervals. Sound is an option in this program.
In these drills the user is asked either to
identify the size and quality of the interval by
typing in the information, or to supply a missing
note for a specified interval above or below a
given note. There are eight lessons in this
program, the first of which requests only the
numeric size of the intervals. Lessons 2 through
8 drill not only the size of intervals, but their
quality as well (major, minor, perfect, augmented,
and diminished).

"Scales and Key Signatures" provides drill in
building major and minor scales with or without
key signatures, as well as drill in building key
signatures, by moving notes and/or accidentals on
the staff with a clef displayed on the screen.
Sound is an option in this program. The lessons
of the program include major scales without key
signatures, major key signatures, natural minor
scales without key signatures, minor key
signatures, a review of major and minor key
signatures, harmonic minor scales, and melodic
minor scales (ascending form only).

"Musical Terms" provides practice in recognizing
the English, French, Italian, and German

equivalents of common music terms. The user may choose among sets of musical terms concerned with tempo, changes of tempo, the character of performance, dynamics, or musical instruments. The user may also choose to provide the foreign equivalent of English terms, or give the English equivalent of foreign terms. In this program the user selects an appropriate response among four multiple choice answers.

Evaluation

Although the documentation for this set of programs is somewhat sparse, the instructions are clear, within each program, and can be bypassed by users already familiar with them. There is some ambiguity in the instructions for "Scales and Key Signatures" regarding whether to enter the accidentals before or after the note on the staff. The prompts vary from one program to the next, but they are consistent within each program, as are the methods of response. Almost all the programs allow second tries but no hints. After a second wrong response is made, the program presents the correct answer. The user may quit a program at any time by pressing the <Q> key.

The programs are factually correct and logically organized. Informative tutorials are found in most of the reference sections included in each program. "Scales and Key Signatures" is one of the few available programs which actually asks the user to construct a key signature. Most merely ask for identification.

It is unfortunate that the program relies on the Apple speaker for its sound. The use of a synthesizer card would improve the sound. And, both the documentation and the instructions within the program neglect to inform the Apple IIe user that the <CAPS LOCK> key must be depressed in order for the program to accept the user's responses.

***

Basic Musicianship Skills II by Allen Winold, John
William Schaffer, Chris Payne, and Susan Tepping.
Indiana University Audio-Visual Center, 1984.

Hardware: Apple II+ or Apple IIe with a minimum
of 48K, DOS 3.3, one disk drive, and monitor.

Cost: $35.00

Publisher's suggested audience: None stated.

Documentation: Brief pamphlet describing the
programs and providing operating instructions.

Description

This program provides drill and practice in
hearing and notating aural pitch patterns. The
user may design a custom lesson or work with the
lessons already prepared by the authors. If one
chooses to design his or her own plan, one must
select the number of notes played in each pattern
(1 to 7), select the tempo of the patterns (slow-
90, medium-120, or fast-150), decide whether the
response will be scale degree numbers, solfeggio
syllables, or moving notes on a staff with or
without key signatures, choose treble or bass
clef, decide whether to have the program change
keys every question, every third question, or
every fifth question, whether to work with
patterns with triadic pitches, pitches from the
major scale or from the harmonic minor scale,
whether to select patterns with ranges of a fifth,
of an octave (tonic to tonic), or of an octave
(dominant to dominant), decide the maximum
interval range from stepwise motion only to an
octave (with gradations in between), and choose
the number of questions desired (1 to 30).

If the user selects the preset lessons, (s)he is
asked to select the degree of difficulty ("very
easy," "easy," "challenging," or "very
challenging"), and to select the type of response
(as stated above).

During each exercise, the various computer keys
employed in the program are displayed along the
bottom of the screen. In exercises which use
them, accidentals are displayed across the top of
the screen. The user chooses an appropriate

accidental by moving the left and right arrow
keys. Depending upon the user's choice of
response, either the scale degree numbers or
solfeggio syllables are displayed on the screen
and are selected by using the <A> and <Z> keys to
move the cursor up and down on the screen. Once
the selection has been made, the program notates
the pitch on the staff with clef.

Evaluation

The program is factually correct and logically
organized. Although the documentation is somewhat
sparse, the instructions are clear, within the
program, and can be bypassed by users already
familiar with them. When placing notes on the
staff without a key signature there is some
ambiguity regarding whether to enter the accidentals
before or after one enters the note on the staff.
The prompts are consistent, as are the methods of
response. The program allows second tries, but no
hints. After a second wrong response is made, the
program presents the correct answer. The user may
quit the program at any time by pressing the <Q>
key.

It is unfortunate that the program relies on the
Apple speaker for its sound. The use of a
synthesizer card would improve the sound. And,
both the documentation and the instructions within
the program neglect to inform the Apple IIe user
that the <CAPS LOCK> key must be depressed
throughout the program in order for the program to
accept the user's responses.

* * *

CAMUS (Computer Assisted Music Units in Solfege):
Melodic Dictations by Colette Jousse Wilkins and
Richard Stern. CONDUIT, 1986.

Hardware: Apple II+, IIe, or IIc with a minimum
of 64K, single disk drive, monitor; Mountain
Computer MusicSystem (synthesizer cards) or Apple
speaker can be used for sound production. An
amplifier and headphones may be desirable. Also
available for the IBM-PC, IBM-XT, IBM-PC jr., DOS
2.1 - 3.1, 128K, one 360K disk drive, color

graphics adaptor, monitor. The IBM version uses only the internal speaker of the computer for sound production.

Cost: $150 for a package of four disks, or each disk for $50.

Publisher's suggested audience: High school and university level, and advanced music students.

Documentation: A User's Guide provides information about how to operate the software and how to make responses; it also includes a summary with an appendix containing the notation of all 400 melodic dictations. Grade levels are proposed for each disk, and descriptions of the dictations on each disk are provided.

Description

Melodic Dictations consists of four disks containing ten groups of ten dictations each for a total of 400 dictations. Instead of being generated by a computer program, the dictations have been written by the author to ensure their musicality.

The melodies on disk 1 are considered to be "very easy to easy" by the author. They may be up to 12 notes long, contain 2nds and 3rds, and may have time signatures of 2/4, 3/4, 4/4, 3/8, or 6/8. They employ the tonic triad, use all major keys and most of the minor keys.

The author considers the melodies on disk 2 to be of "easy to medium difficulty." They may be up to 15 notes long, employ most diatonic intervals with occasional chromatic alteration, contain triadic patterns, and use all the major keys and most of the minor ones. The time signatures employed are 2/4, 3/4, 4/4, 3/8, 4/8, 5/8, 6/8, and 7/8.

The melodies on disk 3 are rated "medium difficult to difficult." They may be up to 18 notes long, include all intervals and modulations within the circle of fifths, and employ all major and minor keys. Syncopations are included and the time signatures used are 3/2, 4/2, 2/4, 3/4, 4/4, 5/4, 6/8, 9/8, and 12/8.

The atonal melodies on disk 4 are considered to be
"difficult to very difficult" by the authors.
They contain compound intervals and difficult
rhythms. The time signatures employed are the
same as those on disk 3 with the addition of 3/16,
5/16, and 6/16.

On each disk the user may select a unit from one
to ten and then a particular dictation among the
ten melodies within that unit by pressing a letter
<A> through <J>.

Each dictation exercise displays a staff, clef
(treble or bass), and meter signature on the
screen. The key signature is not given, nor is
the user told what the key is. Instead, the
program provides the pitch "A"=440. From this
pitch, the user must determine the first note of
the exercise. Included on the screen are the
various commands necessary for the user to enter
responses. The user may <H>ear the dictation as
many times as needed, hear <A>=440 at any time,
hear the <T>empo established at any time, <P>lay
his or her melody as notated up to this point,
<I>nsert notes, <D>elete notes, and place bar
lines with the <L> key. Notes are entered with
the number keys, accidentals with the <8>, <9>,
and <0> keys, and rhythmic values with the bottom
row of the computer keyboard. These values
include whole notes to sixteenth notes and dotted
notes.

As the user enters a note, a cursor moves to the
next note in both the pitch and rhythm entry
modes. None of these exercises has time
constraints. When the user has completed a
melody, the <RETURN> key is pressed for an
evaluation. The program displays the user version
and the program version for comparison and also
provides a percentage score for the pitches and
one for the rhythm. There is no long-term record
keeping on the disk.

Evaluation

This series of programs is logically organized and
factually correct. The user controls the pace of
the exercises as well as their difficulty level.
Despite the fact that the melodies are pre-
composed rather than randomly composed or even

selected randomly, the programs have replay value
due to the large number of dictations contained in
them. The prompts are clear and consistent
throughout, as are the methods of response. The
screen becomes somewhat cluttered with the music
notation, the display of the commands necessary to
enter responses, and various prompts displayed all
at once.

The graphics of the music notation are very good
(although beams are not used), and the sound
coming from the Mountain Computer MusicSystem
cards is also quite good. Errors do not lead to
hints. The programs are not personalized, nor is
a game format used. The scoring provides some
motivation. The user may exit an exercise or a
unit any time by pressing <Q>, or get the
instructions at any time by typing <?>. The
instructions are included within the program and
may be bypassed by those already familiar with
them.

The procedure for entering bar lines may bother
some users. The program draws bar lines
immediately following the note directly above the
cursor. However, because the program also
automatically moves the cursor forward after each
note is entered, the user must move the cursor
back one note each time (s)he wants to notate a
bar line. This feature should not be one of great
concern, however, since the placement of the bar
lines is merely for visual aid and does not affect
grading.

One small inconsistency was discovered. Sometimes
the user must press the <O> key in order to place
the note entered in the proper octave. At other
times, the program automatically places the note
in the register in which it was played.

***

Cat Steps Interval Tutorial by Virgil Hicks (the
University of Akron Series), Wenger Corporation,
1981, 1982, 1985, version 2. This program is now
part of The Music Class: Fundamentals, from The
Music Class Series.

Hardware: Apple II, Apple II+, or Apple IIe, one
disk drive, video monitor.   (Sound comes only from
the Apple speaker; the program does not use the
ALF board.)   Also available for the Commodore 64,
one disk drive and monitor.

Cost: $59 (same for both Apple and Commodore
versions).

Publisher's suggested audience: Beginning: no
previous music experience.

Documentation: Brief descriptive pamphlet.

Description

Cat Steps Interval Tutorial provides instruction
in counting the size of intervals between notes.
An imaginary cat makes paw prints representing the
number of steps in an interval.   A musical staff
is displayed without a clef sign.   Each cat step
is made either on a line or space on the staff.
The tutorial includes other animation and is
interactive.   Instruction, practice, and a test on
intervals are provided.

At the end of the test, the user's score is
displayed with the total number of questions, the
number correct, and a percentage score.   The
program then provides a rating, "E" for excellent,
"G" for good, or "N" for needs improvement, and
encouragement to continue.   A Manager Utility is
available for student record keeping and for
setting standards for student ratings.

Evaluation

The program is factually correct, and the graphics
are fair.   The prompts are clear and consistent.
Errors made by the user in the tutorial and in the
test lead to hints and repeated tries.   Scoring
provides some motivation, although the program is
not personalized in any way.

There are no instructions within the program; the
user learns how to respond to prompts while going
through the tutorial.   The user must go through
the tutorial in order to get to the test.   This
makes the replay value of the program somewhat
questionable.

It is unfortunate that the sound of this program
is routed through the Apple speaker. If this
program is used in a classroom setting, the sound
will be heard by everybody in the room, not just
the user.

* * *

Catch the Key by Brian R. Moore (Moore Music
Series), Micro Music Software Library, published by
Temporal Acuity Products, Inc., version 1.1, 1983.

Hardware: Apple II computer with a minimum of 48K
memory, 3.2 or 3.3 Disk II drive with controller,
video monitor; MMI DAC music card and headphones
required.

Cost: $150

Publisher's suggested audience: Third grade to
twelfth grade students.

Documentation: A user's guide includes the
learning objectives of the program, a summary,
prerequisite skills and knowledge, and operating
instructions.

Description

Presented in game format this program drills
students in the identification of key signatures
which are displayed on the screen according to
parameters selected by the user. In the "Tutor"
mode the user is not timed; in the "Game" mode the
user must attempt to beat the clock. If the user
does not make his response quickly enough,
accumulated points begin going up in puffs of
smoke displayed on the screen. The user may
select from among the following parameters:
treble, bass, grand staff, alto, or tenor clef;
major keys, minor keys, or both; and 0 to 7 sharps
and/or flats.

Responses are entered by typing letter names <A>
through <G> for the keys, <F> for flat, and <S>
for sharp. An instructional module is included on
the diskette. Sound effects (which can be turned
off) accompany each response. If the response is

wrong, the user hears a low, descending glissando;
correct responses receive fanfare-like chords and
congratulatory remarks such as "Move over
Beethoven." At the end of each session a score
card is displayed showing the number of rounds,
number of examples, number of points, number of
bonus points, and the total number of points.

Evaluation

This program is logically organized and factually
correct, and the graphics and sound are quite
good. The instructions are clear, within the
program and can be bypassed if they are not
needed.   The <I>nstructions which the user may
review during the "Tutor" part of the program list
the use of the <N> key to designate "natural."
Yet the program itself does not require the user
to type this additional descriptor for those key
signatures not using a sharp or a flat.   Errors
lead to repeated tries, but not hints. After the
third attempt, pressing the <ESC>ape key provides
the correct answer.

Methods of response are not consistent throughout
the program. When selecting the options listed
above, the user is not required to use an "enter"
key, either the <RETURN> key or the <SPACE BAR>.
However, after typing each key signature response,
the user must hit the <SPACE BAR> in order to
"enter" the answer. While this allows the user to
change his answer before it is entered, it also
slows the response time.

***

Chord Mania by David B. Williams, Julia Schulze,
and David L. Shrader, Micro Music Software
Library, published by Temporal Acuity Products,
Inc., version 1.0, 1981.

Hardware: Apple II computer with a minimum of 48K
memory, 3.2 or 3.3 Disk II drive with controller,
video monitor; MMI DAC music card and headphones
required.

Cost: $125

Publisher's suggested audience: Seventh grade to
adult.

Documentation: A user's guide includes the
objectives of the program, a summary, prerequisite
skills and knowledge, operating instructions, and
instructions for changing any options.

Description

In game format, Chord Mania drills both aural and
visual identification of triads and seventh
chords. The program provides practice in chord
quality identification as well as identification
of chord inversion. In visual mode a four-voice
chord is displayed; the user must identify the
chord by selecting the correct chord quality
and/or the correct inversion from the multiple
choices shown on the screen. After the chord has
been successfully identified, the program plays
the chord for the user. The aural mode is similar
except that the program will initially sound the
chord without notation. When the chord is
identified correctly, the program displays it in
notation for the user. The user is timed in this
program by an hour glass graphically displayed on
the screen with "sand" trickling through it.

Options allow the user to practice alone or with a
friend, to choose aural or visual identification,
to select the chord qualities and inversions to be
practiced, and the chord qualities and inversions
on which to be tested. The user may also choose
to play as an amateur, semi-professional or
professional. The manner in which the points are
accumulated depends upon the user's selection of
one of these difficulty levels. The program keeps
a running scoreboard of progress, showing the
number of rounds played, total points, bonus
points, and grand total. There is no long-term
record keeping on the disk.

An instructional module is included on the
diskette. The arrow keys are used to select
multiple choice answers and the <SPACE BAR> must
be used in order to enter each answer.

Evaluation

The graphics and sound are good in this program, with the exception of some of the low notes which are hard to distinguish. The prompts are clear and consistent, and the use of the hour glass offers the user a visual means by which to calculate how much time is left to enter responses. Instructions are clear and within the program and can be bypassed if not needed. However, instructions are not available during the program should the user need to review them. The program also requests the user's name at the beginning of each session and personalizes each session with statements such as "Good Luck, (name of user)."

This program provides a series of instructor options which allow the instructor to preset many of the parameters of the program. The instructor can select which chord qualities and which inversions will be used in each drill, whether the chords will be identified in the aural or the visual mode, whether the identification task will involve chord quality, chord inversion, or both, and what the difficulty level will be. These options would then be shut off during the program and unavailable to the student.

The large number of choices the user must make before the program begins becomes somewhat cumbersome. First, the types of chords (major, minor, diminished, augmented triads, major-major, major-minor, minor-minor, half diminished, and fully diminished seventh chords) to be drilled or tested must be selected; then root position and various inversions of each of these chords must be selected before the drill can be started. In the aural identification mode, the chords are only played once for the user to identify. Rehearings cannot be requested. Lastly, when one of the drills ends, the program does not take the user back to the main menu screen so that he can choose a different drill. In order to change drills, the user must reboot the disk.

The program lacks specific information regarding the use of the <CAPS LOCK> key on the Apple IIe computer. In order to respond to certain prompts at the beginning of the program, make selections

regarding the types of chords to to be drilled,
and enter responses during the program, the <CAPS
LOCK> key must be depressed. Neither the written
documentation nor the prompts and instructions
within the program inform the user about this
necessity.

***

Clef Notes by G. David Peters, Electronic
Courseware Systems, Inc., 1983.

Hardware: Commodore 64 or 128, one disk drive,
monitor (color monitor optional). Also available
for Apple II+, IIe, or IIc with at least 48K, or
Apple IIc with at least 128K, one disk drive, and
monitor, or the IBM-PC or IBM-PC JR. with at least
128K, one 360K double-sided disk drive, color
graphics board, and monitor.

Cost: $39.95

Publisher's suggested audience: None stated.

Documentation: Brief description on back of
diskette box.

Description

This program drills the user on the identification
of notes in treble, bass, alto, and tenor clefs.
The user may choose drills involving an isolated
clef or a combination of clefs. A musical staff,
clef, and note are displayed on the screen along
with a pitch name. In each drill the user moves
the note to the correct line or space of the pitch
requested by pressing the up and down cursor keys.
The "Challenge Test" has two levels: treble and
bass clefs or all four clefs. In the test the
staff, clef, and note are displayed and the user
must identify the note by moving the right and
left cursor keys to select a pitch among multiple
choice letter names "A" through "G" displayed
beneath the staff.

After the user has completed ten consecutive
correct answers, the program provides a percentage
score, how long the test took in seconds, and

whether the user was placed in the "Hall of Fame."
The program includes instructor options for
student record keeping. Individual student
records include the student's first and last
scores, the time in seconds of the student's first
and last session, the average score and the
average time of each session.

Evaluation

The graphics in this program are good, and the
program is logically organized and factually
correct. The program also includes notes on
ledger lines both above and below the staff for
all clef drills. Instructions appear within the
program and can be bypassed if not needed. The
user may review the instructions during the
program and end the program any time. On the
Commodore, for instance, this can be done by
pressing the <Fl> key. The screen is uncluttered,
and the prompts are clear and consistent. <H>elp
screens provide short tutorials on names of notes
in various clefs.

The program displays the word "yes" for correct
answers and "no" for wrong ones. Errors made by
the user do not lead to hints. However, the user
can continue to reenter answers until (s)he enters
the right one. A running tabulation in the lower
right corner of the screen keeps track of the
number of notes tried, the number correct, and the
number to go.

The program requires two different methods of
response, and this feature may prove to be a
negative one for some users. In each drill, the
user responds by matching a location on the staff
with a note given at random by the program, while
in the test the user must respond by matching the
name of a pitch with a location designated on the
staff. In addition, the slow response of the
program to the user's pressing of the cursor keys
(in the Commodore version) often causes the cursor
to go past the intended location on the staff; for
users in a hurry, this will result in a wrong
answer.

***

Composers and Their Works by David Williams, Al
Blackford and Julie Schulze, Micro Music Software
Library, published by Temporal Acuity Products,
Inc., 1982, version 2.0.

Hardware: Apple II series computer with a minimum
of 48K memory, 3.2 or 3.3 Disk II drive with
controller, video monitor; (MMI DAC music card and
headphones required only if sound effects are
desired).

Cost: $70

Publisher's suggested audience: Fourth grade to
adult.

Documentation: A user's guide includes the
objectives of the program, a summary, prerequisite
skills and knowledge, operating instructions, and
instructions for changing any options.

Description

In game format, this program provides drill and
practice in identifying composers, spelling
composers' names, and recalling their names given
certain information.   The user may select among
three methods of drill, three speed levels, and
six categories of composers.

In "Select-a-Composer," information about
significant works, dates, and nationality are
displayed on the screen and the user must select a
composer among the multiple choice answers
provided.   In "Spell-a-Composer," the name of a
composer appears briefly on the screen and then
disappears; the user must type the name with
absolutely correct spelling.   In "Recall-a-
Composer," information about specific works,
dates, and nationality is again displayed, and the
user must type the composer's name with absolute
precision without benefit of multiple choice
answers or seeing the composer's name displayed
even briefly.

While the user may select the speed (slow, medium,
or fast) of the response time, the program
automatically adjusts the speed during the drill
based upon the user's performance.

The user may choose among six sets of composers organized by musical period: composers to the early 18th century, Classical composers to Beethoven, Romantic composers, Post-Romantic composers, 20th Century composers Part I, or 20th Century composers Part II.

When the user quits, a "Report Card" is displayed providing level attained, speed, number of tries, number correct, and the percentage of correct responses. There is no long-term record keeping provided on the disk.

Evaluation

The sound effects (although optional) in this program are good; their only purpose is to provide motivation when the user's response is correct (fragments from musical literature in major keys, fanfares) and to admonish when the response is incorrect (fragments from musical literature in minor keys). The program uses a personalized approach by providing comments to the user followed by his or her name.

The program is factually correct. The instructions are clear, within the program, and can be bypassed if not needed. However, instructions cannot be recalled during the program if the user requires some review. The program presents clear and consistent prompts, and the screen is neat and uncluttered. The program allows second tries if an answer is incorrect, although it does not provide any hints. After the second wrong answer, the program provides the correct one.

One has to question the publisher's suggested audience for this program. It is unlikely that much of the information about many of the composers listed, let alone some of the composers' names, would be familiar to many fourth grade children. Furthermore, the typing skills required in order to enter responses, especially in timed drills such as these, go beyond not only the skills of fourth grade children, but also beyond the typing abilities of most adults. Since running out of time counts as an error, many novice typists, no matter how thorough their

musical knowledge, would find the program very
frustrating.

The program lacks specific information regarding
the use of the <CAPS LOCK> key on the Apple IIe
computer. In order to respond to certain prompts
at the beginning of the program and in order to
type the spelling of composer's names in the spell
and recall sections of the program, the <CAPS
LOCK> key on the Apple IIe must be depressed.
Neither the written documentation nor the prompts
and instructions within the program inform the
user about this necessity.

***

Descending...Ascending Intervals by Penny Pursell,
Electronic Courseware Systems, Inc., 1985.

See Hear Today...Play Tommorow.

***

Diatonic Chords by James P. McCarthy and Donald
Para, (The Western Michigan Dictation Series),
Micro Music Software Library, Temporal Acuity
Products, Inc., 1984, version 2.21.

Hardware: Apple II computer with minimum of 48K
memory, 3.3 DOS, Disk II drive with controller,
video monitor; MMI DAC music card and headphones
required.

Cost: $150

Publisher's suggested audience: Secondary and
university.

Documentation: A user's guide includes teaching
objectives, prerequisite skills and knowledge, as
well as details about the program.

Description

This program provides drill and practice in taking
harmonic dictation. After choosing one of six

chord categories and a progression number within the category, the user hears the key established and the exercise played as often as the user deems necessary and at any time in the program. The user is then asked to complete the bass and soprano lines and then the Roman numerals and inversions for each chord. The inner voices are not entered. The first chord is always notated for the user. The progressions use major and minor keys through four sharps and flats with one exception, D flat Major.

The six categories of chords are: primary triads (19 progressions), first inversion triads (15 progressions), second inversion triads (14 progressions), dominant sevenths (14 progressions), secondary triads (15 progressions) and review (21 progressions). The authors state that the progressions are not generated randomly for musical and pedagogical reasons. All progressions are in four voices and seven chords long. The documentation lists the complete scores for these exercises for the teacher's use.

The user must use a "code" to enter answers, but <H>elp is available at any time for the mechanics of note entry. In addition to entering the note name and accidental, if necessary, the user must also enter an octave number for each pitch. These are constantly displayed on the right side of the musical staves on the screen. When entering chord functions, the user types normal figured bass symbols: 7, 6, 43, 65, etc. They are displayed vertically on the screen beneath the chord. After the soprano and bass notes are entered successfully and the Roman numeral and figured bass numbers entered correctly, the program plays the chord and notates it on the screen, including the inner voices. There is no scoring, although the user is congratulated when exercises are completed successfully, with a comment about how many times the user heard the exercise.

Evaluation

The graphics of the musical staff and notes are quite good in this program. However, intonation problems were noted in the playing of some of the chords. The screens are neat and uncluttered, and the prompts are clear and consistent. The program

does not provide the correct answers when the bass
and soprano entries are being made. Instead, the
authors encourage experimentation. The user does
have the option of seeing the correct Roman
numeral and figured bass answers if a response is
wrong three or more times. No hints are given in
either case.

When the user types an "illegal" entry (whether it
was a typing error or not!), the program provides
feedback to that effect, a helpful aspect of this
program.

All the chords in the program, including minor and
diminished ones, are represented by upper-case
Roman numerals. There is one inconsistency in the
method of entering figured bass numbers: whenever
a diminished triad in first inversion is entered,
it must be entered as a "D6" rather than just "6."
This is also the way it is notated on the screen.
These two features may be bothersome to some
users.

***

Dictation I by John E. Hatmaker, Wenger
Corporation, 1985.

See Music Drills: Ear Training Series Part III:
Dictation I.

***

DoReMi by Bruce Benward and David Williams, Micro
Music Software Library, 1982, published by
Temporal Acuity Products, Inc., 1982, version 3.0.

Hardware: Apple II computer with 48K memory, 3.2
or 3.3 Disk II drive with controller, video
monitor; MMI DAC music card and headphones
required.

Cost: $75

Publisher's suggested audience: Third grade to
university, although the author states that the
program was created for college freshmen.

Documentation: A user's guide includes teaching
objectives, prerequisite skills and knowledge, as
well as details about the program.

Description

In game format, DoReMi provides drill and practice
in identifying aurally the individual degrees of a
major scale.   The program offers four levels from
which the user may choose.   Level 1 requires the
user to identify one scale degree; each successive
level adds one more note to the requirement.   For
each exercise, the program plays a major scale.
As each degree of the scale is played, the
solfeggio syllable and the scale degree number are
displayed horizontally on the screen.   Following
the scale a randomized sequence of from one to
four notes taken from the scale is played.   The
user is asked to identify this note or sequence of
notes.   Response(s) are registered by using the
left and right arrow keys to select the
appropriate syllable and scale degree number among
the syllables displayed on the screen and then the
<SPACE BAR> to enter the answer.

When the user errs, a short tutorial is employed
automatically.   The user must err in order to hear
the scale played again.   The user is informed that
his or her response is wrong, told what scale
degree (s)he chose, the wrong choice is played,
the right answer is played, and the user is given
two more chances.   If, after three attempts, the
answer is still wrong, the program highlights the
correct response and plays it.

The user is congratulated when his responses are
correct.   After each exercise the program displays
how many sets the user has attempted and how many
(s)he has missed.   Attempts and misses are
cumulative until the user leaves a level.   At this
point the user may continue at the same level or
quit by pressing the <ESC>ape key.   Quitting takes
the user back to the menu where a new level can be
selected or the user can quit the entire program.
The program does not provide a utility for record
keeping.

Evaluation

This program is logically organized and factually
correct. The instructions are within the program
and may be bypassed by those already familiar with
them. The user may quit the program at any time
by pressing the <ESC>ape key. Should the user
require the instructions during the drill, (s)he
may <ESC>ape to the main menu and then select the
instructions.

The instructions are not very informative; they
merely inform the user to use four keys in the
program, the left and right arrow keys, the <SPACE
BAR>, and the <ESC>ape key. Although the methods
of response are consistent throughout the program,
the drills lack any prompts.

Errors on the part of the user do lead to repeated
tries, but no hints. The program requests the
user to enter his or her name at the beginning of
the program, and this name is used thereafter to
personalize the drills. Responses are followed by
both positive and negative feedback. "C'mon so-
and-so, you can do better," "Sorry so-and-so, your
answer is wrong," or "Second time, pretty good"
are examples of the encouraging feedback offered
by the program.

The fact that the program employs no musical
notation may be bothersome to some users. The
documentation for this program states that the
user may hear the major scale of each exercise as
many times as needed. This statement was found to
be false.

***

Double Reed Fingerings by Anne Miller, Electronic
Courseware Systems, Inc., 1985.

Hardware: Commodore 64 or 128, one disk drive,
monitor (color monitor optional). Also available
for Apple II+ or IIe with at least 48K, or IIc
with at least 128K, one disk drive, and monitor.

Cost: $39.95

Publisher's suggested audience: None stated.

Documentation: Brief description on back of
diskette box; a brief pamphlet regarding teacher
options is included.

Description

The purpose of this program is to review and drill
four problem oboe fingerings and four problem
fingerings on the bassoon. The program states
that it will be most beneficial to those who know
oboe fingerings from low B chromatically to C
above the staff and/or to those who know bassoon
fingerings from low E to middle C. A musical
example is displayed, and the user is asked to
decide whether or not a particular fingering such
as forked F is required. The user responds by
typing <Y> for yes and <N> for no. If the
response is <Y>, the user must indicate which note
makes the forked F necessary by moving a cursor
under the appropriate note.

In the half-hole exercises the user indicates
whether each note of an exercise requires half-
hole (by pressing <H>) or does not require half-
hole (by pressing <O>).

When mistakes are made, the program automatically
reviews the situations in which a particular
fingering is required.

The user may choose to work with oboe or bassoon
fingerings. The options for the oboe fingerings
are forked F, left hand E-flat, half-hole, and
octave keys. The choices for bassoon fingerings
are whisper key, half-hole, alternate F-sharp,
and alternate G-sharp. The user may choose to
review or go directly to exercises, and may choose
how many exercises (1-9).

After completing the exercises chosen, the program
tells the user how many were attempted and how
many were correct. Instructor options include a
file which gives the instructor the ability to
keep student records (up to a maximum of 50
scores) and the ability to delete all student
records once the file becomes full.

Evaluation

This program is logically organized and factually correct. Instructions are clear, within the program (for each fingering problem), can be bypassed by those familiar with the program, and can be recalled during the program. Each problem fingering includes a review (which can be bypassed) in addition to exercises. Information about prerequisite skills and knowledge is included in the program rather than in the documentation. The program allows the user to "quit" at any time. On the Commodore, the <Fl> key takes the user back to the main menu.

The prompts are clear and consistent. User errors receive no hints, merely encouragement to try again. If the user errs a second time on the same problem, the program automatically goes to a review screen.

The methods of response are not consistent throughout. For example, in certain exercises the user's response is automatically "entered" by merely pressing the appropriate response key, while in other exercises, the user must press the <RETURN> key after pressing the response key in order to "enter" the response. The user is never informed when this is necessary and when it is not. Furthermore, the program assumes that the user knows how to operate the cursor keys on the Commodore. To move the cursor right and down is no problem; however, the user must use the <SHIFT> key with the right cursor in order to move left, and the <SHIFT> key with the down cursor in order to go up.

The best part about this program is that it does not try to have the user attempt to press various keys on the computer keyboard simulating fingerings on the oboe or the bassoon!

* * *

Ear Challenger: An Aural-Visual Game by Chris Alix and Stephen Walker, Electronic Courseware Systems, Inc., 1981, 1983, 1984.

Hardware: Commodore 64 or 128, one disk drive, monitor (color monitor important to this program). Also available for Apple II+ or IIe with at least 48K, or IIc with at least 128K, one disk drive, and monitor.

Cost: $39.95

Publisher's suggested audience: None stated.

Documentation: Brief description on back of diskette box.

Description

This program is an aural-visual game designed to increase the user's memory of a series of pitches that are taken from the seven diatonic pitches of a major scale. Each pitch is accompanied by a different color bar displayed on the screen. (A color monitor is probably important to this program.) The program plays a note and displays the color bar. The user plays back what was heard by pressing number keys 1 through 7 representing the seven diatonic scale degrees. As each pitch of the series is added, the program plays the whole series starting from the beginning, and the user must play back the entire series from the very first note. A counter at the bottom of the screen keeps the user informed about which pitch in the series has just been added. The user may choose among seven difficulty levels: 5, 10, 15, 20, 25, 30, or 35 note strings of pitches! <H>elp (instructions) is available from the difficulty selection page.

When the user is successful, a series of sirens go off and (s)he is congratulated. When an error is made the program informs the user which note in the series was missed.

Evaluation

The instructions for this program are clear and within the program and the method of response is consistent throughout. Errors do not lead to hints or second tries. The program is accurate and factually correct. It can also be addicting!

***

Ear Training Skills by Penny Pursell, Electronic
Courseware Systems, Inc., 1985.

See Hear Today...Play Tomorrow.

***

Early Music Skills: A Note Recognition Game by
Lolita Walker Gilkes, Electronic Courseware
Systems, Inc., 1984.

Hardware: Commodore 64 or 128, one disk drive,
monitor. Also available for Apple II+ or IIe with
at least 48K, or Apple IIc with at least 128K, one
disk drive, and monitor, or the IBM-PC or IBM-PC
JR. with at least 128K, one 360K double-sided disk
drive, color graphics board, and monitor. This
program is also available in a MIDI version for
the Commodore 64 or 128 and Apple II+ or IIe with
Passport Design MIDI interface card; or for the
Commodore 64 or 128, Apple II+ or IIe, or IBM-PC
with Roland MIDI interface card and a MIDI-
compatible music keyboard or synthesizer.

Cost: $39.95

Publisher's suggested audience: None stated.

Documentation: Brief description on back of
diskette box.

Description

Early Music Skills provides brief tutorials and
drills in four fundamental music reading skills.
The drills are in game format, and the concepts
are presented both aurally and visually. The
drills have no time constraints, and each drill
has its own "Hall of Fame" with space provided for
three names. Each drill requires that a certain
number of items (usually 10 or 12) be completed
before a score is given or before the user can be
eligible to be placed in the "Hall of Fame." The
user may leave a drill at any point and return to
the index by pressing the <Fl> key.

In "Line and Space Notes," the user must decide whether a note displayed on a staff with treble clef is on a line or a space. Responses are made by typing the <L> and the <S> keys. The notes are sounded as they are notated.

"Line and Space Numbers" asks the user whether a note displayed on a musical staff with treble clef is on a line or space and on what number line or space the note is located. The <L> and <S> keys and the number keys are used to make responses.

"Up and Down" drills the user's ability to recognize whether four-, three-, or two-note strings of notes in stepwise motion are moving up or down. In the first part the user sees the notes on the staff and hears them played simultaneously. In the second part the user only hears "invisible notes" and must identify the direction on an aural basis. After a response is made the notes are placed on the staff. The <U> and the <D> keys are used to respond. In order to be placed in the "Hall of Fame" the user must do the "invisible notes" drill.

"Stepping and Skipping" drills recognition of notes stepping up or down, or notes skipping up or down. Notes are displayed on the staff and sounded as they are displayed. The user uses the number keys to select from multiple choice answers: step up, step down, skip up, or skip down.

Different sound effects are produced for correct or incorrect responses. A score is given after each session and the user is told when he is placed in the "Hall of Fame." Other than the "Hall of Fame," there is no record keeping utility on the disk.

Evaluation

This program is logically organized and factually correct. Instructions, although brief, are provided within each drill and can be bypassed by users familiar with them. The game format, as well as sound effects and positive verbal messages after each correct response, provide the program with motivation.

Mistakes do not lead to hints or repeated tries,
and the methods of response are not consistent
throughout. Sometimes the user must type a letter
in order to respond, while at other times a number
must be typed. The graphics of musical notation
and the sound used in the program are of poor
quality in the Commodore version. The computer is
capable of providing much better quality in both
regards.

***

Elements of Music by John M. Eddins and Robert L.
Weiss, Jr., Electronic Courseware Systems, Inc.,
1981, 1983, 1984. A series of three disks
entitled Note Names Drill, Keyboard Note Drill,
and Key Signature Drill.

Hardware: Commodore 64 or 128, one disk drive,
monitor (color monitor optional). Also available
for Apple II+ or IIe with at least 48K, or Apple
IIc with at least 128K, one disk drive, and
monitor, or the IBM-PC or IBM-PC JR. with at least
128K, one 360K double-sided disk drive, color
graphics board, and monitor. Keyboard Note Drill
is also available in a MIDI version for the
Commodore 64 or 128 and Apple II+ or IIe with
Passport Design MIDI interface card; or for the
Commodore 64 or 128, Apple II+ or IIe, or IBM-PC
with Roland MIDI interface card and a MIDI-
compatible music keyboard or synthesizer.

Cost: Comes as a complete set of three disks for
$99.95 or $39.95 each for Note Names Drill,
Keyboard Note Drill, and Key Signature Drill.

Publisher's suggested audience: The publisher
states that these are entry level programs for use
by children or adults.

Documentation: Brief description on back of
diskette box; a pamphlet regarding instructor
management options is included.

Description

The program utilizes a drill and practice format
in each of three sections: pitch identification,

key signature identification, and keyboard note
identification. Each section provides drill
exercises and a test; the user may choose timed
drill (1 to 99 seconds) or untimed drill. Every
test consists of 20 items and allows the user only
5 seconds in which to answer each item.

In Note Names Drill, pitches are displayed at
random in both treble and bass clefs (the clefs
are also randomly picked); the user responds by
pressing the letter name of the note on the
computer keyboard. The user must do 20 exercises
per drill in order to receive a score.

Keyboard Note Drill asks the user to identify the
correct location on a piano keyboard (displayed on
the screen) of randomly selected notes in either
bass or treble clef. The <A> and the <S> keys are
used to move the cursor on the keyboard. The user
must do 20 exercises per drill in order to receive
a score.

In Key Signature Drill, key signatures are
displayed in bass and treble clefs. The user is
asked to identify both the major and minor keys
using the same key signature. The user types the
letter name of the key being identified using <+>
and <-> for sharp and flat respectively. The user
must do 10 exercises per drill in order to receive
a score.

Progress reports are presented to the user at the
completion of each session, whether the session
was a drill or a test. A summary displays the
number correct and a percentage score. The
instructor may also keep track of student progress
through the use of a student records file.

Evaluation

The graphics of musical notation in these programs
are good, and the programs are factually correct
and logically organized. The instructions are
clear, within the program, and can be bypassed by
those already familiar with them. The
instructions can be reviewed during the program by
pressing the <H> key (for help). By pressing the
<Fl> key, the user can quit the program any time
and return to the index at the beginning.

Finding the loading instructions for this disk is
not easy. One has to pull a card out of the
sleeve covering the diskette box and turn it over
to find the instructions. The card does not look
as though it is removable, and nowhere in the
documentation is the user informed of this
necessity.

The keyboard displayed in Keyboard Note Drill is
only two octaves in length, and identifying a note
in any octave will work. It is unfortunate that
register is not important in the program because
the user acquires no sense of relative distance
between the various notes flashed on the screen.
Since octave placement is not a factor in the
program, the display of a one octave keyboard
would be sufficient.

It is not clear why the <A> and <S> keys are used
to move the cursor in the keyboard drill, rather
than the left and right arrow keys.

***

Find That Tune by Penny Pursell, Electronic
Courseware Systems, Inc., 1985.

See Hear Today...Play Tomorrow.

***

Flute Fingerings by David G. Schwaegler, Wenger
Corporation, 1984. Part of the Wind Instrument
Fingerings Series which includes five woodwind
programs (flute, oboe, clarinet, bassoon, and
saxophone) and five brass programs (trumpet,
French horn, trombone, baritone horn, and tuba).

Hardware: Apple II, II+, IIe, or IIc, one disk
drive, video monitor. Also available for the
Commodore 64 or 128, one disk drive, and monitor.

Cost: $29 for each program, or $99 for a set of
five.

Publisher's suggested audience: Beginning,
intermediate and advanced levels are available on
the disk.

Documentation: Brief descriptive pamphlet.

Description

This program provides drill and practice in
matching appropriate flute fingerings with notes
displayed on the musical staff with treble clef.
A note is displayed on the staff (or on ledger
lines), and the user enters the correct fingering
by marking a flute fingering chart, i.e., by
pressing certain computer keyboard keys which
represent the keys on the flute. The range of the
notes drilled in the program includes all notes,
and enharmonic spellings as well, from middle C to
C three octaves above middle C.

A diagram of the keys of the flute is displayed
vertically on the left side of the screen with
various letters and characters from the computer
keyboard printed on each key. On the right side
of the screen a diagram of the left hand is
displayed, indicating which finger of the hand
controls which keys represented on the chart on
the left. Each key acts as a toggle; when it is
pressed it is displayed in reverse video,
indicating that the key is part of the fingering
entered by the user. When it is pressed again, it
goes back to normal, or open.

The user may choose among three programs on the
disk. "Fingering Drill", with three levels
(beginning, intermediate, and advanced) has no
time constraints and allows the user to get help
with correct finger placement. The "Game," with
the same three levels, times the user with a
clock; the user may choose from three speeds.
(The Commodore version uses a mallet and a gong
instead of the clock.) In "Note Names Drill", a
note appears on the staff and the user must type
in its letter name (no second tries).

The disk also has a "toolkit", accessed by a
password, which allows the teacher to create a
student records file (for up to twelve students),
preset drill levels, preset the speed of the game,
and edit the preset fingerings by allowing

selection of primary and alternative fingerings
for the notes.

Evaluation

The graphics in this program are good, and the
prompts are consistent throughout, as are the
methods of response. The instructions are
included in the program and can be bypassed by
users who are already familiar with them. Part of
the instructions are displayed on the screen
during the drill and game, which, in addition to
the musical staff, clef, note, and the diagram of
the instrument keys, makes the screen quite
cluttered.

In an attempt to emulate the actual hand positions
on the instrument, the user is instructed to place
his or her hands on the computer keyboard with
each finger on a certain key. This is rather
awkward and seems unnecessary at first, because
the program only allows the fingering to be
entered one key at a time anyway. Once the user
starts the "Game," however, it becomes apparent
that in order to keep up with the clock, one's
hands must be over the appropriate keys at all
times. The display of the flute key diagram
presented vertically on the screen may be
confusing to some users, since most flutes today
are of the transverse variety.

***

Foreign Instrument Names by David Williams, Al
Blackford and Julie Schulze, Micro Music Software
Library, published by Temporal Acuity Products,
Inc., 1981.

Hardware: Apple II series computer with at least
48K memory, 3.2 or 3.3 Disk II drive with
controller, video monitor; (MMI DAC music card and
headphones required only if sound effects are
desired).

Cost: $50

Publisher's suggested audience: Fourth grade to
university.

Documentation: A user's guide includes the
objectives of the program, a summary, prerequisite
skills and knowledge, operating instructions, and
instructions for changing any options.

Description

In game format, this program provides drill and
practice in identifying foreign musical instrument
names from descriptions, spelling their names, and
recalling them when given their descriptions. The
user may select among three methods of drill,
three speed levels, and three sets of foreign
musical instrument names.

In "Select-a-Name," a description of a foreign
musical instrument is displayed on the screen, and
the user must select the appropriate name
among the multiple choice answers provided. In
"Spell-a-Name," the name of a musical instrument
appears briefly on the screen and then disappears;
the user must type the name with absolutely
correct spelling. In "Recall-a-Name," a
description of a foreign instrument is again
displayed, and the user must type the name with
absolute precision without benefit of multiple
choice answers or seeing the name displayed even
briefly.

The response time (slow, medium, or fast) can be
selected by the user. However, the speed will
automatically increase or decrease during the
drill based upon the user's performance.

The user may choose among three sets of foreign
musical instrument names: an Italian set, a
French set and a German set.

When the user quits, a "Report Card" is displayed
providing level attained, speed, number of tries,
number correct, and the percentage of correct
responses. There is no long-term record keeping
provided on the disk.

Evaluation

The sound effects (although optional) in this
program are good; their only purpose is to
provide motivation when the user's response is
correct (fragments from musical literature in

major keys, fanfares) and to admonish when the
response is incorrect (fragments from musical
literature in minor keys). The program uses a
personalized approach by providing comments to the
user followed by his or her name.

The program is factually correct. Instructions
are clear, within the program, and can be bypassed
if not needed. However, instructions cannot be
recalled during the program if the user requires
some review. The program presents clear and
consistent prompts, and the screen is neat and
uncluttered. The program allows second tries if
an answer is incorrect, although it does not
provide any hints. After the second wrong answer,
the program provides the correct one.

One has to question the publisher's suggested
audience for this program. It is unlikely that
many of the foreign musical terms listed would be
familiar to many fourth grade children.
Furthermore, the typing skills required in order
to enter responses, especially in timed drills
such as these, go beyond not only the skills of
fourth grade children, but also beyond the typing
abilities of most adults. Since running out of
time counts as an error, many novice typists, no
matter how thorough their musical knowledge, would
find the program very frustrating.

In order to respond to certain prompts at the
beginning of the program and in order to type the
spelling of the instruments in the spell and
recall sections of the program, the <CAPS LOCK>
key on the Apple IIe must be depressed. Neither
the written documentation nor the prompts and
instructions within the program inform the user
about this necessity.

***

FourTrak by David M. Kusek and John L. Borowicz,
Passport Designs, Inc., 1983.

Hardware: Apple II (with Applesoft Firmware
card), Apple II+ or Apple IIe, one disk drive with
controller, Soundchaser Computer Music

System (Mountain Computer MusicSystem and Passport
Designs Klavier), amplifier, speakers or
headphones, video monitor, and game paddles.

Cost: Software included with the Klavier.

Publisher's suggested audience: None stated.

Documentation: Includes an informative, detailed
user's guide.

Description

FourTrak is the basic Soundchaser software,
providing an eight-voice, digital synthesizer with
live performance as well as recording
capabilities. Each voice has two digital
oscillators with independent wave form, envelope,
and modulation controls. The system provides ten
"presets", or timbres, and newly-created timbres
can also be saved. Wave forms can be created by
drawing them on the screen or by indicating the
strength of each of 16 partials on a bar graph. A
sequencer, operating like a tape recorder, plays
back whatever the user plays on the keyboard. It
provides sound-on-sound recording, allows the user
to change presets after recording, as well as
allowing speed change without change in pitch.

The "Main Preset Screen" allows the user to
control volume, change presets, change the tuning,
change the register, control the envelope (attack,
decay, sustain, and release) of the left and right
channels individually, and control the amplitude
modulation as well as the frequency modulation.
Ten presets (either those which come with the
disk, or others that the user has created and
stored on the disk) are immediately available to
the user while in this mode. This section of
Fourtrak is used for live performance.

Additional timbres (wave forms) can be created by
using the "WaveMaker." This can be done using two
different methods: by harmonic (Fourier)
synthesis, selecting the partials to be used (from
the fundamental and the first fifteen overtones)
and controlling their amplitudes on a bar graph,
or by drawing the wave form on the screen. Both

of these methods involve the use of game paddles,
and both methods provide separate wave forms for
each (left and right) channel. Once wave forms
are constructed they can be saved in "Master"
files.

The "Sequencer" provides four recording tracks,
each of which may have its own preset or timbre.
The user enters music by playing the "klavier,"
and can have the music played back. Tracks are
entered one at a time; as additional tracks are
played, the user can hear the previous tracks.

The sequencer has an eight-voice limit; if the
user places four voices on each of two tracks, the
other tracks cannot be used. Once the tracks are
entered they can be stored as "Traks" files.

In "Sequencer" mode, the user may load various
"Traks" files, change the presets of the tracks by
loading various "Master" files of presets
(timbres) and assigning them to individual tracks,
and change the tempo without affecting the pitch
of the tracks.

Evaluation

Although the instructions are not included within
this program, the written documentation is very
thorough and the prompts on the screen are clear
and consistent. The system is fairly easy to use,
and, of course, becomes easier with familiarity.
Some users may find the use of hexadecimal numbers
to represent the values of various parameters on
the "Main Preset Screen" somewhat forbidding, but
there really is no need for concern. The system
is enjoyable to use.

* * *

French Horn Fingerings by David G. Schwaegler,
Wenger Corporation, 1984. Part of the Wind
Instrument Fingerings Series which includes five
woodwind programs (flute, oboe, clarinet, bassoon,
and saxophone) and five brass programs (trumpet,
French horn, trombone, baritone horn, and tuba).

Hardware: Apple II, II+, IIe, or IIc, one disk
drive, video monitor. Also available for the
Commodore 64 or 128, one disk drive, and monitor.

Cost: $29 for each program, or $99 for a set of
five.

Publisher's suggested audience: Beginning,
intermediate and advanced levels are available on
the disk.

Documentation: Brief descriptive pamphlet.

Description

This program provides drill and practice in
matching appropriate French horn fingerings with
notes displayed on the musical staff with treble
clef. A note is displayed on the staff (or on
ledger lines), and the user enters the correct
fingering by marking a French horn fingering
chart, i.e., by pressing certain computer keyboard
keys which represent the valves on the French
horn. The range of the notes drilled in the
program includes all notes, and enharmonic
spellings as well, from C one octave below middle
C to the C two octaves above middle C.

A diagram of the four French horn valves is
displayed on the left side of the screen with
various letters and characters from the computer
keyboard printed on each valve. On the right side
of the screen a diagram of the left hand is
displayed, indicating which finger of the hand
controls which keys represented on the chart on
the left. Each key acts as a toggle; when it is
pressed it is displayed in reverse video,
indicating that the key is part of the fingering
entered by the user. When it is pressed again, it
goes back to normal, or open.

The user may choose among three programs on the
disk. "Fingering Drill", with three levels
(beginning, intermediate, and advanced) has no
time constraints and allows the user to get help
with correct finger placement. The "Game," with
the same three levels, times the user with a
clock; the user may choose from three speeds.
(The Commodore version uses a mallet and a gong
instead of the clock.) In "Note Names Drill," a

note appears on the staff and the user must type
in its letter name (no second tries).

The disk also has a "toolkit", accessed by a
password, which allows the teacher to create a
student records file (for up to twelve students),
preset drill levels, preset the speed of the game,
and edit the preset fingerings by allowing
selection of primary and alternative fingerings
for the notes.

Evaluation

The graphics in this program are good, and the
prompts are consistent throughout, as are the
methods of response. The instructions are
included in the program and can be bypassed by
users who are already familiar with them. Part of
the instructions are displayed on the screen
during the drill and game, which, in addition to
the musical staff, clef, note, and the diagram of
the instrument keys, makes the screen quite
cluttered.

In an attempt to emulate the actual hand positions
on the instrument, the program instructs the user
to place his or her hands on the computer keyboard
with each finger on a certain key. This is rather
awkward and seems unnecessary at first, because
the program only allows the fingering to be
entered one key at a time anyway. Once the user
starts the "Game," however, it becomes apparent
that in order to keep up with the clock, one's
hands must be over the appropriate keys at all
times.

***

General Music Terms by David Williams, Al
Blackford and Julie Schulze, Micro Music Software
Library, published by Temporal Acuity Products,
Inc., 1981.

Hardware: Apple II series computer with a minimum
of 48K memory, 3.2 or 3.3 Disk II drive with
controller, video monitor; (MMI DAC music card and
headphones required only if sound effects are
desired).

Cost: $70

Publisher's suggested audience: Fourth grade to adult.

Documentation: A user's guide includes the objectives of the program, a summary, prerequisite skills and knowledge, operating instructions, and instructions for changing any options.

Description

In game format, this program provides drill and practice in identifying musical terms from their definitions, spelling the terms, and recalling them when given their definitions. The user may select among three methods of drill, three speed levels, and among six categories of terms.

In "Select-a-Term," a definition of a musical term is displayed on the screen, and the user must select the appropriate term among the multiple choice answers provided. In "Spell-a-Term," a musical term appears briefly on the screen and then disappears; the user must type the term with absolutely correct spelling. In "Recall-a-Term," a definition of a musical term is again displayed, and the user must type the term with absolute precision without benefit of multiple choice answers or seeing the term displayed even briefly.

The response time (slow, medium, or fast) can be selected by the user. However, the speed will automatically increase or decrease during the drill based upon the user's performance.

The user may choose among six sets of musical terms: melodic terms, harmonic terms, terms about instrumental forms and styles, terms about vocal forms, rhythmic and notational terms, and terms about tone color and dynamics.

When the user quits, a "Report Card" is displayed providing level attained, speed, number of tries, number correct, and the percentage of correct responses. There is no long-term record keeping is provided on the disk.

Evaluation

The sound effects (although optional) in this program are good; their only purpose is to provide motivation when the user's response is correct (fragments from musical literature in major keys, fanfares) and to admonish when the response is incorrect (fragments from musical literature in minor keys). The program uses a personalized approach by providing comments to the user followed by his or her name.

The program is factually correct. The instructions are clear, within the program, and can be bypassed if not needed. However, instructions cannot be recalled during the program if the user requires some review. The program presents clear and consistent prompts, and the screen is neat and uncluttered. The program allows second tries if an answer is incorrect, although it does not provide any hints. After the second wrong answer, the program provides the correct one.

One has to question the publisher's suggested audience for this program. It is unlikely that many of the musical terms in this program would be familiar to many fourth grade children. The typing skills required in order to enter responses, especially in timed drills such as these, go beyond not only the skills of fourth grade children, but also beyond the typing abilities of most adults. Since running out of time counts as an error, many novice typists, no matter how thorough their musical knowledge, would find the program very frustrating.

The program lacks specific information regarding the use of the <CAPS LOCK> key on the Apple IIe computer. In order to respond to certain prompts at the beginning of the program and in order to type the spelling of music terms in the spell and recall sections of the program, the <CAPS LOCK> key must be depressed. Neither the written documentation nor the prompts and instructions within the program inform the user about this necessity.

***

GUIDO Music Learning System developed by Fred
Hofstetter, Office of Instructional Technology,
University of Delaware, 1985, version 6.0.   This
software was developed for PLATO and is also
called MicroGUIDO.

Hardware: Control Data Corporation Viking 110
terminal with touch-sensitive screen; CDC 8-inch
disk drive; University of Delaware Sound
Synthesizer; headphones.   An IBM-PC version of
GUIDO has been released in 1987.   The software is
packaged on two 5 and 1/4-inch diskettes and is
controlled by a mouse instead of the touch-
sensitive screen in the Control Data version.   The
IBM-PC version requires a minimum of 256K, two
360K double-sided disk drives, color graphics
board, and monitor.   The IBM-PC version uses
either the University of Delaware Sound Card or
a MIDI compatible sound system.

Cost: Contact the Office of Instructional
Technology, The University of Delaware for
information.

Publisher's suggested audience: Collegiate music
majors.

Documentation: The Control Data version offered
very scant documentation.   However, the IBM-PC
version includes a lengthy, detailed student
manual and a separate instructor's manual.

Description

The programs in GUIDO (Guided Units of Interactive
Dictation Operations) provide competency-based
drill and practice in five areas of musical
dictation.   Each area contains a series of units
ranging from simple to quite complex material.
Each unit requires the user to provide a certain
number of consecutive correct responses before the
unit can be satisfactorily completed.   In melodic
dictation, for instance, the user might have to
complete four out of five exercises successfully
in order to complete a unit.   Successful
completion usually means getting 85% of the
example correct.   GUIDO places an asterisk next to
the units successfully completed in the menu of
units for each area.

Some drills require the user to complete each
exercise within a certain time limitation. In
some of the interval dictation units, for example,
the user is given only four seconds to respond.
Most units in all drills allow the user to hear
the example as many times as needed without
penalty.

The instructor may control many aspects of these
programs by changing the parameters in the
competency tables, levels of difficulty, titles of
units, contents of units, and allowable student
options. Among other parameters, instructors may
change the order of the units, the amount of time
allowed for response, the melodic ranges of the
various exercises, how many times a user may hear
each example, and what percentage of the exercises
must be correct in order for the user to complete
a unit successfully.

"Interval Dictation" provides 27 units of drill in
the aural recognition of intervals. The program
plays an interval and the user responds by
touching the box on the screen that contains the
interval (s)he thinks was played. In most units,
users can control how the intervals are played
(melodically up, down, or played harmonically),
whether the intervals are played with fixed upper
or lower note (or with randomly selected starting
note), whether the intervals played will be
compound, simple, or both, and how long the notes
of each interval will be played. In the remaining
units, practice and review units, these parameters
are preset. There is no musical notation
displayed in the interval units. Users can hear
the intervals again.

In "Melodic Dictation," GUIDO displays a musical
staff with clef (treble or bass), key signature,
and the first note of the exercise, and plays a
melody of pitches of equal duration. The user
enters the melody one note at a time by touching
the appropriate boxes with the letter names of the
musical alphabet displayed on the screen. Certain
units employ solfeggio syllables instead of letter
names. As they are touched (if correct), the
pitches are sounded and notated on the staff.
Users can control the tempo and hear the melody
played again. "Melodic Dictation" provides 32
units progressing from short, scalewise melodies

in major keys to modal melodies, modulating
melodies, chromatic melodies, atonal melodies, and
twelve-tone rows.

"Chord Qualities" consists of 42 units in which
GUIDO plays chords, and the user touches boxes on
the screen in order to indicate the quality and
inversion of each chord played. The user can hear
the chord again, make GUIDO pause while the chord
is studied, control whether the chord is
arpeggiated or played harmonically, and change the
length of time the chord is played. After each
chord is identified correctly, it is notated in
four parts on a grand staff and displayed on the
screen. "Chord Quality" units progress from major
and minor triads in root position to all types of
triads and seventh chords in root position and all
inversions, and to ninth, eleventh, and thirteenth
chords.

In "Harmonic Dictation," the program plays four-
part harmonic progressions in chorale style, and
the user responds by entering each of the four
voices and the Roman numeral and figured bass
analysis of each chord. The voices are entered by
touching boxes with letter names displayed on the
screen. Analysis is entered by touching boxes of
Roman numerals (small or large case), as well as
figured bass numbers and symbols displayed in
boxes on the screen. As correct notes are
entered, they are notated on a grand staff
displayed on the screen. Analysis symbols are
also displayed on the screen beneath the chords
they represent. Users can change the tempo of the
dictation, change from chorale style to more
arpeggiated styles, adjust the volume of each of
the four voices, and hear the dictation repeated.
The student can also select the order in which
(s)he wants to enter the answers; soprano first,
bass second, analysis third, or some other order.
The 34 "Harmonic Dictation" units progress from
tonic and dominant triads in root position and in
major keys to dominant and non-dominant seventh
chords, secondary dominants, the Neapolitan sixth,
and augmented sixth chords.

"Rhythmic Dictation" provides 40 units in which
GUIDO plays a rhythmic pattern from two to four
measures in length. The entire pattern is played
on the same pitch. The user enters each rhythmic

value of the pattern by touching boxes displayed
on the screen which correspond to the note values
that were played. As correct answers are entered
they are notated without a staff on the screen.
The user may hear the pattern repeated and
controls the tempo at which the pattern is played.
If preparatory beats are needed, the user can have
the tempo established by selecting the "metronome"
box displayed on the screen. The units progress
from undivided beat values in simple meters
through regular and borrowed divisions in simple
and compound meters, as well as quintuplets and
sextuplets in simple and compound meters.

Evaluation

The graphics of musical notation and the sound in
these programs are of the highest quality. The
user may choose among five different sounds for
any of the areas of dictation: clarinet,
harpsichord, pipe organ, reed organ, bells, or a
special sound for rhythmic dictation. (The IBM-PC
version provides over twenty different sounds from
which the user may choose.) The programs are
logically organized and allow the instructor to
change the order of materials if it is deemed
necessary.

Instructions are available and can be seen at any
time within any of the programs. The methods of
response are consistent within each program.
However, prompts to the user are almost entirely
lacking. With the exception of some very subtle
arrows pointing to the the area where the next
note should be entered, there are no prompts at
all. These same small arrows are also used when
the user makes errors; they usually provide hints
that the user's pitch response was too low or too
high. The competency-based scoring procedures
provide obvious motivation to the programs.

The replay value of these programs relies on the
fact that the intervals and chord quality examples
are all selected randomly by the programs. The
melodic, harmonic, and rhythmic exercises are all
composed randomly, within certain limitations
built into the programs, while the user waits.

There are a few negative features of these
programs. In the melodic and harmonic dictation

programs, the tonality of each exercise is never established, and in the rhythmic dictation program, the tempo is not set before the exercise unless the user specifically requests it. Some users may be concerned that the melodic dictation units do not include rhythm, while others may be upset by the fact that the user must precede any sharped or flatted note by pressing a box with the appropriate accidental, even when that accidental appears in the key signature. Occasionally the title of a unit does not correspond to the material presented in the unit. Not being able to predict certain answers based on the title of the unit may be very disconcerting to many users.

The most important negative aspect of the Control Data version of these programs is the fact that the interval and chord quality examples which include notes in the extreme high or low registers are virtually impossible to identify because of the quality of the electronically produced sound in these registers. When a user is about to identify the last interval of a series which will qualify him or her for successful completion of a unit, and (s)he is unable to identify the interval because it occurs in an extremely low register, (s)he becomes frustrated. Identifying such an interval erroneously causes the correct answer counter to restart at zero.

***

Harmonious Dictator by J. Timothy Kolosick and David B. Williams, Micro Music Software Library, 1981, published by Temporal Acuity Products, Inc., 1983, version 2.1.

Hardware: Apple II, II+, or IIe computer with a minimum of 48K memory, 3.2 or 3.3 Disk II drive with controller, video monitor; MMI DAC music card and headphones required.

Cost: $150

Publisher's suggested audience: Seventh grade to adult.

Documentation: A user's guide includes teaching
objectives, prerequisite skills and knowledge, as
well as details about the program.

Description

Harmonious Dictator drills the aural recognition
of chord progressions (harmonic dictation),
providing the user with practice in hearing the
functional relationships of chords within a key.
All diatonic chords and their inversions, selected
seventh chords, and secondary dominants are used.
The program employs all major keys up to six
sharps and six flats and minor keys up to four
sharps and six flats. Each chord progression is
from three to six chords in length. The user
selects a difficulty level from nine different
levels, chooses to have the program self-adjust
the level of difficulty to match his or her
ability or to lock the program at a particular
level, and decides whether to work in major or
minor keys or both.

During the program a grand staff is displayed on
the screen with key signature, the first chord
notated, and its Roman numeral and inversion
analysis provided. The user hears an ascending
major or harmonic minor scale played to establish
the key. Roman numerals one through seven and
figured bass inversion symbols are displayed in
two rows on the bottom of the screen. After
hearing the progression played twice, the user
selects first a Roman numeral and then a figured
bass symbol for each of the remaining chords in
the progression. The selection is made through
the use of the left and right arrow keys and the
<SPACE BAR> for entering each response. As soon
as the user has correctly identified both the
Roman numeral and the inversion, the program
notates the chord on the staff and plays it. The
user may press <R> to hear the progression again
(although points will be subtracted from the score
for each additional playing), press <E> to have
the key reestablished, and press <Q> to quit if a
progression is too hard.

The chords included in the nine levels of
difficulty are: 1) I, IV, V (and ii in minor
keys); 2) ii, vi, iii, diminished ii, and I and V
in first inversion; 3) ii and vii in first

inversion and I and V in second inversion; 4) V7
and ii7 in root position, V7 in first inversion,
and vii in second inversion; 5) ii7 in first
inversion, vi7 and I7, and IV in first inversion;
6) IV7 and iii7, I7 in first inversion, and IV7
in third inversion; 7) iii and vi in first
inversion, vi7 in first inversion, and V7 in third
inversion; 8) I7 and ii7 in third inversion, V7
in second inversion, and vii7 in first inversion
(only in minor mode); 9) IV7 in third inversion,
vi7 in third inversion and secondary dominants
(only in major mode).

After each progression is completed the user is
shown a "report card" which displays the number of
points subtracted for errors or additional
hearings, the total score in points, and a
percentage rating. When a session is finished the
following data is displayed on the screen:
starting difficulty level, ending difficulty
level, starting length of the progression, ending
length of the progression, total chords heard,
total chords notated, and overall competency in
the form of a percentage. The program does not
provide a record keeping utility.

Evaluation

The graphics of the musical notation and the sound
are good in this program. The program is
factually correct and logically organized. The
instructions are clear, within the program, and
can be bypassed by those users already familiar
with them. Although the program is not
personalized, the game format and the scoring
provide motivation. There are no prompts once the
user is working on an exercise; if the user has
not gone through the instructions (s)he will not
know what to do. Wrong answers lead to many
chances to try again, but no hints.

When the time comes for the user to select a
difficulty level, (s)he is given a choice of (1)
simple to (9) complex. No further information
about the levels is available within the program.
One must look in the documentation in order to
make an intelligent decision regarding a starting
level.

The program has one rather aggravating feature.
After the Roman numeral has been selected and
entered successfully, the user is ready to select
a figured bass symbol for the inversion. If a
mistake is made in choosing the inversion, the
user must start all over again and reenter the
Roman numeral, something that has already been
judged to be correct.

One nice feature of the program is that it uses
both upper case and lower case Roman numerals for
major and minor respectively, and the "degree"
sign for diminished chords.

It is unfortunate that both the documentation and
the instructions within the program neglect to
inform the Apple IIe user that the <CAPS LOCK> key
must be depressed in order to make any responses.

***

Harmony Drills: Set I by Bruce Benward and J.
Timothy Kolosick, Micro Music Software Library,
1981, published by Temporal Acuity Products, Inc.,
1982, version 2.2.

Hardware: Apple II series computer with at least
48K memory, 3.3 Disk II drive with controller,
video monitor; MMI DAC music card and headphones
required.

Cost: $90

Publisher's suggested audience: High School to
adult.

Documentation: A user's guide includes
prerequisite skills and knowledge, as well as
details about the program.

Description

This program drills aural recognition of diatonic
chord progressions from simple tonic and dominant
root position chords to more complex patterns
using all diatonic chords in root position and
tonic chords in second inversion. The user is
asked to provide only the Roman numeral and

inversion for each progression, not the musical
notation. Each chord progression is four or five
chords in length. While the program can be used
independently, it can also be used as a supplement
to Bruce Benward's text, Ear Training, A Technique
for Listening, Wm. C. Brown, publisher.

The progressions are pre-composed, systematically
ordered, and provide increasingly more difficult
patterns. The program is divided into five
levels. The twenty progressions in Level 1
include tonic and dominant in root position and
first inversion, and tonic in second inversion.
Level 2, with twenty progressions, uses tonic,
subdominant, and dominant in root position only.
Level 3 uses tonic, supertonic, and dominant in
root position only in fifteen progressions. The
twenty progressions in Level 4 use tonic,
supertonic, subdominant, dominant, and submediant
in root position and first inversion, and tonic in
second inversion. Level 5, with twenty
progressions, uses all diatonic chords in root
position and first inversion, and tonic in second
inversion.

The program displays a menu of Roman numeral and
chord inversion choices, establishes the key, and
then plays a chord progression. Only three keys
are used to respond. The left and right arrow
keys are used to point to the appropriate chord
symbol and inversion for each chord in the
progression, and the <SPACE BAR> is used to enter
the user's response. The user may hear the
progressions as many times as needed, may have the
key established any time, may see the correct
answer, including the actual musical notation and
the chord symbols, if needed, and can continue in
the preset sequence or jump ahead.

After all chords are entered the program indicates
which ones are correct and which are incorrect.
However, no score is kept.

Evaluation

This program is factually correct and logically
organized. The instructions are clear, within the
program, and can be bypassed by those users
already familiar with them. The prompts are clear
and consistent, as are the methods of response.

The user may hear the progression repeated and try
as many times as needed to give the correct
response without fear of penalty, and there are no
time restraints. However, without being
personalized and without a game format, this
program relies heavily on the user's ability to be
self-motivated.

It is unfortunate that both the documentation and
the instructions within the program neglect to
inform the Apple IIe user that the <CAPS LOCK> key
must be depressed throughout the program in order
to make any responses.

***

Hear Today...Play Tomorrow by Penny Pursell,
Electronic Courseware Systems, Inc., 1985. A
series of three disks entitled Ear Training
Skills, Descending/Ascending Intervals, and Find
That Tune.

Hardware: Commodore 64 or 128, one disk drive,
monitor (color monitor optional). Also available
for Apple II+ or IIe with at least 48K, or IIc
with at least 128K, one disk drive, and monitor.

Cost: $39.95 for each disk; $99.95 for the set of
three disks.

Publisher's suggested audience: None stated.

Documentation: Brief description on back of
diskette box; brief pamphlet regarding instructor
management options.

Description

This set of programs provides drill and practice
in melodic fragment dictation, aural
identification of intervals, constructing
intervals, and matching the notation of a melody
with its sound. Each disk provides several
difficulty levels and record keeping capabilities
for the instructor. All the programs use the
left/right and up/down cursor keys, allow the user
to hear exercises repeatedly by pressing the <R>
key, and allow the user to quit the program by

pressing the <F1> key. At the end of each set of
exercises the program provides the user's current
score by stating how many exercises were attempted
and what the percentage of correct answers was.
Each set of exercises insists that twenty problems
be completed with 80% accuracy.

Ear Training Skills provides drill in the aural
identification and notation of intervals and
melodic fragments. Each of the six levels on the
disk use only the treble clef; each level also
includes instructions.

In Levels 1 and 2, the user hears simple five-note
melodic fragments using stepwise motion and tonic
triad arpeggiation in C Major. The staff, clef,
and middle C are displayed on the screen. The
user enters scale degree numbers under the staff
and then places the corresponding notes on the
staff using the cursor keys.

In Level 3, the program plays a diatonic interval
and displays a staff, clef, and the bottom note
(always the tonic) of the interval on the screen;
theee user types in the name of the interval by
typing a number from 1 to 8 (interval quality is
not required in this program), and then places the
second note in the proper location on the staff by
using the cursor keys. The user may choose the
major key or keys to be used in this level from
key signatures up to five sharps and five flats.

Level 4 provides an option to review diatonic
intervals and then plays five-note C Major melodic
patterns including all diatonic intervals. The
user enters the scale degree numbers under the
staff provided on the screen, and then notates the
corresponding pitches on the staff through the use
of the cursor keys.

Level 5 continues the drills of levels 1, 2, and
4, but also allows the user to choose major keys
up to five sharps and flats to be used in the
drills. After a short tutorial on the scale
degree numbers in minor keys, Level 6 allows the
user to choose minor keys up to five sharps and
flats for the exercises which follow.

Descending/Ascending Intervals provides drills in
the aural identification and notation of
intervals, as well as practice in melodic and
rhythmic dictation. The programs on this disk
only drill the numeric size of the interval, not
its quality.

Level 1 plays descending diatonic intervals in
major scales with the tonic being the first note.
The user may choose to work in major keys up to
five sharps and five flats. A staff, clef, and
first note of the interval are displayed on the
screen. After hearing the interval, the user
identifies its size by pressing a number key and
then notates the second note by using the cursor
keys.

The exercises in Level 2 include both ascending
and descending diatonic intervals in major keys in
the bass clef. Level 3 continues the exercises of
Level 2, but in treble clef.

Level 4, "Write That Tune," provides three types
of dictation: pitch only, rhythm only, or pitch
and rhythm combined. The melodic material used is
based on familiar children's songs such as
"Twinkle Twinkle" or "Are You Sleeping," is
usually eight measures long, always in the key of
C Major, and always in treble clef. In the pitch
dictation section, staves, clef, bar lines, and
the rhythmic values for each measure are
displayed. After hearing the whole tune and then
each phrase, the user enters the pitches by using
the cursor keys. In the rhythmic dictation
section, pitches of each measure are displayed as
whole notes. After hearing the melody and then
each phrase, the user enters the rhythmic values
for each pitch by selecting from a range of note
values displayed on the bottom of the screen. In
the dictations involving both pitch and rhythm,
the pitches are entered first and then the
rhythmic values using the same procedures listed
above.

In Find That Tune the user sees three melodies or
portions of melodies displayed on the screen.
These melodies are either familiar children's
tunes in Level 1, or isolated phrases from
familiar works in Level 2. The program then plays
a melody, and the user must select the melody

notated on the screen which matches the melody
heard. The program may play a melody which is not
on the screen, in which case the user selects the
"None of the above" option. Level 1, the beginner
level, uses only melodies in treble clef, while
Level 2, the intermediate level includes melodies
in bass and treble clefs. In Level 2, a melody
notated on the screen in treble clef will not be
accepted as an answer when that same melody is
played in the bass clef.

Evaluation

The graphics of musical notation are fair
(although pairs of eighth notes are not beamed),
and the sound is quite good in these programs.
However, the operating instructions, both in the
documentation and within the program, are
inadequate. While the prompts are consistent,
they are not clear. In Ear Training Skills, the
user is never instructed to enter all the scale
degree numbers before pressing <RETURN>, and then
to place all the pitches on the staff before
pressing <RETURN> again. The instructions lead
the user to think that the <RETURN> key should be
pressed in order to enter each scale degree number
and after each pitch is placed on the staff.

In the interval identification section of Ear
Training Skills the user is asked to type in the
name of the interval. There is no prompt,
however, telling the user to type in the word
"unison" or "octave" (the way they are introduced
in the tutorial), or just a number from 1 through
8. Find That Tune asks the user to provide his or
her response by entering a letter from "A" to "D."
However, when (s)he does this nothing happens;
none of the instructions informs the user that he
must press the <RETURN> key in order to enter each
answer.

For the most part, these programs are factually
correct, although a mistake was noted in the
notation of one of the melodies in Find That Tune.
User errors lead to second tries, but no hints are
given. After the second error, the program
provides the correct response. The method of
response is not consistent throughout. While most
responses are "entered" by pressing the <RETURN>
key, the user must press the <SPACE BAR> in order

to enter the rhythmic values in "Write That Tune."
In order to change from "pitch only" dictation to
either of the other types of dictation in "Write
That Tune," the user must press the <F1> key,
taking him or her all the way back to the main
menu.

While the exercises are randomly generated, one
would have to question the replay value of Find
That Tune. The number of melodies or melodic
phrases is so limited that the tunes are repeated
quite often.

***

Interval Drillmaster by Gerald W. Chastain,
CONDUIT, 1985.

Hardware: Apple II+, IIe, or IIc with a minimum
of 48K, single disk drive, and monitor; ALF
synthesizer card (although the sound may be sent
through the Apple speaker). Headphones and an
amplifier may be desirable.

Cost: $75

Publisher's suggested audience: Grade school,
high school, junior college or college level
students.

Documentation: Includes a "Student Guide,"
"Instructor's Notes," and a copy of the "Self-
Evaluation Sheet" for duplication. Operating
instructions are included.

Description

Interval Drillmaster is an interval dictation
program. This program consists of a graduated
series of drills and tests in identifying and
constructing ascending and descending intervals in
bass and treble clef. Compound intervals (those
greater than an octave) are not included, all
intervals are played melodically, and no double
accidentals are included. While there are eleven
levels of exercises, each level can be used for
interval identification or for notating the second

note of the interval. The user has the option of
taking each level as a drill or as a timed test.

The opening menu allows the user to sign on,
enroll for the first time, or use the program
without enrolling. The user then chooses to work
in melodic interval identification or melodic
interval dictation. The levels from which the
user may choose include the following: 1)
ascending perfect unisons and fourths, and major
seconds and sevenths; 2) ascending minor and major
thirds, tritones, major sixths, and perfect
octaves; 3) ascending minor thirds, perfect
fifths, and minor sixths and sevenths; 4)
descending perfect unisons and fourths, and major
seconds and sevenths; 5) descending minor and
major thirds, tritones, major sixths, and perfect
octaves; 6) descending minor thirds, perfect
fifths, and minor sixths and sevenths; 7)
ascending and descending major seconds, sixths and
sevenths, and perfect fourths; 8) ascending and
descending minor seconds, major thirds, tritones,
and perfect octaves; 9) levels 7 and 8 combined;
10) ascending and descending minor thirds, sixths,
and sevenths, and perfect fifths; and 11) all the
intervals both ascending and descending.

"Melodic Interval Identification" plays intervals
for the user to identify by choosing (using the
arrow keys) the appropriate interval from a
multiple choice list.

In "Melodic Interval Dictation," whether the user
chooses to be drilled or to be tested, a staff,
clef, and first note of the exercise are displayed
on the screen. After hearing the interval, the
user selects the line or space (using the arrow
keys) on which the second note belongs and chooses
an accidental, if necessary, which is also
displayed on the staff.

An "Error Report" can be requested. This report
provides information regarding the intervals
missed and whether they were ascending or
descending. The user can then see and hear each
error.

The drill exercises offer immediate feedback. If
an error is made, the user is given a second
chance and provided with information regarding the

mistake; "No, too small" is a typical response.
The wrong interval will then be played. After a
second wrong answer, the program provides the
correct answer. If the user chooses the timed
tests, he must identify or notate the interval
within ten seconds. The user must do 48 exercises
and supply 34 correct responses in order to
complete a level. No feedback is provided until
all the exercises are completed or until the user
requests an "Error Report."

Through "Summary Reports," the user can keep track
of his or her progress on self-evaluation forms
included in the "Student Guide." In addition, the
disk provides a record keeping utility for up to
85 students.

Evaluation

This program is logically organized and factually
correct. While the prompts are consistent, they
are not very clear unless the user reads the
documentation. The graphics of music notation are
only fair, and the sound, even when using the ALF
synthesizer card, is not remarkable.

One of the nicer features of this program is that
the user has a great deal of control over the
order of the materials. Not only can the user
select varying levels of difficulty, but (s)he can
also build his or her own set of exercises. The
user can choose ascending or descending intervals,
which intervals are to be drilled, and how much
time should be allotted. One can leave a drill or
test at any time and choose some other activity.
In the timed test drills, the user may accelerate
the ten second pace by pressing <C> in order to
proceed to the next example before the allotted
time has expired.

One feature of the program may be bothersome to
some users. While the list of responses is
displayed vertically on the screen, one must use
the left and right arrow keys to make selections.

The documentation and the instructions within the
program neglect to inform the Apple IIe user that
the <CAPS LOCK> key must be depressed throughout
the program.

* * *

Interval Mania by David B. Williams, Julia
Schulze, and David L. Shrader, Micro Music
Software Library, 1980, published by Temporal
Acuity Products, Inc., 1981, version 2.3.

Hardware: Apple II series computer with at least
48K memory, 3.2 or 3.3 Disk II drive with
controller, video monitor; MMI DAC music card and
headphones required.

Cost: $150

Publisher's suggested audience: Fourth grade
to adult.

Documentation: A user's guide includes teaching
objectives, prerequisite skills and knowledge, as
well as details about the program and information
about teacher options.

Description

In game format, this program drills the user in
the aural and visual identification of musical
intervals. An hour glass with running sand
provides the game with incentive, the object being
to identify correctly as many intervals as
possible before time runs out. At each session
the user chooses the visual or aural mode of
presentation, selects the sizes and qualities of
the intervals to be worked on, chooses to work in
the treble clef, bass clef or the grand staff, and
chooses whether to play as an "Amateur," "Semi-
professional," or "Professional." This latter
selection determines how many points will be
awarded for each correct response. Amateurs
receive more points per correct answer than do
professionals. Once the variables are defined,
the program picks the intervals at random. The
intervals are played both harmonically and
melodically at random and are played only once
before they are to be identified.

In the visual mode the program displays an
interval on a staff with clef sign and sounds the
interval. The user chooses the correct interval
size and the correct interval quality by using the
left and right arrow keys to point at multiple
choice answers. The choices on the left side of
the screen include abbreviated interval quality

terms, "MAJ/MIN/DIM/AUG/PRF." The choices on the
right side of the screen are the numbers, one
through eight, signifying the size of the
interval. After the arrow is moved to the quality
or size of interval desired, the user presses the
<SPACE BAR> to enter the answer. The aural mode
is similar except that the program sounds the
interval without displaying the notation. Only
after the correct size and quality is identified,
will the program display the interval in notation.
The choices for quality in the aural mode are
"MAJ/MIN/PRF/TRITONE."

As responses are made, sound effects are played
informing the user that answers are right or
wrong. The program keeps a running scoreboard of
progress on the screen showing the following:
rounds played, total points, bonus points, and
grand total.

Evaluation

The program is logically organized and factually
correct, and the graphics of musical notation and
the hour glass are good. The sound, on the other
hand, is only fair. It is especially difficult to
discern the pitch of intervals played in low
registers.

The instructions are clear, within the program,
and may be bypassed by users already familiar with
them. Instructions cannot be requested during the
game, however, and with only an "arrow" blinking
on the screen, a user unfamiliar with the program
would not know what to do. Errors lead to two
more tries, but no hints. After the third wrong
answer, the program displays the correct answer.

The method of response is consistent throughout
the program. For a timed game, however, the
procedure of having to move the arrow to the
desired quality, hit the <SPACE BAR>, wait for the
program to move the arrow to the right side of the
screen, then move the arrow again to the desired
interval size, and hit the <SPACE BAR> a second
time is very time consuming and costs the user
points.

One feature of the program allows the teacher to
"preset" each of the parameters in the game. The

teacher can decide what sizes and qualities of
intervals the students will identify, whether the
drill will be visual or aural, what clefs will be
used, and what the difficulty level will be.

It is unfortunate that both the documentation and
the instructions within the program neglect to
inform the Apple IIe user that the <CAPS LOCK> key
must be depressed throughout the program in order
to enter any responses.

***

Intervals by Vincent Oddo, Electronic Courseware
Systems, Inc., 1984.

See Aural Skills Trainer.

***

Italian Terms by David Williams, Al Blackford and
Julie Schulze, Micro Music Software Library,
published by Temporal Acuity Products, Inc., 1981.

Hardware: Apple II series computer with at least
48K memory, 3.2 or 3.3 Disk II drive with
controller, video monitor; MMI DAC music card and
headphones required only if sound effects are
desired.

Cost: $50

Publisher's suggested audience: Junior high to
university.

Documentation: A user's guide includes the
objectives of the program, a summary, prerequisite
skills and knowledge, operating instructions, and
instructions for changing any options.

Description

In game format, this program provides drill and
practice in identifying Italian musical terms from
their definitions, spelling the terms, and
recalling them when given their definitions. The

user may select among three methods of drill, three speed levels, and three categories of Italian musical terms.

In "Select-a-Term," a definition of an Italian musical term is displayed on the screen, and the user must select the appropriate term among the multiple choice answers provided. In "Spell-a-Term," a musical term appears briefly on the screen and then disappears; the user must type the term with absolutely correct spelling. In "Recall-a-Term," a definition of an Italian musical term is again displayed, and the user must type the term with absolute precision without benefit of multiple choice answers or seeing the term displayed even briefly.

While the user may select a response time (slow, medium, or fast), the program automatically increases or decreases the speed based upon the user's performance during the drill.

The user may choose among three sets of Italian musical terms: terms for tempo and dynamics, expressive terms, and directions for performers.

When the user "quits," a "Report Card" is displayed providing level attained, speed, number of tries, number correct, and the percentage of correct responses. There is no long-term record keeping.

Evaluation

The sound effects (although optional) in this program are good; their only purpose is to provide motivation when the user's response is correct (fragments from musical literature in major keys, fanfares) and to admonish when the response is incorrect (fragments from musical literature in minor keys). The program uses a personalized approach by providing comments to the user followed by his or her name.

The program is factually correct. The instructions are clear, within the program, and can be bypassed if not needed. However, instructions cannot be recalled during the program if the user requires some review. The program

presents clear and consistent prompts, and the
screen is neat and uncluttered. The program
allows second tries if an answer is incorrect,
although it does not provide any hints. After the
second wrong answer, the program provides the
correct one.

One has to question the publisher's suggested
audience for this program. The typing skills
required in order to enter responses, especially
in timed drills such as these, go beyond not only
the skills of junior high students, but also
beyond the typing abilities of most adults. Since
running out of time counts as an error, many
novice typists, no matter how thorough their
musical knowledge, would find the program very
frustrating.

The program lacks specific information regarding
the use of the <CAPS LOCK> key on the Apple IIe
computer. In order to respond to certain prompts
at the beginning of the program and in order to
type the spelling of Italian terms in the spell
and recall sections of the program, the <CAPS
LOCK> key must be depressed.   Neither the written
documentation nor the prompts and instructions
within the program inform the user about this
necessity.

***

Jazz Dictator by J. Timothy Kolosick, Dan Haerle
and David B. Williams, Micro Music Software
Library, published by Temporal Acuity Products,
Inc., 1985, version 1.42.

Hardware: Apple II, II+, or IIe computer with a
minimum of 48K memory, 3.3 Disk II drive with
controller, video monitor; MMI DAC music card and
headphones required.

Cost: $150

Publisher's suggested audience: Secondary and
university.

Documentation: A user's guide includes teaching
objectives, prerequisite skills and knowledge,
operating instructions, and details about the
program.

Description

In game format, this program drills aural
recognition of chord progressions with chords of
equal duration in jazz style. The user identifies
the Roman numeral function of each chord as well
as individual chord qualities. In later levels,
the user must also decide whether the bass note
has been altered or remains diatonic. The user
must choose among multiple choice answers. The
program uses major and minor keys through four
flats and four sharps; the progressions are from
four to six chords in length. The user may choose
from nine levels of complexity. Chords included
are major sevenths, minor sevenths, dominant
sevenths, half-diminished sevenths, and fully-
diminished sevenths. All the chords are in root
position. The major and minor seventh chords may
have added ninths, while the dominant sevenths
always have added ninths and sometimes
thirteenths. The user identifies only the quality
of the triad with its seventh, disregarding ninths
and thirteenths.

The user selects one of the nine levels to begin
working, decides whether the levels will be self-
adjusting based on his or her performance or
locked at one level, chooses major or minor keys
or both, and decides whether or not to have sound
effects. The program displays a grand staff with
clefs, the first chord notated on the staff and
correct analysis under it, a list of chord-quality
names and a list of Roman numerals for the roots
of the chords. Left and right arrow keys are used
to select answers and the <SPACE BAR> is used to
enter responses. The user may rehear the
progression, by pressing the <R> key, or re-
establish the sound of the tonal center, by
pressing <E>, at any time. After a progression is
completed, the program displays the present level
in which the user is working, the error points,
the number of rehearings the user required, the
score up to that point and a percentage score.
There is no record keeping on the disk.

Evaluation

The graphics of musical notation and the sound are good in this program. The program is logically organized and factually correct. The instructions are clear, within the program, and can be bypassed by those familiar with them. The prompts are clear and consistent, as are the methods of response. Mistakes lead to second tries as well as hints displayed on the screen, such as "Wrong Quality" or "Wrong Roman Numeral." The sound effects following a right answer are different than those following a wrong answer.

The user may quit during the program, but only after completing an exercise. If the user is perplexed and cannot finish an exercise, (s)he must enter dummy answers in order to get to a place in the program which allows him or her to quit and go back to the index and choose another level. The user cannot review the instructions during the program.

***

Key Signature Drill, by John M. Eddins and Robert L. Weiss. Electronic Courseware Systems, Inc., 1981, 1983, 1984.

See Elements of Music.

***

Key Signature Drills by George Makas, Micro Music Software Library, 1981, published by Temporal Acuity Products, Inc., 1982, version 1.1.

Hardware: Apple II, II+ or IIe computer with at least 48K memory, 3.2 or 3.3 Disk II drive with controller, video monitor; MMI DAC music card and headphones required.

Cost: $60

Publisher's suggested audience: Fourth grade to university.

Documentation: A user's guide includes the
learning objectives of the program, a summary,
prerequisite skills and knowledge, and operating
instructions.

Description

This program provides drill and practice in aural
and visual identification of key signatures, as
well as a game requiring the aural identification
of key signatures under time pressures. "Aural
identification" in this case means identifying a
key signature displayed on the screen after
hearing a scale played in the key, and determining
whether the key signature represents a major or a
minor key. In both the drills and the game, the
user chooses the tempo at which the scale is to be
played.

In "Aural Identification," after the user enters a
number from five to thirty (to indicate the tempo
of the scale), a grand staff with key signature in
both clefs is displayed on the screen. The user
hears a major or a harmonic minor scale played;
(s)her then identifies the key signature by
entering a letter name, <A> through <G>, then <F>,
<S>, or <N> (for flat, sharp, or natural), and a
<J> for major or an <N> for minor. The user may
hear the scale played again by pressing the <R>
key and may quit at any time by pressing <ESC>ape.

Each exercise in "Visual Identification" also
displays the grand staff and a key signature in
both clefs. The user is also asked to indicate
the tempo of the scale. Instead of playing a
scale, however, the scale of the exercise is
notated on the grand staff. The key signature is
identified by using the same keys as those
employed in "Aural Identification." The scale is
not played until after the user responds with the
correct key and mode.

The third program is a game requiring aural
identification of key and mode with time
constraints. First, the user chooses among
"Amateur," "Semi-professional," or "Professional"
to indicate the tempo of the playing of the scale.
This program is self-adjusting. If the user
responds correctly less time is given to answer on

the next exercise; more time is given when the
user errs.

The user's score is continually displayed on the
screen. When the user quits, the percentage
correct is displayed along with the number of
items attempted. Record keeping is not included
on the disk.

Evaluation

This program is factually correct and logically
organized. Although the instructions address only
the aural identification aspect of the program,
they are clear, within the program, and can be
bypassed by users already familiar with them.
Prompts informing the user what keys to press in
order to respond are displayed on each screen and
are clear and consistent. However, their
inclusion makes the screen somewhat cluttered.

Errors on the part of the user do not lead to
second chances or hints. When a mistake is made,
the program immediately displays the correct
answer.

The use of the letters <J> to indicate major and
<N> to indicate minor may bother some users.
Furthermore, the <S>, <F>, and <N> keys are not
only used to enter sharp, flat and natural
responses, but the letters produced by these keys
are actually printed on the screen. Thus a user's
response for C-sharp minor appears on the screen
as "CSN." If the user makes a mistake, the
program displays such statements as "Your answer
was AN Major, the correct answer is CN Major."

Indicating the speed or tempo of the exercises
using the numbers 5 through 30, with the lower
number being the faster tempo, seems inappropriate
in a program aimed at musicians. Musicians are
more familiar with metronome markings, which
get smaller as the tempo becomes slower.

It is unfortunate that both the documentation and
the instructions within the program neglect to
inform the Apple IIe user that the <CAPS LOCK> key
must be depressed throughout the program in order
to make responses.

***

Keyboard Note Drill, by John M. Eddins and Robert
L. Weiss. Electronic Courseware Systems, Inc.,
1981, 1983, 1984.

See Elements of Music.

* * *

Keyboard Note Reading/Keyboard Speed Note Reading
by Virgil Hicks (the University of Akron Series),
Wenger Corporation, 1981. This program is now
included in The Music Class: Note Reading, part
of the Music Class Series.

Hardware: Apple II, II+, or IIe with a minimum of
64K, one disk drive, video monitor, game paddles;
ALF synthesizer card, headphones optional (the
sound can be routed through the computer's
internal speaker). Also available for the
Commodore 64 or 128 and in a MIDI version.

Cost: $69 (same for both Apple and Commodore
versions).

Publisher's suggested audience: Elementary:
beginning music students; Intermediate: students
who can read basic music.

Documentation: Brief descriptive pamphlet
includes a summary, operating instructions, and
instructions for changing any options.

Description

"Keyboard Note Reading" provides drill and
practice in translating musical notation to the
keyboard. The user may choose to be drilled on
treble clef, bass clef, treble and bass clef, or
treble and bass clef with ledger lines. A grand
staff is displayed with a piano keyboard displayed
beneath it. A note is displayed on the staff and
the user moves the cursor to the proper key on the
keyboard by turning the game paddle. When a
mistake is made, arrows appear pointing either to
the left or to the right, indicating that the note
requested is either to the right or to the left of

the one the user has indicated. The program
insists on the proper register.

"Keyboard Note Speed Reading" provides a speed
game for naming keyboard notes in the same manner
as above. The user can choose among seven speed
levels from Lento to Presto. The program
continuously displays the number of correct and
incorrect responses. The program provides a
Manager Utility for student record keeping
(optional) and for setting standards for student
ratings. The user must locate twenty notes in
order for the score to be saved by the record
keeping program.

Evaluation

The program is logically organized and factually
correct. The instructions are within the program
and cannot be bypassed. (They are very brief
anyway.) However, in order to see the
instructions during the program, the user must go
back to the main menu. Going back to the main
menu is also the way in which the user can quit
the program. The difficulty level of the program
is adjustable by the user by choosing from among
the various speed levels of the drill. These
choices are made using musical tempo terms.

The program also allows passwords in addition to
student names for long-term record keeping.

***

LISTEN! A Music Skills Program by Vincent Oddo,
Electronic Courseware Systems, Inc., 1985. The
programs on this disk are also found in Aural
Skills Trainer, a series of three disks:
Intervals, Basic Chords, and Seventh Chords.

Hardware: Commodore 64 or 128, one disk drive,
monitor (color monitor optional). Also available
for Apple II+ or IIe with at least 48K, or Apple
IIc with at least 128K, one disk drive and
monitor, and the IBM-PC or IBM-PC JR. with at
least 128K, 360K double-sided disk drive, color
graphics card, and monitor.

Cost: $39.95

Publisher's suggested audience: None stated.

Documentation: Brief description on back of diskette box.

<h2 align="center">Description</h2>

This single diskette presents three programs designed to increase one's ability to hear intervals, basic chords (triads), and seventh chords. After hearing an interval, triad, or seventh chord (depending on the program chosen), the user provides a response by pressing one of the number keys on the computer keyboard. A chart on the screen designates which number keys on the keyboard represent various answers. The user can ask to have the interval, chord, or seventh chord played again by pressing <H>, and can also "escape" to the main menu by pressing <F1>. There are no time constraints.

In "Intervals," after hearing an interval played, the user selects the correct quality and numerical size. The user may choose among the following: "melodic-harmonic ascending," in which the interval is played first melodically, then harmonically, "melodic/harmonic descending," or "harmonic." The user then chooses how many (s)he wants to hear (10-50), and the speed at which the intervals are to be played (slow, medium, or fast). Speed does not apply to harmonic intervals. The intervals from a minor second to a perfect octave, including the tritone, are listed across the bottom of the screen with the number key used to represent them.

In "Basic Chords" the user responds to arpeggiated chords played by the program by selecting their chord quality (aug., dim., major, or minor) in "Root Position Chords" and chord quality and inversion (first or second) in "Inversions of Chords." The user also chooses the number of chords to be played (10-50), the speed at which the triads are to be arpeggiated (slow, medium, fast), and also the direction in which the triads are to be arpeggiated (up or down).

In "Seventh Chords," the user responds to
arpeggiated seventh chords played by the program
by selecting chord quality (M/m, dim, m/m, half-
diminished) in "Root Position" and chord quality
and inversion (6/5, 4/3, and 2) in "Inversions."
The user chooses the number of chords he wants to
hear (10-50), the speed at which they are to be
arpeggiated (slow, medium, or fast), and the
direction of the arpeggiation (up or down).

Each program displays the correct answer when an
incorrect answer is given, and displays the number
of exercises attempted and the number correct at
the top of the screen during the drill. At the
end of each session a score page indicates the
number attempted, the number correct, the percent
correct and a letter grade. It further displays
each interval or chord missed and how often it was
missed. Top scorers are placed in a "Hall of
Fame" with room for three names. One of the three
is erased every time a new name gets in!

Evaluation

The sounds produced by this program are quite
good. The instructions are clear, within each
program, and can be bypassed by those already
familiar with them; however, the instructions
cannot be reviewed during any of the drills. The
prompts are clear and consistent, as are the
methods of response. The program does not allow
repeated tries when mistakes are made. Instead it
says "No" and provides the correct answer. The
user may hear the item, whether interval or chord,
as many times as needed by pressing <H>.

Entering responses by using the number keys on the
computer keyboard is somewhat confusing in these
programs. The numbers designating particular
intervals, for example, do not have anything to do
with the numbers representing the sizes of the
intervals. Many users may find it hard to
associate the <5> key with a perfect fourth, or
the <+> key with a major seventh. The
instructions list the symbols "+" for augmented
and "0" for diminished, but state that they will
not be used as responses in the interval program.

Instead, one of the choices is "TT," representing
the tritone; no further explanation of this symbol
is provided.

***

The Magic Musical Balloon Game by Sally Monsour
and Charles Knox, Micro Music Software Library,
1982, published by Temporal Acuity Products, Inc.,
1984, version 1.1.

Hardware: Apple II, II+, or IIe computer with a
minimum of 48K memory, 3.3 Disk II drive with
controller, video monitor; MMI DAC music card and
headphones nice, but not required. The program
can be set to use the Apple speaker instead of the
DAC board.

Cost: $25

Publisher's suggested audience: Kindergarten to
third grade.

Documentation: A user's guide includes teaching
objectives, prerequisite skills and knowledge, as
well as details about the program.

Description

Presented in game format, this program provides
drill and practice in identifying melodic
direction by ear. The user is presented with a
short melody consisting of four fragments or
phrases. The user hears each fragment (consisting
of from three to six notes) and must decide
whether the fragment ascends, descends, or stays
on the same note. Responses are entered by
pressing the <U> key for up, the <D> key for down,
or the <S> key for same. A graphic balloon is
displayed on the screen while the various
fragments are played. When the user's response is
correct, the balloon moves in the direction of the
fragment, flying over mountains, telephone poles,
houses, high rise buildings, fences, and barns,
graphically displayed on the screen.

There are three games on the disk. Each game
consists of four melodies and each melody is made
up of four short directional fragments. In the
third game, the user's correct answers appear as
a series of notes (ascending, descending, or
repeated) placed on a five-line staff. As the
user responds to each fragment successfully, a
treble clef sign is displayed in the upper right
corner of the screen. If the direction of all
four phrases is identified correctly, there will
be four treble clef signs displayed on the screen.
At the end of each game, the user is given a score
which shows the number of phrases played (sixteen)
and tallies the number of correct responses. A
record keeping utility is not included on the
disk.

Evaluation

This program is logically organized and factually
correct. The instructions are clear, within the
program, and may be bypassed by those users
already familiar with them. The games allow
second tries, but no hints. Even if the user
misses the first time, but is successful on his
second response, the answer is counted as correct,
and a treble clef sign appears on the screen. The
prompts are clear and consistent, as are the
methods of response.

While the game format provides incentive to users
working on the program, there is no attempt at
personalization. The user also lacks control over
the pace of the program. For some users, the pace
will be too slow, for others it will be too fast.
It is also not possible to leave the program at
any time, nor is there an opportunity to indicate
which game the user is interested in playing.
Except for an opportunity given the user at the
end of each game to repeat the game or go on, the
user must experience this program from beginning
to end.

It is unfortunate that both the documentation and
the instructions within the program neglect to
inform the Apple IIe user that the <CAPS LOCK> key
must be depressed throughout the program in order
to make any responses.

***

Major Scale Tutorial/Minor Scale Tutorial by
Virgil Hicks, published by Wenger Corporation (the
University of Akron Series), 1981. These two
programs are now part of The Music Class:
Fundamentals, from The Music Class Series.

Hardware: Apple II, II+, or IIe, one disk drive,
video monitor, game paddles, ALF synthesizer card,
headphones (although sound can be routed through
the computer's internal speaker). Also available
in a MIDI version.

Cost: $69

Publisher's suggested audience: Elementary:
beginning music students; Intermediate: students
who can read basic music.

Documentation: Brief descriptive pamphlet gives a
summary, operating instructions, and instructions
for teacher options.

Description

Major Scale Tutorial explains the structure of the
major scale as a combination of whole and half
steps. The user constructs the C, F, and G major
scales on a treble staff as part of the tutorial.
The tutorial is followed by a drill in which major
scales are randomly selected for the user to
construct. The user must "notate" accidentals
while constructing the scale; but once the scale
is finished, the program places them into a key
signature. A piano keyboard is displayed
throughout each session.

Minor Scale Tutorial explains the structure of the
natural, melodic, and harmonic minor scales.
After the user has constructed one of each, the
next scales are randomly selected for student
construction. A piano keyboard is displayed.

Evaluation

The method of response is consistent throughout;
notes are entered on the staff with a game paddle,
while sharps and flats are entered by pressing the
<S> and <F> keys. Errors lead to repeated tries,
but no hints. Motivation is provided by scores
listing the number of attempts versus the number

of correct answers, as well as by a "Hall of Fame" which lists users with high scores. At the end of each session the program provides the user with a percentage score. The program provides a Manager Utility for student record keeping and setting standards for student ratings.

The program is factually correct and logically organized. Among its strengths is the fact that it goes beyond mere scale identification and actually involves the user in scale construction. The program has replay value because it chooses the scales for construction at random. The program's Manager Utility provides teacher options which include the following: student record keeping for up to 125 students, individual sign-ons and passwords, setting or changing standards necessary for inclusion in the "Hall of Fame," and changing the sound production from the Apple speaker to the ALF synthesizer card.

The program has several weaknesses. The tutorial cannot be bypassed; the user must go through it in order to get to the drill. While the user may quit the drill at any time, the program does not state how many scales must be constructed in order for the score to be saved in the record keeping part of the program. If only a few are attempted the score is not recorded. The user is never told that (s)he must enter the accidental before entering the note (trial and error solves this). The program only involves constructing scales in the treble clef. The teacher would have to assist younger students who might have trouble reading the tutorial. The screen is somewhat cluttered with piano keyboard graphics, staff, instructions, and scoring all on the screen at once. One annoying feature is that each time the text on the bottom of the screen changes, the entire screen is erased, and the user must wait while the graphics of the piano keyboard and musical staff are displayed again and the new text finally appears on the screen.

***

MAPLE (Music Applications Programming Language
Extension) by John Miller, Electronic Courseware
Systems, Inc., 1985, version 1.1.

Hardware: Commodore 64 or 128, one disk drive,
monitor (color monitor optional).

Cost: $99.95

Publisher's suggested audience: None stated.

Documentation: Extensive manual with tutorial,
introduction, and reference section.

Description

MAPLE is an extension of the V2 BASIC language
built into the Commodore 64 and is a music
applications development system. MAPLE adds 29
additional key words, most of which relate to the
playing and scoring of music. Originally devised
to facilitate the creation of music instructional
and music tutorial programs, MAPLE is a system for
programming sound and music notation and can be
used by composers. It assumes a working knowledge
of the BASIC programming language and a
familiarity with the rudiments of music notation
and terminology. It provides the programmer with
the ability to incorporate sound and notation
graphics into BASIC programs. For example,
"STAVES T,6" creates a musical staff with treble
clef on screen row 6. "KEYSIG 2,+" indicates a
key signature of two sharps to be placed on the
staff.

The reference section of the documentation
includes descriptions of the architecture and
some of the inner workings of the MAPLE system,
memory maps, important accessible memory
locations, and a section on the redefined
character set. The set contains music notational
symbols including notes, rests, accidentals, and
chord quality symbols.

Evaluation

Creating sounds on the Commodore 64 or 128 in
BASIC is a time-consuming venture and involves
many POKE statements. The Commodore 64 and 128

have built-in synthesizers which provide the user
with three separate voices. The pitch, attack,
decay, sustain, release, duration, volume, and
waveform (triangle, sawtooth, pulse, or noise) can
be controlled for each of the three voices.
Creating the graphics necessary to produce good
musical notation using BASIC is equally time-
consuming. By extending the BASIC language built
into the Commodore, MAPLE alleviates much of the
effort in creating these musical sounds and
notation.

The codes employed in this system for representing
notes, rhythmic values, ties, accidentals, and key
signatures seem quite logical. The notation and
the sounds produced through the system are very
good. The notational convention that accidentals
do not have to be reiterated within a measure, for
example, is observed, and the user can also
control the direction of the stems on various
notes.

***

Melodic Error Detection and Correction by Virgil
Hicks (the University of Akron Series), Wenger
Corporation, 1981, 1982, 1985. This program is
now included in The Music Class: Ear Training,
part of the Music Class Series.

Hardware: Apple II, II+, or IIe with at least
64K, one disk drive, video monitor, ALF
synthesizer card, headphones optional (the sound
can be routed through the computer's internal
speaker). This program is also available in a
MIDI version.

Cost: $99

Publisher's suggested audience: Intermediate:
students who can read basic music; advanced:
students ready to compose or arrange music.

Documentation: Brief descriptive pamphlet
includes a summary, insufficient operating
instructions, and instructions for changing any
options.

Description

This ear training program provides practice in
detecting and correcting pitch errors in melodic
phrases. A melodic phrase is displayed in
notation on the screen and then played for the
user with no errors, one error, or two errors.
The user must locate each error, and correct each
one. The user may select from eleven program
levels which include melodies with the following
characteristics:

1) Stepwise melodies in major keys;
2) Major and minor thirds in major keys;
3) Melodies beginning on tones other than tonic;
4) Melodies using perfect fourths and fifths;
5) Melodies based on primary harmonies and dominant
   sevenths;
6) Melodies based on tonic, supertonic, subdominant,
   and dominant;
7) Melodic studies in the minor scale;
8) Melodies containing large leaps;
9) Melodies using chromaticism;
10) Melodic studies using tritones;
11) Modal melodies.

Errors are identified by moving the cursor with
the arrow keys and then pressing <RETURN> to mark
them. If the melody is correct the user merely
presses <C>orrect. Incorrect pitches must be
corrected either <U>p or <D>own in half-step
increments. The program is presented in a game
format. The student begins with 12 points for
each melody. Two points are deducted for each
incorrect answer while identifying errors. While
the user may hear the incorrect melody played as
often as necessary, one point is deducted for each
replay. The program provides a Utility Manager
for student record keeping (optional) and setting
standards for student ratings if the default
standards are unacceptable.

Evaluation

The graphics of the staff and notes are fine. The
prompts are consistent and so are the methods of
response. Instructions for each level can be
bypassed, and the program can be ended at any

time. The user can change the order of the
materials by selecting from the menu of levels
which, unfortunately, are not described or
defined. One has to read the written
documentation in order to determine the
characteristics of the melodies at each level.

Another unfortunate aspect of the program is
discovered when the user tries to get help during
the program. While <I>nstructions can be accessed
during the error identification part of the
program, no such instructions are available when
the user is attempting to correct the wrong
pitches, a time when the user most desperately
needs them! The written documentation offers no
help on this problem either. The program goes to
the first erroneous note and begins sustaining an
incessant pitch. Without instruction at this
point, and without the benefit of knowing whether
the pitch sounding is the notated pitch or the
wrong pitch, the user does not know what to do.
After several wrong moves, the program provides a
help screen displaying the word "correct" with a
long dash and a shorter dash either above or below
it. Without instruction, trial and error reveal
that the short dash represents the user's note,
and that by moving it to the same line as the long
dash, the user corrects the pitch.

***

Melodic/Rhythmic Dictation by Virgil Hicks (the
University of Akron Series), published by Wenger
Corporation, 1981, 1982, 1985. This program is
now included in The Music Class: Ear Training,
part of the Music Class Series.

Hardware: Apple II, II+, or IIe with a minimum of
64K, one disk drive, video monitor, ALF
synthesizer card, headphones optional (the sound
can be routed through the computer's internal
speaker); game paddle or joystick optional.

Cost: $99

Publisher's suggested audience: Intermediate:
students who can read basic music; or advanced:
students ready to compose or arrange music.

Documentation: Brief descriptive pamphlet
includes a summary, insufficient operating
instructions, and instructions for changing any
options.

Description

Melodic/Rhythmic Dictation provides drill and
practice in both melodic and rhythmic dictation.
The user may select from the following twelve
units:

1) Stepwise melodies, unmeasured; 2) melodies
including thirds, unmeasured; 3) melodies
beginning on tones not tonic; 4) melodies
with minor seconds through perfect fifths;
5) melodies based on major triads; 6) melodies
based on chord outlines; 7) melodies using
diatonic triads and scalewise motion;
8) melodies using minor scale forms and primary
triads; 9) melodies using all intervals;
10) melodies using chromaticism and minor scale
forms; 11) melodies using chromaticism and
tritones; and (12) modal melodies.

The program displays a musical staff, clef sign,
key signature, time signature, and the first note
of each melody. The tempo is regulated by the
student, and the melody may be repeated without a
scoring penalty. Through the use of the game
paddle (certain keys on the keyboard can be
substituted), the user moves a note up or down on
the staff in order to enter the pitches of the
melody. After all the pitches are entered, the
program erases wrong ones for the user to try
again, or states that all the pitches are correct.

All pitches must be correct before the rhythm can
be entered. Each pitch is then assigned a
rhythmic value by moving the cursor in order to
highlight a note value or bar line from a
selection displayed on the screen. Only correct
note values are accepted.

At the end of a unit, scores are displayed in
percentages based on correct versus attempted
answers. Separate scores are kept for both
melodic and rhythmic dictation in each unit. A

utility manager is included for student record keeping (optional) and for setting standards for student ratings. Ten melodies must be completed for the score to be saved in the record keeping program.

Evaluation

This is an educationally sound program, logically organized, and factually correct. The graphics and sound (through the ALF synthesizer card) are very good, with the exception of the program's inability to beam eighth notes, dotted eighth and sixteenth, etc. When a melody requires more than one line, the clef sign is transferred to the second staff, but not the key signature.

The programs come on two disks, with levels one through six on the first disk, and levels seven through twelve on the second. Each item on the menu of the first disk is numbered to coincide with the number of the level, while on the second disk, the numbering on the menu starts all over again with number 1 and does not coincide with the number of the level. This inconsistency is somewhat disconcerting to the user.

No instructions, either in the program or in the documentation, provide the user with any information on entering the rhythmic values of the notes. When the user presses <H>elp for information, the program merely provides the correct answer.

***

Melodious Dictator by David B. Williams, Micro Music Software Library, 1980, published by Temporal Acuity Products, Inc., 1983, version 3.0.

Hardware: Apple II, II+, or IIe computer with 48K memory, 3.2 or 3.3 Disk II drive with controller, video monitor; MMI DAC music card and headphones required.

Cost: $150

Publisher's suggested audience: Fourth grade to
adult.

Documentation: A user's guide includes the
objectives of the program, a summary, prerequisite
skills and knowledge, and operating instructions.

Description

Presented in game format, this program drills
students in hearing single line melodic fragments
and "notating" them on the treble clef staff.
(The program provides the key signature.) After
listening to the tonic triad arpeggiated and the
melodic fragment played twice, the user "notates"
the pitches on the staff using a graphic
representation of a piano keyboard displayed on
the screen. The left and right arrow keys are
used to move an arrow on the screen, pointing to
the notes on the keyboard. Once the arrow is
positioned over the appropriate key, the <SPACE
BAR> is pressed to enter the answer. The user may
hear the melodic fragment by pressing the <R> key,
but each time this is done points are taken off
the score. Pressing the <N> key causes the names
of the lines and spaces to be displayed on the
musical staff, as well as the letter names of the
keys to be displayed on the piano keyboard.

The melodic fragments use key signatures ranging
from 0 to 3 sharps or flats, including major and
minor keys. There are six ability levels from
which to choose ("tone-deaf" (1) to "super-ear"
(6)). These difficulty levels are based upon the
length of the melody (2-9 notes) and the size of
the skips employed (minor 2nd to octave). Once
the program begins, it self-adjusts the level of
difficulty based upon the user's performance.

When a session is finished the following data is
displayed on the screen: starting difficulty
level, ending difficulty level, starting length of
melody, ending length of melody, total notes
notated, total notes correct, and overall
competency in the form of a percentage score.
There is no long-term record keeping as an
instructor option.

Evaluation

The instructions are clear, within the program,
and may be bypassed by users already familiar with
them. There are reminders regarding which keys to
press displayed on the screen between each
exercise. While the prompts are clear and
consistent, the methods of response are not. When
answering questions before the drill begins, the
user must press the <RETURN> key in order to enter
a response. However, in the drill itself, the
<SPACE BAR> must be used in order to enter each
answer. The user may leave an exercise by
pressing the <Q> key. The user may also press the
<O> key to choose a different level. However,
this can only be done after an exercise is
completed. Errors lead to repeated tries, but no
hints.

The menu from which the user selects a starting
level does not provide descriptions of the
material at each level, nor are the levels
described in the documentation or instructions.
It is difficult to know what level to choose. The
graphics of the musical notation are very poor in
this program. The staff lines are very far apart,
and the note heads, as well as the sharps and
flats employed in the key signatures, are not in
proportion with the staff lines.

The documentation for the program states that the
melodic fragments are from two to seven notes in
length. Experience with the program, however,
indicates that many fragments are eight or even
nine notes long. In like manner, the
documentation states that all of the fragments
begin on the tonic or the dominant. This
statement is also not true. The fragments often
begin on scale degrees other than the tonic or
dominant.

In addition, it is unfortunate that the user may
not press a key and have the tonic triad
arpeggiated additional times while working on an
exercise. This arpeggiation is played only once
before the fragment is played, and the user never
is given an opportunity to hear it again.

The sound effect of a low descending glissando
following a user error is extremely annoying. The

program is not personalized, nor does it provide
much motivation and or positive reinforcement.

It is unfortunate that both the documentation and
the instructions within the program neglect to
inform the Apple IIe user that the <CAPS LOCK> key
must be depressed throughout the program in order
to make any responses.

                         ***

Micro-Baritone by William R. Higgins and David B.
Williams, Micro Music Software Library published
by Temporal Acuity Products, Inc., 1983, version
2.0. Part of the Micro-Brass Series Instrument
Tutors which includes Micro-Trumpet, Micro-French
Horn, and Micro-Tuba.

Hardware: Apple II series computer with at least
48K memory, 3.2 or 3.3 Disk II drive with
controller, video monitor; MMI DAC music card and
headphones required; Micro-Brass Valve Simulator
($70).

Cost: $70; or $295 for the series of four titles,
including the Micro-Brass Valve Simulator.

Publisher's suggested audience: Third grade to
university. The author states that the program is
for "beginners through advanced/intermediate brass
instrument players and for college music education
majors."

Documentation: A user's guide includes the
objectives of the program, a summary, prerequisite
skills and knowledge, and operating instructions.
The documentation also includes detailed
instructions for installing the Micro-Brass Valve
Simulator.

Description

This program provides drill and practice in
associating fingerings on the baritone horn with
pitches notated on a musical staff. The user may
choose to work in the bass clef or the treble clef
(two different disks are provided) and in either a
tutor mode or a game mode. The user enters

answers by pressing the valves on a valve
simulator, a device held in the user's hand.

After the user has chosen one of eight levels of
difficulty, and the tutor mode rather than the
game, the "Tutor" displays a note on a musical
staff with bass clef (or treble clef, if the user
chooses), a graphic display of the three baritone
valves, and the name of the note for which the
user must provide the fingering. The note is
sounded as it appears, and the user enters his or
her response by pressing the appropriate valves on
the valve simulator along with the "enter" button
on the simulator. There are no time constraints
in the "Tutor," and the user may work at his or
her own pace. If the response is correct, the
program plays a "correct" tune along with a
positive statement, such as "Right," or "Keep
going," or "Of course." If the response is
incorrect, the program plays a "wrong" tune,
prints the correct fingering at the bottom of the
screen, displays the correct fingering on the
animated valves on the screen, and provides a
comment such as "You're kidding," or "Think," or
"Sorry."

The "Game" is very much like the "Tutor" with a
few differences. After the user has selected a
game speed (slow, medium, or fast) and a
difficulty level, the program not only displays
the staff, clef and note, but also an hour glass.
Depending upon which game speed was selected, the
user has between 3 and 18 seconds in which to
enter the fingering of the note on the Micro-Brass
Valve Simulator. The object of the game is to
provide the fingering for as many notes as
possible before time runs out. The program does
not accept common alternate fingerings for notes.
If the fingering is correct, a response is
displayed, a tune is played, and points are added
to a visual score. If the wrong fingering is
indicated twice, the correct fingering is shown on
the graphic valves and printed on the bottom of
the screen. Pressing the <F> key (for "freeze")
allows the user to take a break during the game.

The descriptions of the eight levels of
difficulty, defined in both the documentation and
within the program, include the ranges and the
number of accidentals employed at each level: (1)

Cl to C2 with no accidentals, (2) Cl to C2 with
one sharp or flat, (3) B-flat 1 to E2 with two
sharps or flats, (4) A-flat 1 to G3 with three
sharps or flats, (5) A-flat 1 to G3 with four
sharps or flats, (6) A-flat 1 to A-flat 3 with
five sharps or flats, (7) G-flat 1 to C3 with six
sharps or flats, and (8) G-flat 1 to C-sharp 3
with seven sharps or flats. The information
regarding the accidentals is accurate; however,
since this information is the same for each of the
instruments in the Micro-Brass series, the octave
numbering is meaningless. While level one of
Micro-Baritone starts in a narrow range, level
eight employs pitches from the E below the bass
clef staff to the B-flat above middle C. The user
picks a level to start, and the program adjusts
the level according to the user's responses during
both the tutor and the game modes.

Evaluation

The graphics and the sound in this program are
very good, the prompts are clear and consistent,
as are the methods of response, and the program is
logically organized. Errors lead to repeated
tries, but no hints. The instructions are clear,
within the program, and may be bypassed by those
users already familiar with them. The program
asks the user to type his or her name at the
beginning. This name is used throughout the
program to personalize motivational remarks.

One cannot tell by looking at the graphic display
of the baritone valves whether they are numbered
from left to right or from right to left. While
some experimenting quickly clears up this
confusion, numbering the valves on the screen
would be helpful. The program would appeal to a
broader audience if it included a baritone with a
fourth valve and if it also drilled alternate
fingerings.

It is unfortunate that both the documentation and
the instructions within the program neglect to
inform the Apple IIe user that the <CAPS LOCK> key
must be depressed throughout the program in order
to make any responses.

***

<u>Micro-French Horn</u> by William R. Higgins and David
B. Williams, Micro Music Software Library,
published by Temporal Acuity Products, Inc., 1983,
version 2.0.   Part of the Micro-Brass Series
Instrument Tutors which includes   <u>Micro-Trumpet</u>,
<u>Micro-Baritone</u>, and <u>Micro-Tuba</u>.

Hardware: Apple II series computer with 48K
memory, 3.2 or 3.3 Disk II drive with controller,
video monitor; MMI DAC music card and headphones
required; Micro-Brass Valve Simulator ($70).

Cost: $70; or $295 for the series of four titles,
including the Micro-Brass Valve Simulator.

Publisher's suggested audience: Third grade to
university.   The author states that the program is
for "beginners through advanced/intermediate brass
instrument players and for college music education
majors."

Documentation: A user's guide includes the
objectives of the program, a summary, prerequisite
skills and knowledge, and operating instructions.
The documentation also includes detailed
instructions for installing the Micro-Brass Valve
Simulator.

Description

This program provides drill and practice in
associating fingerings on the French horn with
pitches notated on a musical staff.   The program
also provides the sound of the pitches as they are
displayed on the screen.   The user may choose to
work in either a tutor mode or a game mode.   The
user enters answers by pressing the valves on a
valve simulator, a device held in the user's hand.

After the user has chosen one of eight levels of
difficulty, and the tutor mode rather than the
game, the "Tutor" displays a note on a musical
staff with treble clef, a graphic display of the
three French horn valves, and the name of the note
for which the user must provide the fingering.
The note is sounded as it appears, and the user
enters his or her response by pressing the
appropriate valves on the valve simulator along
with the "enter" button on the simulator.   There
are no time constraints in the "Tutor", so the

user may work at his or her own pace. If the
response is correct, the program plays a "correct"
tune along with a positive statement, such as
"Right," or "Keep going," or "Of course." If the
response is incorrect, the program plays a "wrong"
tune, prints the correct fingering at the bottom
of the screen, displays the correct fingering on
the animated valves on the screen, and provides a
comment such as "You're kidding," or "Think," or
"Sorry."

The "Game" is very much like the "Tutor" with a
few differences. After the user has selected a
game speed (slow, medium, or fast) and a
difficulty level, the program not only displays
the staff, clef and note, but also an hour glass.
Depending upon which game speed was selected, the
user has between 3 and 18 seconds in which to
enter the fingering of the note on the Micro-Brass
Valve Simulator. The object of the game is to
provide the fingering for as many notes as
possible before time runs out. The program does
not accept common alternate fingerings for notes.
If the fingering is correct, a response is
displayed, a tune is played, and points are added
to a visual score. If the wrong fingering is
indicated twice, the correct fingering is shown on
the graphic valves and printed on the bottom of
the screen. Pressing the <F> key (for "freeze")
allows the user to take a break during the game.

The descriptions of the eight levels of
difficulty, defined in both the documentation and
within the program, include the ranges and the
number of accidentals employed at each level: (1)
C1 to C2 with no accidentals, (2) C1 to C2 with
one sharp or flat, (3) B-flat 1 to E2 with two
sharps or flats, (4) A-flat 1 to G3 with three
sharps or flats, (5) A-flat 1 to G3 with four
sharps or flats, (6) A-flat 1 to A-flat 3 with
five sharps or flats, (7) G-flat 1 to C3 with six
sharps or flats, and (8) G-flat 1 to C-sharp 3
with seven sharps or flats. The information
regarding the accidentals is accurate; however,
since this information is the same for each of the
instruments in the Micro-Brass series, the octave
numbering is meaningless. While level one of
Micro-French Horn starts in a narrow range, level
eight employs pitches from the E-flat below middle
C to the B-flat above the treble clef staff. The

user picks a level to start, and the program
automatically adjusts the level according to the
user's responses during both the tutor and the
game modes.

Evaluation

The prompts in this program are clear and
consistent, as are the methods of response, and
the program is logically organized. Errors lead
to repeated tries, but no hints. The instructions
are clear, within the program, and may be bypassed
by those users already familiar with them. The
program asks the user to type his or her name at
the beginning. This name is used throughout the
program to personalize motivational remarks.

One cannot tell by looking at the graphic display
of the French horn valves whether they are
numbered from left to right or from right to left.
While some experimenting quickly clears up this
confusion, numbering the valves on the screen
would be helpful. The program would appeal to a
broader audience if it included a French horn with
four valves as well as alternate fingerings.

It is unfortunate that both the documentation and
the instructions within the program neglect to
inform the Apple IIe user that the <CAPS LOCK> key
must be depressed throughout the program in order
for the program to accept the user's responses.

***

Micro-Trumpet by William R. Higgins and David B.
Williams, Micro Music Software Library, published
by Temporal Acuity Products, Inc., 1983, version
2.0. Part of the Micro-Brass Series Instrument
Tutors which includes Micro-French Horn, Micro-
Baritone, and Micro-Tuba.

Hardware: Apple II series computer with 48K
memory, 3.2 or 3.3 Disk II drive with controller,
video monitor; MMI DAC music card and headphones
required; Micro-Brass Valve Simulator ($70).

Cost: $70; or $295 for the series of four titles, including the Micro-Brass Valve Simulator.

Publisher's suggested audience: Third grade to university.   The author states that the program is for "beginners through advanced/intermediate brass instrument players and for college music education majors."

Documentation: A user's guide includes the objectives of the program, a summary, prerequisite skills and knowledge, and operating instructions. The documentation also includes detailed instructions for installing the Micro-Brass Valve Simulator.

Description

This program provides drill and practice in associating fingerings on the trumpet with pitches notated on a musical staff.   See <u>Micro-French Horn</u> for further description.

While level one of <u>Micro-Trumpet</u> starts in a narrow range, level eight employs pitches from the G below middle C to the C two octaves above middle C.   The user picks a level to start, and the program automatically adjusts the level according to the user's responses during both the tutor and the game modes.

Evaluation

The prompts in this program are clear and consistent, as are the methods of response, and the program is logically organized.   Errors lead to repeated tries, but no hints.   The instructions are clear, within the program, and may be bypassed by those users already familiar with them.   The program asks the user to type his or her name at the beginning.   This name is used throughout the program to personalize motivational remarks.

One cannot tell by looking at the graphic display of the trumpet valves whether they are numbered from left to right or from right to left.   While some experimenting quickly clears up this confusion, numbering the valves on the screen would be helpful.   The program would appeal to a

broader audience if it included alternate
fingerings.

It is unfortunate that both the documentation and
the instructions and prompts within the program
neglect to inform the Apple IIe user that the
<CAPS LOCK> key must be depressed throughout the
program in order for the user to make any
responses.

***

Micro-Tuba by William R. Higgins and David B.
Williams, Micro Music Software Library, published
by Temporal Acuity Products, Inc., 1983, version
2.0. Part of the Micro-Brass Series Instrument
Tutors which includes Micro-Trumpet, Micro-French
Horn, and Micro-Baritone.

Hardware: Apple II series computer with 48K
memory, 3.2 or 3.3 Disk II drive with controller,
video monitor; MMI DAC music card and headphones
required; Micro-Brass Valve Simulator ($70).

Cost: $70; or $295 for the series of four titles,
including the Micro-Brass Valve Simulator.

Publisher's suggested audience: Third grade to
university. The author states that the program is
for "beginners through advanced/intermediate brass
instrument players and for college music education
majors."

Documentation: A user's guide includes the
objectives of the program, a summary, prerequisite
skills and knowledge, and operating instructions.
The documentation also includes detailed
instructions for installing the Micro-Brass Valve
Simulator.

Description

This program provides drill and practice in
associating fingerings on the tuba with pitches
notated on a musical staff with bass clef. See
Micro-Baritone for further description.

While level one of <u>Micro-Tuba</u> starts in a narrow
range, level eight employs pitches from the E five
ledger lines below the bass clef staff to the E-
flat above middle C. The user picks a level to
start, and the program automatically adjusts the
level according to the user's responses during
both the tutor and the game modes.

Evaluation

The prompts in this program are clear and
consistent, as are the methods of response, and
the program is logically organized. Errors lead
to repeated tries, but no hints. The instructions
are clear, within the program, and may be bypassed
by those users already familiar with them. The
program asks the user to type his or her name at
the beginning. This name is used throughout the
program to personalize motivational remarks.

One cannot tell by looking at the graphic display
of the tuba valves whether they are numbered from
left to right or from right to left. While some
experimenting quickly clears up this confusion,
numbering the valves on the screen would be
helpful. The pitches played with each note to be
fingered in this program are not in the correct
register for the tuba. The program would appeal
to a broader audience if it included alternate
fingerings.

It is unfortunate that both the documentation and
the instructions and prompts within the program
neglect to inform the Apple IIe user that the
<CAPS LOCK> key must be depressed throughout the
program in order for the user to make any
responses.

***

<u>Mode Drills</u> by George Makas, Micro Music Software
Library, 1981, published by Temporal Acuity
Products, Inc. 1982, version 1.1.

Hardware: Apple II series computer with at least
48K memory, 3.2 or 3.3 Disk II drive with
controller, video monitor; MMI DAC music card and
headphones required.

Cost: $70

Publisher's suggested audience: Junior high to
university.

Documentation: A user's guide includes the
program's objectives, a summary, prerequisite
skills and knowledge, and operating instructions.

Description

The disk includes four drills: the first provides
aural drill in major and three forms of minor; the
second, aural drill of church modes; the third,
visual drill of major and three forms of minor;
and the fourth, visual drill of church modes.   Six
church modes are drilled: ionian, dorian,
phrygian, lydian, mixolydian and aeolian.

In the program, the user chooses the drill on
which to work as well as the speed at which the
scales and modes are played in the aural drills.
The method of response is consistent throughout
and involves entering a number representing the
user's choice from a series of possible answers
presented on the screen.   There are no hints or
second chances; when a mistake is made the program
displays the incorrect answer and the correct
answer, each on a grand staff for comparison.
Motivation is provided by a cumulative percentage
score.   The user may obtain his score at any time
by typing "S," although the score is continuously
displayed on the screen.

Evaluation

The program is logically organized and factually
correct; instructions are clear, within the
program and can be bypassed if not needed. The
graphics of the staff, clefs, and notes are good,
and the sound is decent.   The program has replay
value because it selects the scales for each
exercise at random.   The program can be ended at
any time and takes the user back to the main menu
should (s)he want to choose another drill.   Record
keeping for the teacher is not provided.   One
negative point is that the speed of the scales is
selected from numbers between 10 and 30, with the
lower number being faster, the opposite of
metronome settings.

<u>Mr. Metro Gnome I/Rhythm I</u> by Virgil Hicks (level
I of a series of four Mr. Metro Gnomes in the
University of Akron Series), published by Wenger
Corporation, 1981. This program is now included
in <u>The Music Class: Rhythm</u> in the Music Class
Series.

Hardware: Apple II, II+, or IIe, one disk drive,
video monitor; ALF synthesizer card and headphones
are optional (the sound can be routed through the
computer's internal speaker). Also available for
the Commodore 64, one disk drive and monitor.

Cost: $69

Publisher's suggested audience: Elementary:
beginning music students.

Documentation: Brief descriptive pamphlet
includes a summary, operating instructions, and
instructions for changing any options.

Description

An animated, foot tapping "Mr. Gnome" introduces,
demonstrates, drills and quizzes both the notation
and performance of whole, half, and quarter notes.
Tapping his foot to the beat, Mr. Gnome plays
these note values on his trumpet and then asks the
user to "play" them by tapping any key on the
computer keyboard. Both the sound and the
notation of these notes are presented. In
"Challenge Mr. Gnome," the user can create
rhythmic patterns from 1 to 8 notes long using
whole, half, and quarter notes for performance by
either Mr. Gnome or the user. The user chooses
among the note choices displayed on the screen by
using the arrow keys to highlight his choice.
Each pattern is displayed on a "chalkboard."
After Mr. Gnome gives a tempo of four beats, the
user taps the rhythm on any key. The user's
correct performance earns him points. A written
multiple choice quiz is given regarding Mr.
Gnome's lesson, and the user is also asked to tap
a rhythm quiz of six rhythmic patterns. When the
user chooses the (R)adio from the menu, Mr. Gnome
plays a short tune which uses the rhythmic note
values studied.

"Rhythm I" presents drill and practice with tests
on the material presented by Mr. Gnome. The user
may select a tempo, may ask the computer to play
back what the user tapped along with the correct
pattern for aural comparison, and display the
notation of both the user's pattern and the
correct pattern for visual comparison. Final user
scores are a total of the written and rhythm
quizzes. The program provides a Manager Utility
for student record keeping and for setting
standards for student ratings.

Evaluation

The program is logically organized and factually
correct with the exception of the word "beat,"
which is misspelled as "beet" in one of the
multiple choice answers. Instructions for the Mr.
Gnome tutorial appear on each display rather than
in a separate place in the program, so they cannot
be bypassed. Rhythm I includes instructions
within the program which can be bypassed if the
user is already familiar with them. The user may
end the program at any time by pressing <ESC>ape,
which brings back the menu screen, and may also
get help any time in the program. The sound and
the graphics are good. The student record keeping
program provides for student passwords as well as
for names; however, the user is never informed
that ten exercises must be completed before the
score is saved.

While the prompts in these programs are consistent
throughout, the keys used to input answers change
between "Mr. Gnome" and "Rhythm I," making the
method of response inconsistent. Other than a
score box appearing on the screen there is little
positive reinforcement and no personalization.

While playing rhythmic patterns on the keyboard,
the user may not hold down a key in order to
sustain a long note. If the key is not released
immediately, the program tells the user an error
has been made. The concept of a sustained note is
not reinforced in the performance part of this
program. There is also a definite change of tempo
between the four pulses given by Mr. Gnome and the
pulses accompanying the user's key inputs--the
latter are slower. If a user's performance is
based on the given tempo, the program will

announce that an error has been made.   The visual
comparison of the user's performance and Mr.
Gnome's is not done in musical notation, but
rather with varying length dashes which represent
the time spans between the user's key clicks.
These dashes are hard to interpret.

***

Mr. Metro Gnome II/Rhythm II by Virgil Hicks
(level II of a series of four Mr. Metro Gnomes in
the University of Akron Series), published by
Wenger Corporation, 1981.   This program is now
included in The Music Class: Rhythm in the Music
Class Series.

Hardware: Apple II, II+, or IIe, one disk drive,
video monitor; ALF synthesizer card and headphones
are optional (the sound can be routed through the
computer's internal speaker).   Also available for
the Commodore 64, one disk drive and monitor.

Cost: $69

Publisher's suggested audience: Elementary:
beginning music students.

Documentation: Brief descriptive pamphlet includes
a summary, operating instructions, and instructions
for changing any options.

Description

See Mr. Metro Gnome I/Rhythm I for description and
evaluation.   Mr. Metro Gnome II adds eighth notes
to the rhythm vocabulary of Mr. Metro Gnome I.

***

Mr. Metro Gnome III/Rhythm III by Virgil Hicks
(level III of a series of four Mr. Metro Gnomes in
the University of Akron Series), published by
Wenger Corporation, 1981.   This program is now
included in The Music School: Rhythm, part of the
Music Class Series.

Hardware: Apple II, II+, Apple IIe, one disk
drive, video monitor; ALF synthesizer card and
headphones are optional (the sound can be routed
through the computer's internal speaker). Also
available for the Commodore 64, one disk drive and
monitor.

Cost: $69

Publisher's suggested audience: Intermediate:
students who can read basic music.

Documentation: Brief descriptive pamphlet
includes a summary, operating instructions, and
instructions for changing any options.

Description

See Mr. Metro Gnome I/Rhythm I for description and
evaluation. Mr. Metro Gnome III adds tied notes,
dotted quarter notes, dotted half notes, and
dotted whole notes to the rhythm vocabulary of Mr.
Metro Gnome I and Mr. Metro Gnome II.

***

Mr. Metro Gnome IV/Rhythm IV by Virgil Hicks
(level IV of a series of four Mr. Metro Gnomes in
the University of Akron Series), published by
Wenger Corporation, 1981. This program is now
included in The Music Class: Rhythm, part of the
Music Class Series.

Hardware: Apple II, II+, or IIe, one disk drive,
video monitor; ALF synthesizer card and headphones
are optional (the sound can be routed through the
computer's internal speaker). Also available for
the Commodore 64, one disk drive and monitor.

Cost: $69

Publisher's suggested audience: Intermediate:
students who can read basic music.

Documentation: Brief descriptive pamphlet
includes a summary, operating instructions, and
instructions for changing any options.

Description

See **Mr. Metro Gnome I/Rhythm I** for description and evaluation. **Mr. Metro Gnome IV** adds sixteenth notes to the rhythm vocabulary of **Mr. Metro Gnome I**, **Mr. Metro Gnome II**, and **Mr. Metro Gnome III**.

***

Music Applications Programming Language Extension by John Miller, Electronic Courseware Systems, Inc., 1985, version 1.1.

See **MAPLE**.

***

Music Appreciation: A Study Guide by Joseph E. Koob II, Electronic Courseware Systems, Inc., 1986. Two disks entitled **The Musical Language** and **Music History**.

Hardware: Apple II+ or IIe with a minimum of 48K, one disk drive, and monitor.

Cost: Each disk is $39.95; student disk, $19.95 each; or two disks and the textbook, **Exploring Music Through Experience**, by the same author, for $79.95.

Publisher's suggested audience: The author states that the disks can be used with any music appreciation textbook written for high school or college level students.

Documentation: A brief description of the programs and brief operating instructions are included, along with a bibliography of recommended readings.

Description

The author states that both **The Musical Language** and **Music History** are intended to facilitate the study of music terminology and composers. The material is presented as briefly as possible and

is meant to provide review for students already
familiar with it. Each disk includes a tutorial
section (a review of selected topics) and a quiz
section (containing quizzes on the material
presented in the review). Each quiz presents ten
questions randomly taken from a large pool of
questions. The questions require the user to fill
in blanks in statements by typing a response.
Following the quizzes, a twenty-five question
test, covering all the topics on the disk, may be
taken by the user.

The six topics covered in The Musical Language
include "pitch," "duration," "dynamics," "timbre,"
"melody and harmony," and "form, texture, and
style." Some of the terms included under "timbre"
are overtones, strings, woodwinds, brasses,
percussion, embouchure, single reed, double reed,
vibrato, and pizzicato. Items defined in
"dynamics" are all Italian words for dynamics.
Terms employed in "pitch" include letter names,
staff, clef, ledger lines, accidentals, scales,
key signatures, and relative and parallel keys.
As the author states, these terms are defined
briefly.

The periods of Western music history reviewed in
Music History are Greek, Medieval, Renaissance,
Baroque, Classical, Romantic, and Modern. The
terms and names mentioned for the Greek period
include Apollo, Dionysus, aulos, and one sentence
about Greek modes. Terms and composers in the
Renaissance review include imitative polyphony,
counterpoint, diminution, augmentation, madrigal,
Renaissance musical instruments, Des Prez,
Palestrina, and Lasso. Polytonality, quartal
harmony, microtones, Impressionism, Expressionism,
Schoenberg, Stravinsky, Debussy, Ravel, and Bartok
are reviewed in the Modern period.

An instructor management option is included on the
disk. This option allows the teacher to keep
records for up to fifty people. The disk requires
sign-ons and passwords for various users.

Evaluation

All of the programs on these disks require a lot
of reading. In addition, the user's reading is
slowed by the fact that the text is displayed on

the screen word by word rather than a whole screen
at a time. The review sections of this software
could be presented far more effectively in hard
copy form. On the other hand, because their
questions are generated randomly from a large
pool, the quizzes and tests can be taken a number
of times without having all the questions
repeated.

The prompts are clear and consistent throughout,
and the methods of response are always the same.
Errors do not lead to repeated tries or hints;
there is no scoring or positive reinforcement.
Instructions are included within the program, but
cannot be bypassed by those familiar with them.
The user can end the program anytime by pressing
the <ESC>ape key and is taken back to various
menus where (s)he can choose a different topic.

Typing and spelling are issues in the quizzes.
The programs require accurate spelling of all
responses. Typing skills may be less of a concern
than spelling because there are no time
constraints, allowing non-typists a chance to
enter their responses at their own speed.

The ten-question quizzes and the twenty-five-
question tests provide no feedback until the quiz
or test is completed. Most users will want some
positive or negative feedback before answering all
the items on these quizzes and tests.

Whether the programs are factually correct is
debatable. Many of the terms and concepts
discussed are quite sophisticated. And yet the
definitions of terms and the discussions of
composers are so brief and incomplete that many
users will find them insufficient and far too
sketchy.

                          ***

Music Box Tool Kit, Music Box I, and Music Box II
by Virgil Hicks (University of Akron Series),
Wenger Corporation, 1981. These programs are
included in The Music Class: Music Symbols,
part of the Music Class Series.

Hardware: Apple II, II+, or IIe with at least
64K, one disk drive, video monitor, game paddles
(Apple IIe users may use the open/closed Apple
keys).

Cost: Music Box I and Music Box II, each $59.
Music Box Tool Kit, $119.

Publisher's suggested audience: Elementary:
beginning music students; Intermediate: students
who can read basic music.

Documentation: Brief descriptive pamphlet
including summary, operating instructions,
instructions for changing any options, and
instructions for creating new symbols using the
tool kit.

Description

"Music Box" presents an animated display which
challenges the user to recognize quickly musical
symbols. Musical symbols move across the screen
as the name of a symbol is displayed. If the name
and the moving symbol match, the user presses the
button on the game paddle to open a gate and allow
the symbol into a "correct" bin. If there is no
match and the user does not open the gate, the
symbol automatically flies off the screen. If the
user makes a mistake and either opens the gate for
a mismatch or does not open the gate in time for a
match, the symbol automatically is placed in a
"wrong" bin. There are 20 levels of difficulty;
the higher the difficulty, the less time allowed
for response (the symbols move across the screen
more quickly). The difficulty level automatically
increases or decreases based on correct or
incorrect responses.

In the "Music Box Game" symbols are presented in
game format; the user selects a difficulty level
and stays at the same level for the entire game.
Points and bonus points are scored for possible
inclusion in the "Hall of Fame."

"Music Box for Two" challenges two players to
recognize symbols competitively for the best
score.

Among the symbols included in Music Box I are all note and rest rhythmic values from eighth notes to whole notes, accidentals, sixteenth notes, dotted half notes, and double bar. Among those included in Music Box II are various dynamic symbols, meter signatures, clef signs and tied notes.

"The Tool Kit" allows the instructor to create a special set of music symbols for presentation in the Music Box format. The symbols are drawn on a high resolution grid. As each new symbol is created, it is miniaturized on the top of the screen so that the creator can see what it will look like in the game. Up to four sets of 20 symbols each may be created and stored.

The names of symbols answered incorrectly are given at the end of each session. The program provides a Manager Utility for student record keeping and for setting standards for student ratings. Through this program the instructor controls which set of symbols the students use.

Evaluation

This is a very creative program. The graphics for the most part are good. The tie and the slur look too much alike, and the crescendo looks like an accent because the symbol has to be created in too limited a space. One of the best parts about this program is that it provides the user with the ability to create a group of music symbols from scratch. The procedure for creating the symbols is quite simple.

Instructions are clear and included in the program and can be bypassed if the user is already familiar with them. However, the instructions cannot be accessed once the program is underway. Obviously the game format does not allow repeated tries, nor are hints given when mistakes are made.

A negative point is the fact that the program does not make it clear that ten items must be completed before a score is stored in the record keeping program.

At the end of each session, the incorrect symbol names are displayed vertically on the screen,

i.e., the words are spelled down the page. Young
users may find these words difficult to read.

***

The Music Class: Ear Training, part of the Music
Class Series, published by Wenger, 1987.

Hardware: Apple II, II+, IIe with at least 64K,
one disk drive, video monitor; ALF synthesizer
card optional.

Cost: $49

The software in The Music Class: Ear Training was
formerly marketed under three separate titles.
For description and evaluation see Aural Interval
Recognition, Melodic Error Detection and
Correction, and Melodic/Rhythmic Dictation.

***

The Music Class: Fundamentals, part of The Music
Class Series, published by Wenger, 1987.

Hardware: Apple II, II+, or IIe with at least
64K, one disk drive, video monitor; ALF
synthesizer card optional.

Cost: $39

The software included in The Music Class:
Fundamentals was formerly marketed under two
separate titles. For description and evaluation
see Cat Steps Interval Tutorial/Game and Major
Scale Tutorial/Minor Scale Tutorial.

***

The Music Class: Music Symbols, part of the Music
Class Series, published by Wenger, 1987.

Hardware: Apple II, II+, IIe with a minimum of
64K, one disk drive, video monitor; ALF

synthesizer card optional; game paddles are also optional.

Cost: $39

The software included in The Music Class: Music Symbols was formerly marketed under three separate titles. For description and evaluation see Music Box Tool Kit, Music Box I and Music Box II.

***

The Music Class: Note Reading, part of the Music Class Series, published by Wenger, 1987.

Hardware: Apple II, II+, IIe with a minimum of 64K, one disk drive, video monitor; ALF synthesizer card optional.

Cost: $49

The software included in The Music Class: Note Reading was formerly marketed under two separate titles. For description and evaluation see Note Reading Tutorial/Staff Note Reading and Keyboard Note Reading/Keyboard Speed Note Reading.

***

The Music Class: Rhythm, part of the Music Class Series, published by Wenger, 1987.

Hardware: Apple II, II+, or IIe with at least 64K, one disk drive, video monitor; ALF synthesizer card optional.

Cost: $49

The software included in The Music Class: Rhythm was formerly marketed under four separate titles. For description and evaluation see Mr. Metro Gnome I/Rhythm I, Mr. Metro Gnome II/Rhythm II, Mr. Metro Gnome III/Rhythm III, and Mr. Metro Gnome IV/Rhythm IV.

***

Music Composer by David B. Williams, Micro Music
Software Library published by Temporal Acuity
Products, Inc., 1981, version 2.4.

Hardware: Apple II series computer with at least
48K memory, 3.2 or 3.3 Disk II drive with
controller, video monitor; MMI DAC music card and
headphones or amplifier and speakers required.

Cost: $150

Publisher's suggested audience: Junior high to
university.

Documentation: Includes a detailed user's guide.

Description

With Music Composer the user can compose or play
from one to four voices simultaneously, display
all voices while the music is playing, enter music
notes through a coding system or through an
optional "Graphic Entry" approach, create timbres
through Fourier construction, edit existing
compositions, and save music on disk. The disk
contains a demonstration loop that automatically
plays some selections. The manual includes an
introduction to the commands, as well as technical
sections which explain all commands in detail.

The sound is created by digital synthesis through
the Micro Music DAC card. The tones of the four
voices are generated using a software sampling
technique.

The program comes with seven different timbres or
tone colors; each voice may have a different
tone color. The user can also create additional
timbres with the "Fourier" command. This command
provides the means of constructing wave forms
which are then assigned to one of the seven
timbres, or presets, stored in memory. The user
can choose the number of harmonics (up to 16) in
the spectrum of the sound, as well as the overall
amplitude of the voice during "Play" mode. One
can also choose the relative amplitudes of each of
the harmonics represented in a bar graph.

Although there is a rhythmic delay, the user can
view the music while it is being played. The

music moves across the screen from right to left,
with the screen acting like a window to the score.

There are two methods of composing or entering
music. In the "Graphic" mode, music symbols are
displayed on the screen, and the user uses the
left and right arrow keys to make selections. The
rhythmic value of the note is selected first, then
the pitch, then an accidental (if needed). The
<SPACE BAR> is used to enter the result. The
music is composed in "sets," each vertical
simultaneity representing one set. Composing is
always done from the bottom of the chord up.

The "Literal" mode of entering music is more
efficient and involves entering a series of codes.
"2:1?EF3," for example, enters an eighth note "F"
in the third octave in set 2, voice 1. As the
codes are entered the program notates the note or
rest on a grand staff displayed on the screen.
All accidentals must be added, even if they
appear in the key signature.

Evaluation

Although the codes employed are fairly logical,
most users will want to refer to the manual often
in literal mode. Prompts do appear on the screen,
but the actual codes are not displayed.

The maximum number of sets the Music Composer will
allow in a single piece varies with the number of
voices. If the piece consists of a single voice,
the user may compose 1638 sets, two voices, 1170
sets, three voices, 910 sets, and four voices, 744
sets.

***

Music Composer/Music Maker (cartridge), Commodore
Electronics Ltd., 1982.

Hardware: Commodore 64, video monitor, and a
storage device (either tape cassette or disk
drive) if one wants to store compositions. The
cartridge is placed in the cartridge slot in the
back of the computer.

Cost: $16.97

Publisher's suggested audience: None stated.

Documentation: Includes a brief manual.

Description

The user may use this program to compose pieces
of music with up to three voices. The music is
entered into the computer using a series of
detailed codes. The codes indicate the voice
number (1, 2, or 3), the pitch, the octave or
register, and the rhythmic value of each note.
The disk has a three-voice piece by Bach on it.
The user may hear this piece (and pieces of his
own creation) and see the notation displayed on
the screen while it is being played.

The user may choose a different timbre or
"instrument" for each of the three voices, or have
all voices the same. There are nine timbres from
which to choose: accordion, calliope, "rhythm
sound," harpsichord, organ, harmonica, xylophone,
banjo, and "special." "Special" provides some
special effects, including white noise, pulse,
sawtooth, or triangle wave forms, control over
attack/decay and sustain/release, and filtering.
The filtering capabilities include low pass, high
pass, band pass, low and band pass, low and high
pass, band and high pass, and low, band and high
pass. Additional special effects available
through the editor include vibrato, pulse width
modulation, and ring modulation.

Another option allows the user to convert the
computer keyboard into a piano or synthesizer
keyboard and play it as such. The keys <G>
through <=> on the second row of the keyboard
provide the diatonic pitches for one octave in C
Major, while the <Y>, <U>, <O>, <P>, and <@> keys
on the row above provide the intervening chromatic
pitches.

The music created can be saved to and loaded from
tape on a datasette.

Evaluation

Some sophisticated music and sounds can be created using this software. The program takes advantage of the three-voice synthesizer built into the Commodore 64 and 128. Entering the notes using the codes requires referral to the written documentation. The program itself provides no prompts or instructions for the user. Music making, while awkward on the computer keyboard, can be interesting for those wanting to experiment with different sounds. Obviously, one cannot perform pieces requiring much keyboard facility.

As the user creates or plays music, the program provides its notation on the screen. The "score" moves across the screen from right to left. Unfortunately, the notation is very poor.

Some very nice sounds can be made with this program.

***

Music Composer Quiz by Joseph A. Brownlee, Electronic Courseware Systems, Inc., 1985.

Hardware: Commodore 64 or 128, one disk drive, monitor (color monitor optional). Also available for Apple II+, IIe, or IIc with at least 48K, or Apple IIc with at least 128K, one disk drive, and monitor, or the IBM-PC or IBM-PC JR. with at least 128K, one 360K double-sided disk drive, color graphics board, and monitor.

Cost: $39.95

Publisher's suggested audience: None stated.

Documentation: Brief description on back of diskette box.

Description

This program presents a quiz consisting of 20 questions randomly selected from a "pool" of 100 questions created by the author. Responses are made by typing in the name of a composer. This is

not a multiple choice quiz; the user must come up
with the answers on his own. Users are given
three chances to answer a question successfully
before the correct answer is displayed. After the
first and second unsuccessful tries, hints provide
additional information about the composer in
question. Points are awarded on the basis of how
many tries the user needed to get the right
answer: 5 points for the first try, 3 for the
second, and 1 for the third. The quiz is timed;
the user has 30 seconds to answer each question.
The program provides no sounds or graphics, and it
is not terribly forgiving with regard to the
spelling of a composer's name; spelling has to be
nearly perfect for the program to accept an
answer.

The user may skip questions; however, after the
last question in the quiz, the program returns to
the ones the user skipped and asks them again. As
the user acquires points, they are displayed on
the screen during the quiz, along with the
possible number of points the user could have
attained had all the answers been correct on the
first attempt. The user does not have to wait
until the end of the quiz in order to receive
feedback. Each answer receives a "Correct" or
"Wrong" response.

A "Music Composer Editor" is included on the disk.
This utility, entered by means of a password,
allows the instructor to inspect and edit each
question, each of the hints that accompanies each
question, and the list of possible answers the
program will accept as correct. It also allows
the instructor to create his own questions, hints,
and possible responses by merely replacing some or
all of the ones included on the disk. The
instructor options also include record keeping.

Evaluation

Instructions are clear and included in the
program; however, they cannot be bypassed. A user
already familiar with them must reread them in
order to get into the quiz. Scoring provides
motivation for the user to continue working, or to
do the quiz several times in an effort to better
his or her score. The program is logically
organized and factually correct.

Some of the questions seem quite trivial: "What
classical composer sang in his own operas until he
drank nitric acid and destroyed his voice?" or
"What Baroque composer died of blood poisoning
when he dropped a baton on his foot?"
Fortunately, the "Music Composer Editor" allows
editing and/or replacement of any or all of the
100 questions in the quiz file, which means that
the instructor can tailor the questions and the
hints to the needs of his students.

***

Music Construction Set by Will Harvey, Electronic
Arts, 1983.

Hardware: Commodore 64 or 128, one disk drive,
monitor (color optional), and joy stick or Koala
Pad. Also available for the Apple II and II+, one
disk drive, monitor, with joystick or Koala Pad;
or Apple IIe or IIc, one disk drive, monitor, with
joystick, Koala Pad, or AppleMouse; available for
the IBM-PC, XT, or PC Jr. with color graphics
adaptor, with optional joystick or Koala Pad. The
Apple computers will need an additional sound
source such as the Mockingboard; a printer is an
option for all of the above hardware.

Cost: $19.95

Publisher's suggested audience: None specified.

Documentation: Includes a manual, as well as a
reference card.

Description

The main purpose of this program is to provide the
means for the user to compose music. Using a joy
stick or "Koala Pad" to control an icon of a hand
with a pointing finger, the user can drag notes,
rests, natural, sharp, and flat signs, clef signs,
ties and dots (all displayed) onto a grand staff
displayed on the screen. The user may also make
choices of key (or change the key), time
signature, tempo, timbre, and volume. The program
also gives the user the ability to hear and/or
view everything he has composed starting at any

point, to save his compositions on disk, to
transpose compositions, and to "cut and paste"
sections anywhere in a composition. The notation
of each piece is displayed through a window and
moves across the screen from left to right as it
is being played.

The disk already contains a dozen pieces composed
using the system, including a two-part invention
by Bach, a Pachelbel canon, a movement of a Mozart
piano sonata, and "Turkey in the Straw." Timbre
choices include piano, harpsichord, accordian,
flute, organ, and banjo. Meter choices include
2/4, 3/4, 4/4, and 6/8. A set of icons in the
lower right corner of the screen include a jar of
paste, a pair of scissors, a house, a left arrow,
a right arrow, and a plug. By moving the "hand"
to each of these icons, one chooses to cut or
paste notation, move right or left in the
notation, go back to the beginning of the
notation, or indicate to the program whether the
joystick or the "Koala Pad" is being used.

Evaluation

The graphics of music notation and the sounds
created by this program are very good, although
eighth notes are not beamed. The pieces which
were composed using the system and stored on the
disk indicate that one can compose some very
sophisticated music with this software; however,
it is a very time-consuming undertaking.
Maneuvering notes, rests, and other musical
symbols and placing them on the staff is not easy
with the joystick, and only a little bit better
using the "Koala Pad." Using the mouse in the
Apple version is considerably easier. When one is
ready to listen to a piece, the display of its
notation moves so quickly across the screen that
it is impossible to read.

***

Music Drills: Ear Training Series Part I: Theory
Fundamentals by John E. Hatmaker, Wenger
Corporation, 1985. Part II, Aural Fundamentals,
and Part III, Dictation I, form the other parts of
this series.

Hardware: Apple II, II+, IIe, or IIc with a
minimum of 64K, one disk drive, and video monitor.

Cost: $49, or all three Music Drills: Ear
Training Series disks for $119.

Publisher's suggested audience: First year
college students.

Documentation: A thirty-one page booklet, with
descriptions of each of the programs on the disk,
is included. In addition, a brief syllabus is
provided to help instructors and students use the
lessons with the following texts: Harmony and
Voice Leading Volume I by Aldwell and Schachter
(Harcourt, Brace, Jovanovich), Music in Theory and
Practice, Volume I, by Benward (William C. Brown
Publishers), Tonal Harmony by Kostka and Payne
(Alfred A. Knopf), Elementary Harmony by Ottman
(Prentice-Hall), and Harmony, 4th edition, by
Piston/DeVoto (W. W. Norton).

Description

These programs drill users in the identification
of note names and the identification and
construction of intervals, triads, scales and key
signatures. Except where noted below, the user's
score, consisting of the number of items
attempted, the number correct, and a percentage,
is displayed on the screen after each exercise.
No second chances are allowed when a mistake is
made, and there are no time constraints. Record
keeping for each of the twelve drill programs on
the disk may be kept for up to ten students. By
typing a password, the instructor can access a
series of management options which allow entering
student names and passwords, examining scores,
printing scores either to the screen or to a
printer, and deleting or replacing records.

In "Note Names," the user is asked to identify
notes presented on a musical staff with a clef of
the user's choice, treble, bass, alto, or tenor;
each drill includes notes presented two ledger
lines above and two ledger lines below the staff.
Notes with accidentals are not included in any of
these drills. Note names are entered by typing
the keys <A> through <G>.

In "Intervals," the user chooses either to
identify intervals or to spell them.
Identification is done by selecting an appropriate
label for each interval displayed on the staff
from a list of multiple choice answers also
displayed on the screen. The choices for a
particular interval are always limited to those
associated with the size of the interval notated.
For example, a fifth on the staff would have three
choices listed--augmented 5th, perfect 5th, or
diminished 5th--while a sixth on the staff would
have four choices--augmented 6th, major 6th, minor
6th, or diminished 6th. All the intervals are
notated in the treble clef only. The second drill
asks users to spell intervals either above or
below a note presented on a staff, again with
treble clef only. The user enters the letter name
of the note, <A> through <G>, and <S> for sharp,
<F> for flat, <X> for double sharp, and <D> for
double flat, when applicable.

"Triads" provides two drills, one in the
identification of triad qualities, and one in the
spelling of triads. The identification drill
involves the user in selecting an appropriate
triad quality for a triad notated on the staff
with treble clef only. The selection is made
from a multiple choice list--augmented, major,
minor, or diminished. The spelling drill displays
the root of a triad on a treble clef staff and
asks the user to supply the third and fifth above
the root which will result in a particular quality
triad. The notes are entered by using the letter
keys <A> through <G> and the <S>, <X>, <F>, and
<D> keys for accidentals. Each entry, third and
fifth, is evaluated separately by the program as
it is entered.

Both identification and spelling drills are
included in "Scales." In the identification
drill, scales are notated on two treble clef
staves. The upper staff displays the ascending
and the lower staff the descending form of the
scale. The user is asked to identify the scale by
selecting from a multiple choice list which
includes major, harmonic minor, natural minor, and
melodic minor. The scales are all notated without
key signatures but with accidentals placed where
necessary. The spelling drill displays a treble
clef and first note on the staff and asks for

either the ascending form or the descending form
of a particular scale--major, harmonic, natural,
or melodic minor. The user then must supply scale
degrees 2 through 8 or 7 through 1, in the case of
a descending scale. The notes are entered by
employing the letter keys <A> through <G> and <S>,
<X>, <F>, and <D> for accidentals. Each note is
evaluated individually as it is entered. During
the spelling drill the score is not displayed on
the screen as it is in the other drills on this
disk.

"Keys" provides drills in identifying and
supplying key signatures. In the identification
drill, the user is presented with a key signature
placed on a treble clef staff and provided with
information regarding the mode, either major or minor.
The user is asked to provide the name of the key
by typing the letters <A> through <G> and <S>,
<X>, <F> or <D> for accidentals if the key
requires it. In the second drill, the user is
asked to supply the key signature for a given
major or minor key. The user responds by typing
the number of flats or sharps necessary for the
key in question. The program then places the
correct key signature on the treble clef staff.

Evaluation

The graphics of musical notation are excellent in
all of these programs. Instructions and sample
exercises are clear, are included within each
drill, and can be bypassed by users already
familiar with them. The instructions also inform
the user that mistakes may be erased by employing
either the left arrow key or the <DELETE> key.
The programs are logically organized and factually
correct. The programs lack any personalization,
and rely on scoring to motivate the user. It must
be noted that the user must complete at least 30
exercises (and often more if mistakes are made) in
order to have a score recorded in the record
keeping utility on the disk. The documentation
states that the programs "require the user to
demonstrate a degree of proficiency before they
are completed."

The user may leave a drill at any time by using
the <Q> key, keeping in mind that his or her score
may not be saved if (s)he has not completed enough

exercises. Instructions may be reviewed during
the program by leaving the drill and requesting
them from the menu for that particular drill.
Each drill allows the user to leave the drill and
come back to it by asking if the user would like
his or her place saved.

The prompts are very clear, and the codes required
to enter answers are displayed on the screen at
all times, although this makes the screen somewhat
cluttered.

In the drill involved with supplying key
signatures, the user must enter "0S" in order to
provide an answer of no sharps or flats for the
key of C Major. Trying to enter an answer of
"nothing" by pressing the <SPACE BAR> with no
response will not work.

It is unfortunate that the treble clef is the only
clef used in all the programs except "Note Names."
Certainly college level music software should
include additional clefs.

***

Music Drills: Ear Training Series Part II: Aural
Fundamentals, by John E. Hatmaker, Wenger
Corporation, 1985. Part I, Theory Fundamentals,
and Part III, Dictation I, form the other parts of
this series.

Hardware: Apple II+, or Apple IIe, with minimum
64K, one disk drive, video monitor. The sound
source for these programs can be the Apple speaker
or the cassette output located on the back of the
computer, the ALF synthesizer card, Mountain
MusicSystem cards, or a Passport Type I MIDI. If
the cassette output is used, the publisher
recommends the use of an amplifier.

Cost: $49, or all three Music Drills: Ear
Training Series disks for $119.

Publisher's suggested audience: First year
college students.

Documentation: A thirty-one page booklet, with descriptions of each of the programs on the disk, is included. In addition, a brief syllabus is provided to help instructors and students use the lessons with the following texts: Harmony and Voice Leading Volume I by Aldwell and Schachter (Harcourt, Brace, Jovanovich), Music in Theory and Practice, Volume I, by Benward (William C. Brown Publishers), Tonal Harmony by Kostka and Payne (Alfred A. Knopf), Elementary Harmony by Ottman (Prentice-Hall), and Harmony, 4th edition, by Piston/DeVoto (W. W. Norton).

Description

These programs drill users in the aural identification of isolated intervals, triads, scales and seventh chords. In each of the drills the user can work at his or her own pace. No items are played until the user presses the <P> key. The user then enters his response by selecting an answer from multiple choices displayed on the screen; this is accomplished with the arrow keys and the <SPACE BAR>. Items may be heard again after the answer has been entered. When a mistake is made, the user may hear and see in notation the correct response as well as the wrong one. No second chances are allowed when a mistake is made, and there are no time constraints.

The user's score, consisting of the number of items attempted, the number correct, and a percentage, is displayed on the screen after each exercise. Record keeping for each of the four drill programs on the disk may be kept for up to ten students. Each program requires 24 to 36 completed items before a record will be stored. Users may exit from drills after completing fewer items by pressing <Q>.

By typing a password, the instructor can access a series of management options which allow entering student names and passwords, examining scores, printing scores either to the screen or to a printer, and deleting or replacing records.

In "Intervals," the user identifies the size and quality of each interval heard by selecting an appropriate label for the interval from a list of

multiple choice answers displayed on the screen.
The list includes minor second, major second,
minor third, major third, perfect fourth, perfect
fifth, tritone, minor sixth, major sixth, minor
seventh, major seventh, and octave. The bottom
note of the interval is notated on a treble clef
staff. After pressing <P>, the interval is
played melodically from the bottom up and then
from the top down (and then played harmonically
when the ALF sound synthesizer card is used).
After the user enters an answer, the correct
interval is notated on the staff.

"Triads" provides drill in the identification of
triad qualities. The drill involves the user in
selecting an appropriate triad quality for a triad
arpeggiated both up and down (and played
harmonically when the ALF sound synthesizer card
is used). All the triads are in root position,
and the root is displayed on a treble clef staff.
The multiple choice list includes augmented,
major, minor and diminished. After the user
enters an answer, the correct triad is notated on
the staff.

"Scales" involves the user in the identification
of scale types. After hearing both the ascending
and the descending form of a scale, the user
identifies the scale by selecting from a multiple
choice list which includes major, harmonic minor,
natural minor, and melodic minor. During the
drill the first note of the scale is displayed on
a treble clef staff. After the user enters an
answer, both the ascending and the descending
forms of the scale are notated on a grand staff.
The upper staff displays the ascending and the
lower staff, the descending form of the scale.
The scales are all notated without key signatures
but with accidentals placed where necessary.

"Sevenths" provides drill in identifying various
types of seventh chords. After playing the chord
the program provides the user with multiple
choices including major-major, major-minor, minor-
major, minor-minor, half-diminished, and fully-
diminished seventh chords. Each seventh chord is
arpeggiated both up and down, and after the user
has responded, the correct seventh chord is
notated in the treble clef. Again, all the chords

are in root position, and the root is notated on
the staff at the beginning of the exercise.

Evaluation

The graphics of musical notation are excellent in
all of these programs. The quality of the sound
produced by the programs will vary depending upon
the sound source available to the user.

Instructions and sample exercises are clear, are
included within each drill, and can be bypassed by
users already familiar with them. The programs
are logically organized and factually correct.
The programs lack any personalization, and rely on
scoring to motivate the user.

The user may leave a drill at any time by using
the <Q> key, keeping in mind that his or her score
may not be saved if (s)he has not completed enough
exercises. Instructions may be reviewed during
the program by leaving the drill and requesting
them from the menu for that particular drill.
Each drill allows the user to leave the drill and
come back to it by asking if the user would like
his or her place saved.

The prompts are very clear, and the codes required
to enter answers are displayed on the screen at
all times, although this makes the screen somewhat
cluttered.

It is unfortunate that the treble clef is the only
clef used in all these programs. Certainly
college level music software should include
additional clefs.

***

Music Drills: Ear Training Series Part III:
Dictation I, by John E. Hatmaker, Wenger
Corporation, 1985. Part I, Theory Fundamentals,
and Part II, Aural Fundamentals, form the other
parts of this series.

Hardware: Apple II+, or Apple IIe, with minimum
64K, one disk drive, video monitor. The sound
source for these programs can be the Apple speaker

or the cassette output located on the back of the computer, the ALF synthesizer card, Mountain MusicSystem cards, or a Passport Type I MIDI.   If the cassette output is used, the publisher recommends the use of an amplifier.

Cost: $49, or all three <u>Music Drills: Ear Training Series</u> disks for $119.

Publisher's suggested audience: First year college students.

Documentation: A thirty-one page booklet, with descriptions of each of the programs on the disk, is included.   In addition, a brief syllabus is provided to help instructors and students use the lessons with the following texts: <u>Harmony and Voice Leading Volume I</u> by Aldwell and Schachter (Harcourt, Brace, Jovanovich), <u>Music in Theory and Practice</u>, Volume I, by Benward (William C. Brown Publishers), <u>Tonal Harmony</u> by Kostka and Payne (Alfred A. Knopf), <u>Elementary Harmony</u> by Ottman (Prentice-Hall), and <u>Harmony</u>, 4th edition, by Piston/DeVoto (W. W. Norton).

Description

The programs on this disk provide drills in pitch, rhythmic, and melodic dictation.   In each program the user hears a dictation pattern and is then asked to notate it on manuscript paper.   After finishing the notation, the user can request that the correct pattern be displayed on the screen (by pressing <V>) for comparison with the pattern notated on manuscript paper.   The user may choose the speed of the presentation from fast, medium, or slow, and choose a level of difficulty within each program.   The user may hear the pattern as many times as needed both before and after the correct answer is displayed by pressing <P>.   None of the exercises is composed by the program, but all are randomly selected.   Each program provides a number of sets of varying difficulty; each set contains ten exercises.   There is no scoring or record keeping available.   The user may leave a drill at any point by pressing <Q>.   Whether the user has completed ten exercises or has exited from a set, the program offers the choice of repeating the set, trying another set, or

returning to the main menu to select a different
kind of dictation.

"Pitch Dictation" provides five preset levels of
diatonic pitch patterns. The pitches are all of
equal duration, and there are ten patterns for
each level. After choosing a level, the user sees
a staff with treble clef, key signature, and the
first note. The patterns in level one are all in
major keys with up to three sharps or flats, four
to six notes long, and start and end on the tonic.
In level two, the patterns are in major and minor
keys up to four sharps or flats, six to eight
notes long, and start and end on the tonic. Level
three presents patterns in major and minor keys
with a maximum of four sharps or flats, that are
eight to ten notes long, and start on the tonic,
but end on something other than the tonic. Level
four presents ten- to fourteen-note patterns in
major and minor keys through five sharps or flats,
starting on the tonic, but ending on a note other
than the tonic. Level five presents patterns of
twelve to fifteen notes in major and minor keys
through six sharps or flats, with starting and
ending notes that are not the tonic.

"Rhythmic Dictation" provides five preset levels
of rhythmic patterns graduated in length and
rhythmic complexity. In each pattern the user is
presented a single line staff with a meter
signature. Each exercise is preceded by a measure
of beats to establish the tempo. The number of
beats in this preparatory measure is determined by
the top number of the meter signature; in 6/8
there are six eighth note pulses, and in 3/2 there
are three half note pulses. The pitch used to
establish the tempo is different from the single
pitch used in the rhythmic pattern itself. Level
one presents patterns of six to nine notes in
simple meters (including 5/4, 3/2, 4/8 and more
common ones) and includes whole, half, quarter,
eighth, sixteenth, dotted half, dotted quarter,
and dotted eighth notes. Level two provides
patterns eight to twelve notes in length in simple
and compound meters which include 3/8, 12/16, 5/8,
6/16, along with more common ones. Employing ten-
to sixteen-note patterns in simple and compound
meters, Level three presents exercises with
measures which are less homogeneous. Level four,
again employing simple and compound meters,

provides patterns of from twelve to nineteen notes
with syncopation and ties. Level five presents
fifteen- to twenty-five-note patterns in simple
and compound meters and includes triplets.

"Layer Dictation" provides three preset levels of
melodic patterns graduated by length and
complexity. The patterns include both pitch and
rhythm; the pitches are all diatonic and are
transposed to various major and minor keys. Each
pattern is preceded by a measure of notes to
establish the tempo. Each exercise contains two
layers (levels), the first being a structural
melody and the second an embellishment of the
first. In each exercise a treble clef staff, key
and meter signatures, and the starting pitch
without any rhythmic value are displayed on the
screen. Layer 1 always contains three to eight
notes of quarter and whole note values. The
patterns in Layer 2, Level one, are from seven to
eleven notes long and include common meters and
rhythms, step-wise motion, and leaps within the
tonic triad. Layer 2, Level two, provides
patterns with from nine to fourteen notes
including step-wise and leap motion involving non-
tonic triads with more complex rhythmic activity.
Level three, Layer 2 patterns are from ten to
eighteen notes in length, have ranges of over an
octave, use more complex rhythmic activity, and
include ties.

A special program on the disk allows the creation
of new dictation patterns which can either replace
any or all of the dictation patterns provided on
the original disk or be saved on other disks. All
the patterns are constructed in C Major. The
programs later transpose and/or change the mode of
the patterns automatically and at random. The
written documentation provided with the programs
provides clear instructions regarding the process
by which new patterns are created and stored on
the disks, making it relatively easy for an
instructor to create patterns which suit the needs
of his or her students.

Evaluation

The graphics of musical notation are very good in
these programs; appropriate beaming of rhythmic
values is included. The quality of the sound

produced by the programs will vary depending upon
the sound source available to the user.
Indicating to the programs which sound source is
being used is accomplished very easily. The
programs are logically organized and factually
correct. Instructions and sample exercises are
clear, within each program, and can be bypassed by
those users already familiar with them. Although
the patterns are pre-composed, the programs have
replay value because the patterns undergo
transposition and mode change, as well as
differing order, at random. The prompts are clear
and consistent. There are no hints or repeated
tries because the user is responding on manuscript
paper and is not being judged by the program.

It is unfortunate that the treble clef is the only
clef used in the patterns of these programs. Even
the pattern creation program does not provide for
any other clef. Certainly college level music
software should address other clefs. In addition,
the user must decide the speed of the presentation
of the various patterns very early in the program
before choosing which type of dictation is going
to be drilled. In order to change this speed, one
must leave the drill and go back to the main menu.
The programs would be improved if the user could
change the speed during the drill itself as
difficulty arises.

Another shortcoming lies in the fact that neither
the "Pitch Dictation" nor the "Layer Dictation"
programs establish the key before playing the
pattern in each exercise. Despite the fact that
only diatonic pitches are employed, many of the
patterns, especially the ones which begin and end
on notes other than the tonic, are made more
difficult because they are not heard in a tonal
context. Furthermore, the pitch used to establish
the tempo in the "Layer Dictation" exercises is
the same as the pitch of the first note. This is
disconcerting to some users, who find it difficult
to sort out the beat establishing pitches from the
actual first note of the pattern.

***

Music Flash Cards: Music Comprehension Programs
by Vincent Oddo, Electronic Courseware Systems,
Inc., 1984.

Hardware: Commodore 64 or 128, one disk drive,
monitor (color monitor optional).   Also available
for Apple II+ or IIe with at least 48K, or IIc
with at least 128K, one disk drive, and monitor.

Cost: $99.95 or $39.95 for each of three disks.

Publisher's suggested audience: None stated.

Documentation: Brief description on back of
diskette box.

Description

The three disks included in this series provide
nine programs with drills in identifying note
names, understanding rhythmic values, and
identifying scales, modes, key signatures,
intervals, and triads displayed on the screen.
The methods of response vary with each program.
In some cases, the user types letter names <A>
through <G>, while in others the number keys must
be typed to enter an answer.   Most of the programs
provide the user with a list of multiple choice
answers.   The user chooses an answer from the list
by highlighting it using the arrow keys on the
computer keyboard.   None of the programs allows
second chances.   When an error is made, the
programs state that the answer is wrong and
provide the correct answer immediately.   None of
the programs has any time constraints.

In each program the user chooses how many items
will be included in the drill by typing a number
from 10 to 25.   After the items selected have been
completed, the number of tries, the number
correct, and a percentage score are displayed.   If
the score is high enough (70%), it qualifies the
user to be placed in the "Hall of Fame."

Disk 1:

In "Names of Notes" a note is displayed on a
musical staff with either treble or bass clef.
The user types the letter name that matches the
note.   The user may choose to work with notes in

either treble or bass clef, but not in both in the
same drill.

"Rhythmic Values" displays a note or a rest value
on the screen and provides a list of rhythmic
values. The user chooses among whole, half,
quarter, eighth, sixteenth or thirty-second notes
by highlighting the appropriate value. The user
may choose to be drilled in note values, rest
values, or both in the same drill.

In "How Many" the user is drilled on how many
notes or rests of a smaller value will equal a
larger rest or note value. Responses are entered
by pressing the number keys. The user chooses to
be drilled on note or rest values, but not both in
the same drill. This drill includes dotted half,
dotted quarter and dotted eighth notes and rests
in addition to the values included in "Rhythmic
Values."

"Add/Subtract" displays two note or rest values.
Either the two values are being added together or
one is being subtracted from the other. The arrow
keys are used to select from a table of note or
rest values, the value which equals the answer.
The user may choose to be drilled in note values
or rest values, but not both in the same drill.

Disk 2:

"Major and Minor Scales" provides drill in
identifying types of scales notated in treble clef
and displayed on the screen. Arrow keys are used
to select the type of scale displayed from a list
including major, natural minor, harmonic minor,
and melodic minor. Only the ascending form of the
scale is displayed in each case.

"Modal Scales" provides drill in identifying
various church modes notated in the treble clef
and displayed on the screen. The arrow keys are
used to select the name of the mode displayed.
The choices are ionian, dorian, phrygian, lydian,
mixolydian, aeolian, and locrian.

In "Major and Minor Key Signatures" the user sees
a key signature displayed on a musical staff and
enters the letter name (and an <S> for sharp or an
<F> for flat, as needed) of the key the signature

represents. The user may select drills in treble
or bass clef, in major or minor keys, and key
signatures using flats or key signatures using
sharps.

Disk 3:

"Intervals" displays various intervals on a
musical staff with either treble or bass clef
randomly chosen by the program. With the arrow
keys the user highlights the quality of the
interval displayed; major, minor, diminished, and
augmented are the multiple choices. After
choosing a quality, the user enters the numeric
size of the interval.

In "Basic Chords" the user is asked to identify
the quality of triads notated on a musical staff
displayed on the screen. The arrow keys are used
to highlight the quality of each chord displayed;
major, minor, diminished, and augmented are the
multiple choices. The user may choose to work in
bass clef or treble clef (but not in both in the
same drill), and to work with root position triads
only or inverted triads (major 6, major 6/4, minor
6, or minor 6/4) only.

Evaluation

The graphics of musical notation, especially the
symbol for flats, are not very good in these
programs. The instructions are clear and within
each program; however, they cannot be bypassed by
those already familiar with them. The prompts are
always clear and consistent.

The programs offer no personalization, although
the scoring provides a certain amount of
motivation. The programs do not ask for the user's
name unless his or her score qualifies for the
"Hall or Fame." Users who do not care about the
"Hall of Fame," or who would prefer not to be
included, will find these programs frustrating.
Unless the user is prepared to shut off the
computer and reboot the disk, each program goes
ahead and places qualified users in the hall and
displays the names in the hall. A user must have
made correct responses seventy percent of the time
in order to be qualified. However, in some of the
programs, if the user quits before completing the

number of items selected at the beginning and has
been eighty percent correct, (s)he will be
qualified for the hall. There is a "Hall of Fame"
for each program and for subprograms as well. For
example, a user could be qualified to be placed in
the "Hall of Fame" for Basic Chords-Treble Clef-
Root Position and/or Basic Chords-Bass Clef-
Inversions.

The user is instructed to press the <F1> key in
order to quit a specific program or to press <S>
to see the score displayed. Trial and error
reveals that this can only be done after the user
has entered an answer and before pressing the
<RETURN> key to try another item.

The programs are logically organized with perhaps
one exception. "Intervals" asks the user to enter
the quality of the interval first and then the
size. Most users will want to identify the size
of the interval before figuring out its quality.

For the most part, the programs are factually
correct. Some strange things were discovered in
"Add/Subtract." One item asks the user to add a
dotted eighth note and an eighth note. The
correct answer is not among the multiple choices,
although the program accepts a quarter note as a
correct answer. Another item will not accept an
eighth note as the right answer when an eighth
note is subtracted from a quarter note.

While many of the programs require the user to use
the arrow keys to highlight the answer among
several choices, the movement of the highlight
(actually reverse video) varies considerably
between programs. For example, in "Add/Subtract"
there is such a long delay between the time the
user presses the arrow key and the time that the
highlight actually moves, that one frequently goes
past the intended choice and must move the
highlight backwards.

* * *

Music History by Joseph E. Koob II, Electronic Courseware Systems, Inc., 1986.

See Music Appreciation: A Study Guide.

* * *

Music I: Terms and Notations by Linda Borry Hausmann, Minnesota Educational Computing Corporation, 1982, version 2.2. One of three music theory drill and practice packages; the other packages are Music II: Rhythm and Pitch and Music III: Scales and Chords. These programs were originally written for the Apple II series of computers under the title Music Theory.

Hardware: Atari with 48K memory, single disk drive, video monitor; (small amplifier and headphones may be desired).

Cost: $29

Publisher's suggested audience: Beginning to advanced music students.

Documentation: Includes a 59-page support manual which provides a description of the programs, lists learning objectives, instructs the material to be covered in the programs, and suggests a sequence of instruction for someone using all four of the packages.

Description

The five programs on this disk, "Note Types," "Name the Note," "Enharmonics," "Terms," and "Key Signatures" are described in Music Theory in this index. At the end of each session, the programs in the Atari version provide the user with only the number of exercises attempted and the number correct. A percentage score is not included as it is in the Apple version.

Evaluation

The graphics of musical notation in these programs is superior to that found in the Apple version,

although neither version provides for beams in the
notation of rhythm.

In the Atari version, a flat and a sharp are
entered by typing the <#> sign and the <%> sign
respectively. Having to press the <SHIFT> key in
order to type these signs will be bothersome to
many users.

Unlike the Apple version, the Atari version allows
the user to quit the programs at any point by
pressing the <ESC>ape key twice.

***

Music II: Rhythm and Pitch by Linda Borry
Hausmann, Minnesota Educational Computing
Corporation, 1982, version 2.2. One of three
music theory drill and practice packages; the
other packages are Music I: Terms and Notation
and Music III: Scales and Chords. These programs
were originally written for the Apple II series of
computers under the title Music Theory.

Hardware: Atari with 48K memory, single disk
drive, video monitor; (small amplifier and
headphones may be desired).

Cost: $29

Publisher's suggested audience: Beginning to
advanced music students.

Documentation: Includes a 59-page support manual
which provides a description of the programs,
lists learning objectives, instructs the material
to be covered in the programs, and suggests a
sequence of instruction for someone using all four
of the packages.

Description

The seven programs on this disk, "Aural
Intervals," "Visual Intervals," "Wrong Note,"
"Missing Note," "Counting," "Rhythm," and "Rhythm
Play" are described in Music Theory in this index.
At the end of each session, the programs in the
Atari version provide the user with only the

number of exercises attempted and the number
correct. A percentage score is not included as it
is in the Apple version.

Evaluation

The graphics of musical notation in these programs
is superior to that found in the Apple version,
although neither version provides for beams in the
notation of rhythm.

Unlike the Apple version, the Atari version allows
the user to quit the programs at any point by
pressing the <ESC>ape key twice.

* * *

Music III: Scales and Chords by Linda Borry
Hausmann, Minnesota Educational Computing
Corporation, 1982, version 2.2. One of three
music theory drill and practice packages; the
other packages are Music I: Terms and Notations
and Music III: Rhythm and Pitch. These programs
were originally written for the Apple II series of
computers under the title Music Theory.

Hardware: Atari with 48K memory, single disk
drive, video monitor; (small amplifier and
headphones may be desired).

Cost: $29

Publisher's suggested audience: Beginning to
advanced music students.

Documentation: Includes a 59-page support manual
which provides a description of the programs,
lists learning objectives, instructs the material
to be covered in the programs, and suggests a
sequence of instruction for someone using all four
of the packages.

Description

The five programs on this disk, "Whole-Half,"
"Find the Half," "Triads," "Scales," and
"Sevenths" are described in Music Theory in this
index. At the end of each session, the programs

in the Atari version provide the user with only
the number of exercises attempted and the number
correct. A percentage score is not included as it
is in the Apple version.

Evaluation

The graphics of musical notation in these programs
is superior to that found in the Apple version,
although neither version provides for beams in the
notation of rhythm.

Unlike the Apple version, the Atari version allows
the user to quit the programs at any point by
pressing the <ESC>ape key twice.

***

Music in Theory and Practice Tutor, Volume I, by
Bruce Benward with Brian Moore and David B.
Williams. (A computer-assisted supplement to
Music in Theory and Practice, Volume I, Third
Edition, by Bruce Benward), Micro Music Software
Library, Temporal Acuity Products, Inc., 1985.

Hardware: Apple II, II+, or IIe with a minimum of
48K memory, Disk II drive with controller, video
monitor (monochrome preferred), Micro Music DAC
board, speaker or headphones.

Cost: $350

Publisher's suggested audience: High school or
college music students.

Documentation: A user's guide includes the
objectives of the program, a summary, prerequisite
skills and knowledge, and operating instructions.
This eight-disk set of programs is designed to
accompany Music In Theory and Practice, Volume I,
Third edition, by Bruce Benward, William C. Brown
Publishers, 1985. These programs cannot be used
without the textbook. The documentation includes
a table of contents listing the various programs
on each of the eight disks and linking each to
a particular assignment in the text.

Description

Each of the programs on these disks is linked to a
specific assignment in Benward's text. The user
may proceed through each disk in the order in
which the material is presented or skip around on
the disk by pressing the <ESC>ape key to choose a
different drill from the main menu. In many of
these programs, the user may press <H> to hear
musical examples either from the text or on the
screen. Many of the drills in this series ask
questions and then provide multiple choice
answers. In one of the scale drills, for example,
the user is asked to identify the notes in a
particular scale by choosing among five possible
answers displayed on the screen. Other drills
involve the user in constructing intervals,
triads, or seventh chords or supplying the alto
and tenor voices in a part-writing exercise by
selecting notes from a piano keyboard displayed on
the screen. The selection is made by moving an
arrow on the screen to the appropriate note on the
keyboard with the left and right arrow keys.
Right answers receive short fanfares for sound
effects. When mistakes are made in a particular
drill, the user is usually given a second chance
along with some hints, and then is instructed to
refer to specific pages in the textbook for
review. There are no time constraints in any of
the drills. None of the disks provides a record
keeping utility.

Disk 1 provides drill in naming notes in treble,
bass, tenor, alto, soprano, and mezzo soprano
clefs, drill in identifying the specific octave or
register of given notes, drill in matching
enharmonically equivalent notes, drill in
selecting appropriate meter signatures for notated
melodies, and drill in applying rhythmic notation
rules to confusing or incorrectly notated
measures.

Disk 2 includes drills in constructing major,
natural minor, harmonic minor, and melodic minor
scales, drills in which the user indicates the
major scales or harmonic minor scales in which
given step-wise tetrachords belong, drills in
matching key signatures with parallel and relative
major and minor keys, drills which ask the user to
indicate the scale or authentic mode upon which

given melodies are based, drills in constructing
intervals above and below given notes, and a drill
in identifying the type and size of intervals
between two voices of a canon.

Disk 3 provides drill in constructing major,
minor, diminished, and augmented triads on a piano
keyboard displayed on the screen, drill in
identifying the letter name and accidental of
various degrees of major, harmonic minor, melodic
minor, and natural minor scales, drills in
supplying major and various types of minor keys in
which various triads function and how they
function (Roman numeral), drills in providing the
Roman numeral and figured bass analysis of chords
notated in four parts on a grand staff, drills in
identifying and labeling non-harmonic tones
(passing tones, escape tones, anticipations, pedal
tones, suspensions, neighbor tones, appoggiaturas,
retardations, and changing tones) in short chord
progressions, and drills in harmonizing short
tunes with tonic, subdominant, and dominant
triads.

Disk 4 includes practice in naming the structural
tones of given melodies, practice in finding
parallel phrases, sequences, repeated periods, and
phrase extensions in a Mozart sonata and a
Schubert impromptu, drills in providing the
transposition required for various instruments to
play given actual pitches, drills in filling in
the alto and tenor voices of chorale phrases in
which the outer voices are given, and drills in
providing Roman numeral and figured bass analysis
of chorale phrases. No seventh chords are
included on this disk.

Disk 5 provides drills in Roman numeral and
figured bass analysis of chord progressions and
chorale phrases, drills in providing harmonization
of chorale tunes, drills in identifying the
qualities of seventh chords, and drills in
resolving given dominant and leading tone seventh
chords.

Disk 6 continues to provide drills in
harmonization of given melodies, drills in Roman
numeral and figured bass analysis of chorale
phrases, drills in providing the inner voices of
exercises in which the outer voices are given, and

exercises in which the user is asked to indicate where and when modulations occur.

Disk 7 provides drill in constructing non-dominant seventh chords when the root is given, drills in resolving non-dominant seventh chords, drills in adding inner voices and analysis to chorale phrases involving seventh chords, drills in constructing secondary or applied chords, drills in which the user must specify where in a given piece of music a secondary dominant chord could occur, and drills in identifying what type of seventh chord will result when a particular figured bass symbol is given.

Disk 8 provides drill in analysis of form. The drills stress phrase relationships, key schemes and modulations, harmonic vocabulary, cadence types, and compositional devices such as imitation, sequence, phrase extension, and harmonic elaboration. The remainder of the disk provides drills and exercises in the chord symbols used in popular music and exercises in harmonizations of "popular" tunes.

Evaluation

The idea of providing computer-assisted drill for the assignments in a textbook has a lot to be said for it. As the student works on these drills, (s)he gets immediate feedback, rather than having to wait until the assignments are turned back by the instructor with corrections. Furthermore, this "tutor" provides helpful hints that guide the student to the correct response when wrong ones have been made. The programs also provide the student with the sounds of the exercises, something a textbook alone cannot do, and something which not all students are capable of providing for themselves.

The programs are logically organized and factually correct. The main menu of each disk lists the programs on the disk by letter name and the pages in the text which these programs supplement. The graphics of musical notation are acceptable, and the sound is quite good. Instructions are clear and within each program. Each program may be ended at any time, and the user may return to the

main menu of each disk to select a program out of
the normal order.

A few features of these programs may be
problematic for some users. In the scale
construction program, the user is presented with
five multiple choice answers of letter names for
the scales, rather than their musical notation.
In exercises involving chordal analysis, the Roman
numerals employed are all displayed in large case,
regardless of the quality of the chord. In triad
and seventh chord construction drills, the root is
always displayed in notation on the screen, and
the user is asked to supply the additional notes.
The prompts and instructions are unclear in these
drills, and the user is never informed that (s)he
must first press the <SPACE BAR> in order to
"enter" the given root, before going on to enter
additional notes in the chord.

***

<u>Music Machine</u> (cartridge), Commodore Electronics
Ltd., 1982

Hardware: Commodore 64 or 128 and video monitor.
No disk drive is necessary; the cartridge fits
into the cartridge slot on the back of the
computer.

Cost: $10.97

Publisher's suggested audience: None stated.

Documentation: Includes a brief manual.

Description

The program converts the computer keyboard into a
piano or synthesizer keyboard. The second row of
keys on the computer keyboard, <Q> through <*>,
provide the diatonic pitches in C Major (the range
is a twelfth), while the top row of keys, <2>,
<3>, <5>, <6>, <7>, <9>, <0>, provide the
chromatic pitches.

While the program makes use of the Commodore 64
and the Commodore 128 built-in three-voice

synthesizer, it only permits the use of two voices at any one time. The user can control the tuning of the pitches in microtonal increments should (s)he want to play with other instruments or with a radio or tape. The program also permits the user to perform in six different registers.

The user may choose seven different rhythmic patterns to accompany his or her playing and change the tempo. The user may select "triangular," "sawtooth," "square," or "narrow pulse" wave forms for the pitches themselves. The "keyboard" may be placed in "decay" mode, in which the notes have an initial attack and fall off in amplitude quickly, in "sustain" mode, in which the notes are sustained at original amplitude until the key is released, or in "hold" mode, in which the notes are sustained after the key is released and until the next key is pressed.

The program also provides several effects options. "Glide" provides glissandos between notes. In "Special," each note played is sounded through two voices simultaneously, providing a more complex sound, and "vibrato" can be added.

Evaluation

Music making with this program, while awkward on the computer keyboard, can be interesting for those wanting to experiment with different sounds. Obviously, one cannot perform pieces requiring much keyboard facility.

As the user plays notes, the program provides the notation of the notes on the screen. The "score" moves across the screen from right to left. Unfortunately, the notation is very poor.

The program itself provides no prompts or instructions for the user. One has to refer to the written documentation in order to the use the program at all.

Some very nice sounds can be made with this program, and it is unfortunate that there is no way to save them.

***

Music Made Easy by Sandy Feldstein, Alfred
Publishing Co., 1982, 1984, distributed by
Electronic Courseware Systems, Inc.

Hardware: Commodore 64 or 128, one disk drive,
color monitor (optional). Also available for
Apple II+ or IIe, one disk drive, and monitor. A
small amplifier and headphones may be desirable.

Cost: $29.95

Publisher's suggested audience: None stated.

Documentation: A user's manual presents basic
music theory concepts as well as instructions on
how to use the programs.

Description

This disk consists of eight "tutorials" or
programs, each presenting instruction and drill on
specific basic music theory topics. The sound,
while it may reinforce the learning, is optional
and can be turned off in case the user is in a
crowded room. Most of the drills employed in each
section require that the user get 10 correct
answers in a row before the drilling stops. None
of the drills has any time constraints. During
the drill, the number tried, the number correct,
and the number yet to complete are displayed on
the screen. After completing a drill the user is
told how many he tried in order to complete 10
items in succession without a mistake. There is
no record keeping utility included on the disk.

Section 1 deals with the musical staff, treble and
bass clefs, names of the lines and spaces in the
two clefs, whole, half, and quarter notes,
measures, bar lines, and time signatures. Drills
in this section include asking the user to type
the names of notes in treble and then in bass
clef, asking the user if the stem on a note is on
the proper side of the note and if the stem
direction is correct, asking the user to place
beat numbers within measures, and having him or
her place bar lines in their proper locations.

The grand staff, ledger lines, whole, half, and
quarter rests, 2/4, 3/4, and the dotted quarter
are the topics of Section 2. Drills involve the

user in naming various notes on the grand staff,
numbering beats and placing bar lines in exercises
with rests, and telling how many quarter notes are
in larger notes.

Section 3 covers ties, slurs, repeat signs, first
and second endings, eighth notes and eighth rests.
The drills ask the user to indicate whether a tie
or a slur is being employed in notated examples,
what the order of each measure of a notated
example would be when repeat signs and first and
second endings are employed, and where the bar
lines belong in examples using eighth notes.

In Section 4, dotted quarter notes, flat, sharp,
natural, whole and half steps are discussed. The
user is drilled again in placing bar lines in
notated examples and in naming notes when
accidentals and ties are used.

The chromatic scale, major scale, and key
signatures are covered in Section 5. The user is
asked to construct major scales by typing the
names of the notes (they are then notated on a
treble clef staff), to name the scale that uses a
given key signature, and to type which notes in
the scale get sharped or flatted. The keys of C,
G, F, and B-flat are drilled.

Section 6 deals with dynamics, D.C., D.S., coda,
fine, tempo markings and other music symbols, and
major chords and triads. Drills involve the user
in showing the order of measures in musical
examples in which D.S., D.C., Coda, and Fine are
used. The user is also asked to match musical
terms with definitions, and to spell major triads
with G, D, C, F, and B-flat given as roots. As
the user types the letter names, the program
notates the triads on a treble clef staff
displayed on the screen.

Roman numeral chord function, progressions,
dominant seventh, and inversions, are the topics
of Section 7. Drills involve the user in spelling
the major triads built on I, IV, and V in the keys
of C, G, and F Major, asks the user to spell
dominant seventh chords on G and F, and then to
spell dominant seventh chords in the keys of G, C,
and F Major. This section also asks the user to
spell triads and seventh chords in different

inversions and to notate the I, IV, and V7 chords
using root position or inversions so that the
voice leading is smooth.

Section 8 deals with harmonizing a melody and
introduces passing and neighboring tones. The
drills require the user to provide the chord names
("G," "D7") which would provide the best harmony
for each measure of given melodies, place Roman
numeral analysis under the chords, enter the
chords so that the voice leading is smooth, and
label certain pitches in given melodies with <P>
for passing tones and <N> for neighbor tones.

Evaluation

There are no instructions within any of these
programs, although the prompts on the screen are
usually pretty clear. User errors do not lead to
hints or second tries. When mistakes are made,
the program says no and displays the correct
response immediately. The programs do not attempt
any personalization.

The graphics of music notation are rather poor.
The user cannot go directly to the drills in each
section, but must go through the tutorials first.
These tutorials require a lot of reading, and all
of the prose and musical examples are included in
the written documentation. The menu from which
the user selects a section in which to work does
not include descriptions of each section. In
order to make an intelligent choice of section,
the user must refer to the written documentation.

While the opening of each section informs the user
that one can leave a section by typing any of the
function keys, attempts to do this fail. There is
absolutely no way to leave a section in order to
choose another one, until the section is
completed.

***

Music Maestro by John Paulson, Springboard
Software, 1983.

Hardware: Apple II+, IIe, or IIc, Disk II drive
with controller, video monitor (color optional).
Also available for the Commodore 64 or 128, single
disk drive, and monitor. An amplifier and
headphones may be desired with either the Apple or
the Commodore.

Cost: $34.95

Publisher's suggested audience: Young children.

Documentation: A brief descriptive pamphlet
provides a summary and operating instructions.

Description

Designed for young children, this program provides
a "Picture Menu" consisting of a cycle of four
different screen displays representing each of
four games included on the disk. This menu
enables children to select a game by pressing any
key when they see the picture of the game they
want displayed on the screen. The games introduce
young users to the piano keyboard and the names of
notes in treble and bass clef, as well as provide
the means for children to create music and to test
their pitch memory skills.

"Perform/Record/Playback" enables the child to
play musical notes by pressing the top row of
number keys using three different formats--piano
keyboard, treble clef, or bass clef--each of which
is displayed on the screen at any one time. When
a key is pressed, the letter name of the note is
displayed on either the keyboard or a staff with
one of the clefs. The notes are all diatonic in
the key of C Major. Resulting melodies can be
"recorded," played back, or stored on disk.

In "Guido's Quiz," using the three formats (piano
keyboard, and treble or bass clefs) the child is
asked to identify the note name or the name of the
piano key displayed with a question mark on it.
At first all the note names appear on either the
keyboard or the staff with clef, depending upon
the user's choice. Eventually each note becomes a
question mark, and the user types its letter name.
Finally, isolated notes with question marks or
keys with question marks appear on either the

staff or the keyboard one at a time, and the child must identify them.

"Melody Tutor" loads and plays tunes recorded and stored on the disk in the keyboard format of the "Perform/Record/Playback" program. The disk also provides a number of familiar tunes which are utilized in this program. The child is asked to play back the tune one note at a time using the number keys on the computer keyboard, but always having to start at the beginning for each successive note. "Melody Tutor" approves correct responses; mistakes cause the Tutor to review.

In "Kaleidoscope," as the top row of numbers is used to play a tune created by the child, a graphic design is produced on the screen for each note. These graphics have nothing to do with music notation.

Evaluation

The graphics of musical notation and the quality of the sound are less than adequate in this program. Written instructions appear both in the documentation and within the program. Without these instructions no one, including adults, can work with the program because it does not employ any prompts. Young children will be unable to use this program unless someone who can read explains to them how to operate the software and what the various programs expect them to do.

***

Music: Pitch, Minnesota Educational Computing Corporation, 1984, version 1.0. One of a series of four music theory drill and practice packages; the other packages are Music: Rhythm, Music: Terms and Notation, and Music: Scales and Chords. These programs were originally written for the Apple II series of computers under the title Music Theory.

Hardware: Commodore 64 or 128, single disk drive, video monitor; (small amplifier and headphones may be desired).

Cost: $29

Publisher's suggested audience: Beginning to
advanced music students.

Documentation: Includes a 32-page support manual
which provides a description of the programs,
lists learning objectives, instructs the material
to be covered in the programs, and suggests a
sequence of instruction for someone using all four
of the packages.

Description

The four programs on this disk, "Aural Intervals,"
"Visual Intervals," "Wrong Note," and "Missing
Note" are described in <u>Music Theory</u> in this index.
At the end of each session, the programs in the
Commodore version provide the user with only the
number of exercises attempted and the number
correct.   A percentage score is not included as it
is in the Apple version.

Evaluation

The graphics of musical notation in these programs
is superior to that found in the Apple version,
although neither version provides for beams in the
notation of rhythm. The use of color in the
Commodore version is tastefully done.   However,
this may be offset by the long loading time
required by the Commodore 1541 disk drive.   Given
the rather sophisticated sound capabilities of the
Commodore 64, the sound programmed in the
Commodore version is disappointing and no better
than the sound of the Apple speaker in the Apple
version.

An error was discovered in "Wrong Note."   In one
exercise the notes A-flat down to four D naturals
are notated on the screen.   When the user presses
<P>, the program plays A-flat, D, D, D, E-flat.
After the user chooses the fifth pitch as the
wrong one, the program notates A-flat, D, D, D, D-
flat as the "correct" notation.

After successful completion of each exercise in
"Aural Intervals," "Wrong Note," and "Missing
Note," the program asks the user if (s)he wants to
hear the item again.   Many users who do not want

to rehear something they have already completed,
will be bothered by the fact that they must invest
two key strokes (<N> and <RETURN>) before they can
go on to the next item.

Unlike the Apple version, the Commodore version
allows the user to quit the programs at any point
by pressing the <F1> key twice.

***

Music Printer

See MusicPrinter.

***

Music: Rhythm, Minnesota Educational Computing
Corporation, 1984, version 1.0. One of a series
of four music theory drill and practice packages;
the other packages are Music: Pitch, Music:
Terms and Notation, and Music: Scales and
Chords. These programs were originally written
for the Apple II series of computers under the
title Music Theory.

Hardware: Commodore 64 or 128, single disk drive,
video monitor; (small amplifier and headphones may
be desired).

Cost: $29

Publisher's suggested audience: Beginning to
advanced music students.

Documentation: Includes a 32-page support manual
which provides a description of the programs,
lists learning objectives, instructs the material
to be covered in the programs, and suggests a
sequence of instruction for someone using all four
of the packages.

Description

The three programs on this disk, "Counting,"
"Rhythm," and "Rhythm Play" are described in Music

Theory in this index. At the end of each session,
the programs in the Commodore version provide the
user with only the number of exercises attempted
and the number correct. A percentage score is not
included as it is in the Apple version.

Evaluation

The graphics of musical notation in these programs
is superior to that found in the Apple version,
although neither version provides for beams in the
notation of rhythm. The use of color in the
Commodore version is tastefully done. However,
this may be offset by the long loading time
required by the Commodore 1541 disk drive. Given
the rather sophisticated sound capabilities of the
Commodore 64, the sound programmed in the
Commodore version is disappointing and no better
than the sound of the Apple speaker in the Apple
version.

After successful completion of each exercise in
"Rhythm" and "Rhythm Play," the program asks the
user if (s)he wants to hear the item again. Many
users who do not want to rehear something they
have already completed, will be bothered by the
fact that they must invest two key strokes (<N>
and <RETURN>) before they can go on to the next
item.

Unlike the Apple version, the Commodore version
allows the user to quit the programs at any point
by pressing the <F1> key twice.

***

Music Room, An Instrument Tuning Exercise by Ray
E. Zuber, Electronic Courseware Systems, Inc.,
1984.

Hardware: Commodore 64 or 128, one disk drive,
monitor (color monitor optional).

Cost: $39.95

Publisher's suggested audience: None stated.

Documentation: Brief description on back of
diskette box.

Description

<u>Music Room</u> simulates a situation in which a
musician must tune six different musical
instruments: a piccolo, a violin, a trumpet, a
saxophone, a cello, and a tuba.   Each instrument
must be tuned individually in its own register.
An interactive tutorial about tuning wind and
string instruments is included on the disk.

An electronic tuner and one of the six instruments
are displayed on screen.   The tuner and the
instrument play the tuning note separately and
then together.   The user must determine if the
instrument is sharp or flat and then correct the
problem by adjusting the instrument.   In the case
of the stringed instruments, the choices are to
"loosen" or to "tighten" the string.   In the case
of the wind instruments, the choices involve
"lengthening" or "shortening" the instrument.   One
adjustment does not usually fix the problem, and
the user must adjust several times in order to get
the instrument in tune with the tuner.

The user enters responses by pressing the function
keys.   <F1> is used when the two sounding pitches
are in tune, <F3> to loosen or lengthen, <F5> to
tighten or shorten, and <F7> to hear the two
pitches again.   Every time the user makes a
correct decision, the program responds by
announcing that it is either loosening or
tightening.   The two notes are played again, and
the user must make another decision.   If the user
makes a wrong decision, the program states that it
is wrong and that the instrument is either flat or
sharp, plays the two notes again and waits for the
user's next decision.

After all six instruments have been tuned, the
user is awarded points (out of a possible 1000),
told how long the task of tuning all six
instruments took, and told how many errors were
made.   There is no record keeping.

Evaluation

The graphics, especially in color, are quite good in this program, and the sounds are fair. The prompts are clear and consistent and are displayed at the bottom of the screen throughout the drill. There is no personalization, but the scoring and timing provide motivation and give the program replay value. When the user does well, the program displays terms such as "excellent" and "outstanding."

Although it requires a lot of reading, the tutorial on tuning is quite good and involves the user in responding to some stimuli. It can be bypassed for those wanting to go directly to the drill.

***

Music: Scales and Chords, Minnesota Educational Computing Corporation, 1984, version 1.1. One of a series of four music theory drill and practice packages; the other packages are Music: Pitch, Music: Rhythm, and Music: Terms and Notation. These programs were originally written for the Apple II series computers under the title Music Theory.

Hardware: Commodore 64 or 128, single disk drive, video monitor; (small amplifier and headphones may be desired).

Cost: $29

Publisher's suggested audience: Beginning to advanced music students.

Documentation: Includes a 32-page support manual which provides a description of the programs, lists learning objectives, instructs the material to be covered in the programs, and suggests a sequence of instruction for someone using all four of the packages.

Description

The five programs on this disk, "Whole-Half,"
"Find the Half," "Triads," "Scales," and
"Sevenths" are described in Music Theory in this
index. At the end of each session, the programs
in the Commodore version provide the user with
only the number of exercises attempted and the
number correct. A percentage score is not
included as it is in the Apple version.

Evaluation

The graphics of musical notation in these programs
is superior to that found in the Apple version,
although neither version provides for beams in the
notation of rhythm. The use of color in the
Commodore version is tastefully done. However,
this may be offset by the long loading time
required by the Commodore 1541 disk drive. Given
the rather sophisticated sound capabilities of the
Commodore 64, the sound programmed in the
Commodore version is disappointing and no better
than the sound of the Apple speaker in the Apple
version.

There are errors in the Commodore version of
"Scales." In one exercise, the program plays a
melodic minor scale ascending and the dorian mode
descending and will only accept "natural minor" as
an answer. In another exercise, the ascending
form of the melodic minor scale is played both
ascending and descending, and the program accepts
"melodic minor" as an answer. The program accepts
"phrygian" as an answer for the phrygian mode
played with a raised sixth degree. In still
another case, a natural minor scale is played
ascending with a dorian mode descending, and the
expected answer is "natural minor."

After successful completion of each exercise in
"Whole-Half," "Find the Half," "Triads," "Scales,"
and "Sevenths," the program asks the user if (s)he
wants to hear the item again. Many users who do
not want to rehear something they have already
completed, will be bothered by the fact that they
must invest two key strokes (<N> and <RETURN>)
before they can go on to the next item.

Unlike the Apple version, the Commodore version
allows the user to quit the programs at any point
by pressing the <Fl> key twice.

* * *

Music Symbols by David Williams, Al Blackford and
Julie Schulze, Micro Music Software Library,
published by Temporal Acuity Products, Inc., 1981.

Hardware: Apple II series computer with at least
48K memory, 3.2 or 3.3 Disk II drive with
controller, video monitor; (MMI DAC music card and
headphones required only if sound effects are
desired).

Cost: $70

Publisher's suggested audience: Third grade to
university.

Documentation: A user's guide includes the
objectives of the program, a summary, prerequisite
skills and knowledge, operating instructions, and
instructions for changing any options.

Description

In game format, this program provides drill and
practice in identifying musical symbols displayed
on the screen, spelling the names of the symbols,
and in recalling them when displayed on the
screen. The user may select among three methods
of drill, three speed levels, and between two sets
of musical symbols.

In "Select-a-Symbol," a musical symbol is
displayed on the screen, and the user must select
the appropriate symbol name among the multiple
choice answers provided. In "Spell-a-Symbol," the
name of a musical symbol appears briefly on the
screen and then disappears; the user must type the
name with absolutely correct spelling. In
"Recall-a-Symbol," a musical symbol is again
displayed, and the user must type the name with
absolute precision without benefit of multiple
choice answers or seeing the name of the symbol
displayed even briefly.

While the user may select a response time (slow, medium, or fast), the program automatically increases or decreases the speed based upon the user's performance during the drill.

The user may choose between two sets of musical symbols, one set containing less familiar symbols than the other.

When the user "quits," a "Report Card" is displayed providing level attained, speed, number of tries, number correct, and the percentage of correct responses. There is no long-term record keeping.

Evaluation

The sound effects (although optional) in this program are good; their only purpose is to provide motivation when the user's response is correct (fragments from musical literature in major keys, fanfares) and to admonish when the response is incorrect (fragments from musical literature in minor keys). The program uses a personalized approach by providing comments to the user followed by his or her name.

The program is factually correct. The instructions are clear, within the program, and can be bypassed if not needed. However, instructions cannot be recalled during the program if the user requires some review. The program presents clear and consistent prompts, and the screen is neat and uncluttered. The program allows second tries if an answer is incorrect, although it does not provide any hints. After the second wrong answer, the program provides the correct one.

One has to question the publisher's suggested audience for this program. It is unlikely that many of the musical symbols included in this program would be familiar to third grade children. Furthermore, the typing skills required in order to enter responses, especially in timed drills such as these, go beyond not only the skills of junior high students, but also beyond the typing abilities of most adults. Since running out of time counts as an error, many novice typists, no

matter how thorough their musical knowledge, would find the program very frustrating.

In order to respond to questions at the beginning of the program, as well as to enter responses in the spelling and recall sections of the program, Apple IIe users must have the <CAPS LOCK> key depressed. Neither the documentation nor the instructions within the program inform the user of this necessity.

***

Music Terminology by Vincent Oddo, Electronic Courseware Systems, Inc., 1984.

Hardware: Commodore 64 or 128, one disk drive, monitor (color monitor optional). Also available for Apple II+ or IIe with at least 48K, or Apple IIc with at least 128K, one disk drive, and monitor, or the IBM-PC or IBM-PC JR. with at least 128K, one 360K double-sided disk drive, color graphics board, and monitor.

Cost: $39.95

Publisher's suggested audience: None stated.

Documentation: Brief description on back of the diskette box.

Description

This program provides users with a glossary and a set of drills on the meaning of Italian musical terms having to do with tempo, dynamics, and articulation. The author has chosen Willi Apel's Harvard Dictionary of Music, (second edition, revised and enlarged), Harvard University Press (1969) as the source of the terms and abbreviations used in the programs. The user has five programs from which to choose.

The "Glossary" provides a definition and related information for thirty-five Italian terms. The user may "look up" a term by choosing the "Glossary" from the main menu and then selecting a term about which (s)he wants information. In

addition to the thirty-five terms with lengthy
definitions and information, there are thirteen
terms included in the "Glossary" with briefer
coverage.

"Categories of Terms" is a drill which asks the
user to match a term displayed in a "window" with
an appropriate category in a multiple choice list.
The categories are "tempo indication," "change of
tempo," "manner of performance," "dynamic
indication," or "change of dynamics."

In the "True/False Questions" drill, a musical
term is followed by a definition; the user must
decide if the definition belongs with the term by
pressing <F> for false and <T> for true.

"Multiple-Choice Questions" displays a definition
followed by four multiple choice terms. The user
must choose the term which matches the definition.

In the "Fill-in Questions" drill the user must
type in the term which most closely matches the
definition displayed. Spelling and punctuation
must be absolutely correct.

Each drill has 25 questions, although the user may
"quit" at anytime (by pressing the <F1> key on the
Commodore). None of the drills includes any time
constraints. After the final question of each
drill the user is provided with a list of all the
terms needing review, i.e., all the ones answered
incorrectly, along with a percentage score.

Evaluation

The program is logically organized and factually
correct. The prompts are clear and consistent,
although the methods of response vary from one
drill to the next. Instructions are clear, within
the program, and can be bypassed for users already
familiar with them. Errors do not lead to
repeated tries or hints. A mistake provokes a
"wrong" or "no" message, followed by the correct
answer.

While the "Glossary" contains forty-eight terms,
some defined more briefly than others, the drills
actually use many more. (The author says over
100.) The drills often employ abbreviations of

terms, since in actual musical notation, they are
usually found in abbreviated form. The drills
also use terms related to the ones in the
"Glossary," all of which are discussed in the
individual definitions and related information.
For example, the related information about the
term "tempo" includes "tempo ordinario," "tempo
primo," "tempo giusto," "tempo commodo,"
"l'istesso tempo," and "a tempo."

The drill involving fill-in questions may be
frustrating to young users or to users with
limited typing skills. Unless the musical term is
spelled and typed accurately, the response is
found to be unacceptable. While the other drills
often use abbreviations of terms, the user may
not use abbreviations in the fill-in questions.

***

Music: Terms and Notation, Minnesota Educational
Computing Corporation, 1984, version 1.1. One of
a series of four music theory drill and practice
packages; the other packages are Music: Pitch,
Music: Rhythm, and Music: Scales and Chords.
These programs were originally written for the
Apple II series of computers and entitled Music
Theory.

Hardware: Commodore 64 or 128, single disk drive,
video monitor; (small amplifier and headphones may
be desired).

Cost: $29

Publisher's suggested audience: Beginning to
advanced music students.

Documentation: Includes a 32-page support manual
which provides a description of the programs,
lists learning objectives, instructs the material
to be covered in the programs, and suggests a
sequence of instruction for someone using all four
of the packages.

Description

The five programs on this disk, "Note Types,"
"Name the Note," "Enharmonics," "Terms," and "Key
Signatures" are described in Music Theory in this
index. At the end of each session, the programs
in the Commodore version provide the user with
only the number of exercises attempted and the
number correct. A percentage score is not
included as it is in the Apple version.

Evaluation

The graphics of musical notation in these programs
is superior to that found in the Apple version,
although neither version provides for beams in the
notation of rhythm. The use of color in the
Commodore version is tastefully done. However,
this may be offset by the long loading time
required by the Commodore 1541 disk drive.

In the Commodore version, a flat and a sharp are
entered by typing the <#> sign and the <%> sign
respectively. Having to press the <SHIFT> key in
order to type these signs will be bothersome to
many users.

Unlike the Apple version, the Commodore version
allows the user to quit the programs at any point
by pressing the <Fl> key twice.

***

Music Theory by Linda Borry, Minnesota Educational
Computing Corporation, 1980, version 2.2. The 17
programs included on this disk are available for
the Commodore 64 or 128 (MECC) on four separate
disks entitled Music: Rhythm, Music: Terms and
Notation, Music: Pitch, and Music: Scales and
Chords. These programs are also available for the
Atari, entitled Music I: Terms and Notations,
Music II: Rhythm and Pitch, and Music III:
Scales and Chords. These titles are also listed
in this index.

Hardware: Apple II, II+, or IIe computer with at
least 48K memory, disk drive with 3.3 DOS, video
monitor (small amplifier and headphones may be

desired). Also available for the Commodore 64 or
128, single disk drive and monitor, and for the
Atari 800 XL, single disk drive and monitor.

Cost: $49

Publisher's suggested audience: Beginning to
advanced music students.

Documentation: Includes a 120-page support manual
which provides a description of the programs,
lists learning objectives, provides prerequisites
for each program, instructs the material to be
covered in each program, and suggests a sequence
of instruction for someone using all of the
programs.

Description

This series of seventeen programs provides drill
and practice in several areas of musical skills
and knowledge. Aural skills are drilled in "Aural
Intervals," "Find the Half," "Missing Note,"
"Rhythm," "Rhythm Play," "Scales," "Sevenths,"
"Triads," "Whole-Half," and "Wrong Note," while
knowledge of musical notation and musical
terminology is drilled in "Counting,"
"Enharmonics," "Key Signatures," "Name the Note,"
"Note Types," "Terms," and "Visual Intervals."
Each program provides its own set of instructions
and provides a percentage score at the end of each
user session. None of the programs provides
record keeping on the disk.

"Aural Intervals" provides drill and practice in
the aural recognition of intervals played
melodically. The user selects the intervals to be
practiced and may choose any combination of
intervals from major and minor seconds to perfect
octaves. No compound intervals are included. The
user also selects how the intervals will be
presented--ascending, descending, or both--and
chooses how many intervals will be played at each
session. The program waits until the user
pressses the <RETURN> key before it plays each
interval, allowing the user to work at his or her
own pace. Abbreviations for each interval, such
as "MI2" for minor second, "TRI" for tritone, and
"P5" for perfect fifth, are displayed on the
screen during the drill. The user may press the

<R> key to hear the interval played again. The
program does not allow second tries and displays
the correct answer immediately after a mistake is
made.

In "Counting," an incomplete measure, which can be
completed by adding one note value, is displayed
on the screen. The user selects a note value from
a multiple choice list to complete the measure.
The choices include note values from sixteenth
notes to whole notes, including dotted whole,
dotted half, dotted quarter, and dotted eighth
notes. The user selects the time signature for
each exercise from a list of simple and compound
meters, including, 2/4, 3/4, 4/4, 5/4, 6/4, 3/8,
6/8, 9/8, and 12/8. The user also chooses how
many exercises are to be done for each session.
An arrow on the screen in each exercise indicates
where in the measure the additional note belongs.
The user enters responses with codes such as <DW>
for a dotted whole, <E> for eighth, and <Q> for
quarter.

"Enharmonics" provides drill in the identification
of notes which are equivalent in pitch but which
may be notated differently. In this drill the
name of a note (not its notation) is displayed on
the screen using a "#" for a sharp and a "*" for a
flat. The user responds with the simplest
enharmonic spelling of the given note by typing a
letter name and a <#> or a <*> when necessary.
The user specifies how many exercises to complete
and whether the exercises will include notes with
double sharps or flats or notes with single sharps
or flats. The program allows no second tries and
displays the correct answer immediately after a
mistake has been made.

"Find the Half" is an aural drill in which the
user must find an interval of a half step in a
scalar passage in which all the intervals but one
are whole steps. The user is asked to type in the
order number of the pitch after which the half
step occurs. The user may choose to work with a
series of three, four, or five notes in a set of
problems. The user chooses how many problems are
to be presented per session. No second chances
are provided.

"Key Signatures" provides drill in recognizing major and minor key signatures. The user may choose to work with major keys only, minor keys only, or both major and minor keys. A key signature is displayed on a musical staff with clef sign (treble or bass at random); the user is asked to identify either the major or the minor key that the signature represents. Responses are entered by pressing a letter key from <A> through <G> and a <#> for sharp or a <*> for flat if appropriate. The user has two opportunities to identify it correctly. If the first response is incorrect, (s)he is asked to try again. If a second incorrect response is entered, the correct answer is displayed immediately. Even if the second response is correct, the correct answer is not counted in the final score.

"Missing Note" provides practice in elementary melodic dictation by presenting an aural five-note pattern and a corresponding, but incomplete, visual pattern of four notes. The patterns have no rhythm; all the notes are quarter notes. The user may specify the maximum number of flats or sharps to be used in the key signatures of the patterns, the largest interval to be used, and the number of problems to be attempted. The user identifies the note that is missing from the visual pattern by pressing the letter name--<A> through <G>--of the note. The program does not require the user to enter sharps and flats. The missing notes are all diatonic, so the appropriate sharps and flats appear in the key signatures. The user may study the visual pattern as long as needed before pressing <RETURN> for the first hearing. Additional playings can be heard by pressing <R>. The program does allow second chances, but no hints. If an error is made on the second try, the correct answer is displayed immediately.

"Name the Note" provides practice in identifying notes on a musical staff with either treble or bass clef. The user may choose to work at one of five different levels: (1) treble clef with no sharps or flats or ledger lines; (2) bass clef with no sharps, or flats or ledger lines; (3) a mixture of treble and bass clefs, no sharps or flats or ledger lines; (4) a mixture of treble and bass clefs, no sharps or flats, but some ledger

lines; or (5) treble and bass clefs, some sharps
or flats, and some ledger lines. The user
responds by typing letter names <A> through <G>
and <#> for sharps and <*> for flats. No second
chances are provided; the correct answer is
displayed immediately when a mistake is made.

"Note Types" provides drill in recognizing the
rhythmic values of different notes and rests. The
user may choose to work with notes only, rests
only, or both, as well as how many problems to
attempt. The user first identifies the note or
rest displayed on the screen on a musical staff by
typing a code and then determines the number of
quarter note beats the note or rest is to be held.
The values used in the program are whole, dotted
whole, half, dotted half, quarter, dotted quarter,
eighth, dotted eighth, and sixteenth. The codes
employed include "DQ" for dotted quarter and "E"
for eighth. When designating the number of
quarter note beats in each note or rest value, the
user must use decimal numbers to indicate the
value of certain notes or rests. For example, a
dotted eighth is worth .75 and a dotted quarter is
worth 1.5. There are no second chances in this
program. If a mistake is made, the correct answer
is displayed on the screen immediately.

In "Rhythm," the user is asked to compare a visual
rhythmic pattern with three aural ones. After the
visual pattern is displayed, the user chooses to
hear any one of the three aural patterns while
attempting to determine which of the three matches
the one displayed on the screen. In each
exercise, two measures are displayed; the first is
always a measure of four quarter notes to
establish the tempo. The second measure is the
one used in the comparison. The user may work at
his or her own pace and hear the patterns as often
as required. No second chances are provided. The
correct answer is displayed after one error.

"Rhythm Play" provides practice in performing
rhythm patterns. A pattern is displayed on the
screen in notation; using the <N> key, the user
taps the pattern for the program to judge.
Exercises may be chosen from three levels of
difficulty: (1) three- to five-note patterns with
half, dotted quarter, quarter, and eighth notes,
(2) five- or six-note patterns using quarter and

eighth notes with some syncopation, or (3) six- or
seven-note patterns using dotted quarter, quarter,
eighth, dotted eighth, and sixteenth notes with
some syncopation. Two measures are displayed on
the screen, the first of which consists of four
quarter notes. Although the directions are not
clear, the user taps the four quarters in order to
establish the tempo, and then taps the actual
pattern in the second measure. The user may study
the pattern as long as needed before entering a
response. When a mistake is made, the program
notates the pattern entered by the user for
comparison with the correct one already notated on
the screen. The user can hear the correct pattern
played by pressing <R>.

"Scales" provides practice in identifying aurally
major scales, three types of minor scales, and
four modes (dorian, phrygian, lydian, and
mixolydian). The user may choose to work on major
and minor scales only, or to work with all the
scales and the modes. When the user is ready, the
program plays the scale both ascending and
descending. The user may hear the scale repeated
as many times as needed by pressing <R>. The user
identifies the scale or mode by pressing a number
key representing that scale on the screen. The
program allows one additional try when a mistake
is made. After the second mistake, the correct
answer is displayed on the screen.

"Sevenths" provides practice in the aural
identification of arpeggiated root position major
(major-major), minor (minor-minor), dominant
(major-minor), half-diminished, and fully-
diminished seventh chords. One may choose to work
with major, minor, and dominant seventh chords
only, or to work with exercises employing all five
types of seventh chords. Users may also choose
between a fixed root or a different root for each
chord. Each chord is arpeggiated both up and back
down, and the user may hear this repeated as often
as necessary. The codes necessary for identifying
each type of seventh chord are displayed on the
screen during the drill. The program does not
provide for second chances when mistakes are made.

"Terms" provides drill on the definitions of 57
Italian musical terms associated with performance
directions, dynamics, tempo, and change of tempo.

Three levels of difficulty are available: (1)
most commonly used terms, (2) commonly used terms,
and (3) less commonly used terms. A music term is
printed on the screen below which three possible
definitions are displayed. The user selects the
definition which most closely fits the term and
enters its corresponding letter, <A>, <B>, or <C>.
When the user has completed a session, the score
and any incorrectly defined terms are displayed.
The program does not provide for second chances.

"Triads" provides practice in aural recognition of
arpeggiated major, minor, augmented, and
diminished triads in root position. One may
choose to work with major and minor triads only or
to work with triads of all four qualities. The
triads are arpeggiated both up and down, and the
user may choose a fixed root or a different root
for all triads. The arpeggiated triad may be
heard as often as necessary by pressing the <R>
key. The user enters a response by selecting the
appropriate chord quality and typing its
corresponding number displayed on the screen. The
program does not provide for second chances.

"Visual Intervals" provides practice in
recognizing intervals by sight. The user
specifies the maximum number of sharps or flats to
be used in the key signatures, the combination of
intervals to be practiced (seconds, thirds,
fourths, fifths, sixths, and sevenths), and the
number of problems to attempt. For each problem
two notes are presented on a staff with treble
clef and a key signature. The user has one chance
to identify the interval between the two notes.
Abbreviations for each interval, such as "MI2" for
minor second, "A4" for augmented fourth, and "P5"
for perfect fifth, are displayed on the screen
during the drill. If a mistake is made, the
correct answer is displayed immediately.

"Whole-Half" provides practice in differentiating
aurally whole and half steps played melodically
both up and down. The user is presented with two
pitches and must determine whether the interval
between them is a whole step or a half step. The
program waits for the user to indicate when to
play the interval. The user may hear the interval
played again by pressing <R>. The user decides
how many problems to attempt and enters responses

with the <W> key for whole and the <H> for half
steps. The program does not provide for second
chances.

In "Wrong Note," the user is provided practice in
comparing written and performed pitch patterns.
The program displays a pattern of five notes on
the screen. After the user studies the notes in
the pattern and indicates that (s)he is ready to
hear the pattern, the program plays the pattern
with one wrong note. By pressing <R> the user may
hear the aural pattern as many times as needed.
The wrong note is either a half step or a whole
step off. The first note is always correct, and
the user must identify the wrong note by typing a
number from <2> to <5>, indicating its order
number among the five given pitches. The user may
select how many sharps or flats are to be used in
the key signatures of the exercises, select the
largest interval to be used in each problem, and
select how many problems will be attempted. If
the user makes a mistake, both the correct and the
incorrect patterns are displayed on the screen.
After the user has made a response, (s)he may hear
either the correct pattern or the incorrect
pattern. The program does not provide an
opportunity for second chances.

Evaluation

These programs are logically organized and
factually correct. The instructions are clear,
included in each program, and can be bypassed by
those already familiar with them. However, the
instructions cannot be gotten during a drill, nor
can the user end the program any time. If one
wants to stop, the remaining exercises in a
particular drill must be completed before one can
quit and go back to the menu where a different
drill can be selected.

For the most part the prompts are clear and
consistent in each program. However, in "Rhythm
Play," the user is instructed to "Play the pattern
using the <N> key." There are no further
instructions. One does not know whether to
establish one's own tempo by starting with the first
measure of four quarter notes, or to wait until the
program establishes the tempo so that the user may
proceed to play the pattern in the second measure.

A positive aspect of the programs is that they
allow the user to work at his or her own pace.
There are no time constraints, and the programs
all wait until the user indicates that (s)he is
ready to see or hear the stimulus for the
exercise. Another good feature about these
programs is that each one displays the codes or
abbreviations needed to make responses on the
screen during the drill. In addition, when a
response is not within the acceptable range of
possibilities, these programs tell the user that
his or her answer is invalid. For instance, in
"Visual Intervals," if the user responds by typing
"MA4," the program replies that that answer is
invalid, rather than merely saying it is a wrong
answer.

These programs provide very little in the way of
motivation for the user. There is no
personalization or game format, merely a screen at
the end of each session displaying the number of
exercises attempted, the number correct, and a
percentage score.

Limited to the Apple speaker, the sound in these
programs is not very good, and the graphics of
musical notation are poor. For instance, the
musical staff appears on the screen as five rows
of dots, rather than as five solid lines.

Having to type <#> for sharp and <*> for flat in
some of the programs involved with pitch and key
signatures may be cumbersome to many users. In
order to type these characters, one must not only
press these keys, but also the <SHIFT> key,
creating extra key strokes. <S> and <F> might be
more meaningful to the user.

***

The Musical Language by Joseph E. Koob II,
Electronic Courseware Systems, Inc., 1986.

See Music Appreciation: A Study Guide.

***

Musical Stairs: An Exercise in Interval
Relationships by Stephen L. Walker, Electronic
Courseware Systems, Inc., 1984.

Hardware: Commodore 64 or 128, one disk drive,
monitor (color monitor important to this program).
Also available for Apple II+ or IIe with at least
48K, or Apple IIc with at least 128K, one disk
drive, and monitor, or the IBM-PC or IBM-PC JR.
with at least 128K, one 360K double-sided disk
drive, color graphics board, and monitor. This
program is also available in a MIDI version for
the Commodore 64 or 128 and Apple II+ or IIe with
Passport Design MIDI interface card; or for the
Commodore 64 or 128, Apple II+ or IIe, or IBM-PC
with Roland MIDI interface card and a MIDI-
compatible music keyboard or synthesizer.

Cost: $39.95

Publisher's suggested audience: Young children.

Documentation: Brief description on back of
diskette box.

Description

Musical Stairs is a drill and practice game
designed to introduce intervallic relationships to
young children. The program displays a piano
keyboard and a musical staff with treble or bass
clef and quizzes numeric intervals within one
octave using only the white keys. An interval is
notated on the staff and played for the user, who
answers by using the arrow keys to move the cursor
to the key on the keyboard which represents the
second note of the interval. The second note is
always above the first. The user may choose to
work in treble clef, bass clef, or both. A score
is kept, shown to the user after completion of ten
items, and may qualify the user for the "Hall of
Fame."

The instructions include a brief tutorial. It
begins by playing a C Major scale, and as the
notes are played they are notated on the staff
with treble clef, and their scale degree numbers
are placed on the appropriate keys of the one-
octave piano keyboard. Using several examples,
the tutorial states that an interval between two

notes is found by counting "from the first note to
the second note."

Evaluation

This program does not really drill a student on
the size of intervals. The task the user is asked
to perform is to match a pitch on the staff with a
key on a one-octave piano keyboard displayed on
the screen. While it is true that numbers appear
on the keys as the user moves the cursor up to the
appropriate piano key, these numbers are only
ancillary; the user can perform the assigned task
without the numbers.

Instructions are clear, within the program, and
can be bypassed by those familiar with them.
Positive reinforcement is provided by
congratulatory comments and sound effects when the
user makes correct responses. When mistakes are
made the program allows repeated tries, offers the
user a hint by placing an asterisk below the
correct piano key, but never actually provides the
right answer. The user may leave the drill at any
time by pressing the <F1> key and returning to the
index.

The "Hall of Fame" provides space for twenty
players. The documentation states that the "Hall
of Fame" may be cleared of all data by typing
"DELETE DATA" on the name entry page. Several
attempts to do this failed. The quality of the
graphics of musical notation and of the sounds
produced by the program is less than one should
expect from a Commodore 64.

***

MusicPrinter by Jack M. Jarrett, Micro Music
Software Library, published by Temporal Acuity
Products, Inc., 1986, version 1.0.

Hardware: Apple II+, IIe, IIc or IIGS computer
with 48K memory minimum, 3.3 DOS, Disk II drive
with controller, video monitor, Epson, Okidata,
Imagewriter, or other compatible printer, equipped
with dot-addressable graphics. A long list of

compatible printers and interfaces is included in the manual.

Cost: $149

Documentation: Includes detailed user's manual, as well as a character code chart for quick reference.

Description

Advertised as a "word processor" for music, this program provides the user with the means to create, edit, and print musical scores. The program contains a set of musical symbols or characters which can be generated by the user by typing one- or two-letter "codes." For example, "HU" is the code for a half note with the stem up. The task of placing a particular musical symbol in a particular location on the musical staff involves moving the cursor to the desired location using the arrow keys and entering a character code. While the character codes are quite detailed, they are also logical, intuitive, and fairly easy to remember. Learning to use this music notation "processor" is like learning a word processor; an investment of time leads to familiarity and facility. A "Character Code Chart" and "Function Index" are included with the manual.

The program is strictly a music printer; it does not play music and does not require a synthesizer card, musical keyboard or MIDI interface.

The program allows music to be printed in three different print styles: normal, emphasized (similar to boldface in a word processor), and compressed, which prints characters half as wide as normal. The user can request as many as nine passes for darker, clearer print.

The program allows the creating or editing of a single line or, at most, two staves (for keyboard notation) at a time. Music notation is saved in disk files as either a single line or two staves. The notation is also printed one file at a time. In order to print a score, printing from disk files can be done in automatic sequence of consecutive files.

Lines of notation are not limited to the width of
the monitor screen, but may be from 1 to 175
characters long. When a line does go beyond the
confines of the screen, the screen automatically
scrolls along with the notation. Of course, one
must have a printer which will accommodate longer
lines of notation.

This system automatically adds ledger lines for
notes above or below the staff. Predesigned staff
formats include multiple staff characters such as
piano brackets for double staff keyboard music.
In addition to a very complete set of musical
characters, including thirty-second notes and
beams, upper and lower case alphabetical
characters in three type fonts are included,
allowing the user to add text to the notated
music. The program will also automatically
transpose lines of music.

<h2 style="text-align:center">Evaluation</h2>

The output of this program, both on the screen and
in hard copy is extremely good. Unlike many music
printing programs in which notes are entered via a
piano keyboard (most of which print exactly what
the user played, including notes held a split
second too long or hit unintentionally), this
program allows the user to place notes and other
musical notation exactly where they belong.

An update, version 2.0, 1987, of this software has
become available and can be obtained by sending
the publisher the old version along with $30. The
new diskette has the new version on one side and
the old version on the other, so that files
written under version 1.0 can still be used. The
new version supports a mouse or joystick for
cursor movement. These devices make the placing
of musical symbols on the staff easier and faster.
In addition, the new version will also run on the
Apple IIGS.

***

Name It: Kids' Classics by Bruce Benward and
David Williams, Micro Music Software Library,
published by Temporal Acuity Products, Inc., 1986,
version 3.2.   This program was formerly marketed
as Name That Tune--Ear Training Game for Kids.

Hardware: Apple II, II+, or IIe computer with at
least 48K memory, 3.2 or 3.3 Disk II drive with
controller, video monitor; MMI DAC music card and
headphones required.

Cost: $40

Publisher's suggested audience: Third grade to
university.

Documentation: A user's guide includes teaching
objectives, prerequisite skills and knowledge, as
well as details about the program.

Description

This program provides drill and practice in
identifying aurally the individual degrees of a
major scale.   The program plays a major scale as
many times as the user desires, displaying it
diagonally across the screen as solfeggio
syllables and scale degree numbers.   The program
then plays the tones of a familiar melody one by
one, with appropriate rhythm.   After each melodic
tone is played the user must choose which scale
degree has been played by moving the arrow keys to
select a pitch from the scale degrees displayed on
the screen.   The user does not enter the rhythm.
As the program adds more notes to the melodies, it
always starts back at the beginning, and the user
must reenter all the notes from the beginning.
After about four tones have been entered, the user
is given an opportunity to guess the title of the
melody by choosing among four multiple choice
answers.   If the user is wrong the program
continues to provide melodic tones and gives other
chances to guess the title of the melody.   The
user can request up to 24 melodies (the number
stored in the program).

The program is in game format and keeps track of
the user's right and wrong answers, giving a
running account of progress.

Evaluation

The sound is good in this program; "Twinkle Twinkle," "Old MacDonald," "Row Row Row Your Boat," and "Silent Night" are examples of the familiar tunes used. No musical notation is used in the entire program. A brief tutorial and instructions about the keys to use (left and right arrow keys, the <SPACE BAR>, and the <ESC>ape keys) are within the program and cannot be bypassed. The program requests the user's name and uses it within the program when congratulating or requesting information.

The program always plays the scale from "Do" to "Do" at the beginning of each exercise. Frequently, however, the scale is displayed on the screen from "Fa" to "Fa" or from "Sol" to "Sol" or from "Re" to "Re," depending upon the range of the melody in question. In these cases, the played scale starts on the "Do" within the syllables and scale degree numbers displayed on the screen, plays to the top syllable displayed and must wrap around and complete the scale in the register below where it started. Dividing the scale into two parts, with what should be the upper part now sounding below what should be the lower part, may be confusing to some users.

It is unfortunate that both the documentation and the instructions within the program neglect to inform the Apple IIe user that the <CAPS LOCK> key must be depressed throughout the program in order for the user to enter any responses.

***

Name That Tune--Ear Training Game for Kids by Bruce Benward and David Williams, Micro Music Software Library, Temporal Acuity Products, Inc., 1982, version 3.1.

For description and evaluation see Name It: Kids' Classics.

***

Note Names Drill, by John M. Eddins and Robert L.
Weiss. Electronic Courseware Systems, Inc., 1981,
1983, 1984.

See Elements of Music.

***

Note Reading Tutorial/Staff Note Reading by Virgil
Hicks and Frank Bradshaw (the University of Akron
Series), Wenger Corporation, 1981, 1982, 1985.
This program is now included in The Music
Class: Note Reading, part of the Music Class
Series.

Hardware: Apple II, II+, or IIe with a minimum of
64K, one disk drive, video monitor; game paddles
or joystick are optional; ALF synthesizer card,
headphones optional (the sound can be routed
through the computer's internal speaker). Also
available for the Commodore 64 or 128.

Cost: $69 (same for both Apple and Commodore
versions).

Publisher's suggested audience: Elementary:
beginning music students; Intermediate: students
who can read basic music.

Documentation: Brief descriptive pamphlet
includes summary, operating instructions, and
instructions for changing any options.

Description

Using graphics and sound, "Note Reading Tutorial"
provides instruction about sounds ascending or
descending, how sounds are notated with notes on
lines and spaces, and the names of notes.
Multiple choice questions are interspersed for the
user to answer. The staff and treble and bass
clefs are discussed. "Staff Note Reading"
provides a speed game for locating notes. A note
is displayed on a musical staff with a clef sign.
The user then turns a game paddle or uses a
joystick or uses the arrow keys to choose the
correct letter name of the note. There are six
levels from which to choose: treble clef, bass

clef, treble and bass clef, treble and bass clef
with ledger lines, alto clef, or tenor clef.

The program keeps track of the user's correct
answers during the tutorial and gives a percentage
of correct answers after the tutorial is
completed. During "Staff Note Reading" the number
of correct answers and average response time in
seconds are displayed on the top of the screen.
When the user is finished (s)he is evaluated on
the basis of the average number of seconds it
takes to respond with a correct answer. The
program also provides the teacher with a Manager
Utility for student record keeping and for setting
standards for student ratings. This utility
allows the use of passwords in addition to student
names. A "Hall of Fame" holds the names and
scores of the twenty top scorers.

Evaluation

"Note Reading Tutorial" requires a lot of reading,
which may be a problem for young users. It is
logically organized and even allows the user to go
back several screens if something needs review.
However, some of the statements do not seem
completely accurate. For example, the tutorial
states that "Low notes go down," and "The
direction of low notes is down." At one point in
the tutorial the user is asked to identify the
location of the "G line," but the program will not
accept the bottom line of the bass clef as an
answer. Errors lead to hints and second tries
only in the tutorial, not in the game.

The instructions for "Staff Note Reading" are
clear, within the program, and can be bypassed by
users already familiar with them. Unfortunately
the instructions do not make it clear to the user
that a minimum of ten exercises must be completed
in order to have the score saved by the record
keeping program. The user may end the program any
time.

The sound of the ALF synthesizer card is good, but
the graphics of the clefs signs and notes are not
as good as they could be. The note heads actually
are diamond-shaped rather than round.

***

Note Speller: A Note Recognition Game by Lolita
Walker Gilkes, Electronic Courseware Systems,
Inc., 1984

Hardware: Commodore 64 or 128, one disk drive,
monitor (color monitor optional). Also available
for Apple II+ or IIe with at least 48K, or Apple
IIc with at least 128K, one disk drive, and
monitor, or the IBM-PC or IBM-PC JR. with at least
128K, one 360K double-sided disk drive, color
graphics board, and monitor.

Cost: $39.95

Publisher's suggested audience: None stated.

Documentation: Brief description on back of
diskette box.

Description

In game format this program provides a ten
question quiz in identifying note names in treble
and bass clef staves. Notes are displayed in
four- to seven-note sets, and each set of pitches
presented on the staff spells a word. Under time
pressure, the user must identify the letter names
of the notes and decide what word the letters
spell. When the user indicates (s)he is ready to
spell the word, the notes disappear from the
staff, and the user types the word. The program
plays the notes after they have been identified
successfully. The user may choose to be drilled
in treble clef, bass clef, or the grand staff, and
may choose among three speeds, "adagio,"
"moderato," or "allegro." The faster the word is
spelled, the higher the score. Bonus points are
added for the medium and fast speeds. The user is
asked if (s)he wants long words included in the
quiz. If the user chooses to review notes, (s)he
receives a brief tutorial on the names of the
lines and spaces in the clef chosen at the
beginning. One may choose to have the drills
include ledger lines in the grand staff quiz.

A timer, displayed on the right side of the
screen, reminds the user of the time element of
the quiz. The high score of preceding players and
the user's score are displayed throughout each
session. The user's score is displayed at the end

of the quiz, along with whether or not the score
was high enough to place the user's name in the
"Hall of Fame." Other than the "Hall of Fame,"
the disk does not provide a record keeping
utility. Unfortunately the "Hall of Fame" only
holds three names. As players with better scores
finish the quiz, earlier "Hall of Famers" are
bumped.

Evaluation

This program is logically organized and factually
correct. The graphics of musical notation are not
outstanding, however, and the sounds of the
pitches are not representative of the sound
capabilities of the Commodore 64. The
instructions are within the program and can be
bypassed by those familiar with them. The prompts
are clear and consistent, as are the methods of
response. The program allows no second chances.
If the answer is incorrect, or time has run out,
the user is so informed, and the correct answer is
displayed on the screen.

The user is asked to type his name at the
beginning of the program, but beyond wishing him
or her good luck, the program involves no
personalization thereafter. The instructions go
further than most in telling the user how to erase
typing mistakes by using the left cursor key
(although it is assumed that the user knows that
the <SHIFT> key must be pressed in order to make
the right cursor key a left cursor key on the
Commodore 64). However, when the user attempts to
correct mistakes, the left cursor key does not
work. Typing could be a problem for young users.

* * *

Patterns in Pitch: An Aural-Visual Pitch Program
by Vincent Oddo, Electronic Courseware Systems,
Inc., 1985. This program is available under the
same title, in three levels, the third being the
most difficult.

Hardware: Commodore 64 or 128, one disk drive,
monitor (color monitor optional). Also available
for Apple II+ or IIe with at least 48K, or Apple

IIc with at least 128K, one disk drive, and
monitor, or the IBM-PC or IBM-PC JR. with at least
128K, one 360K double-sided disk drive, color
graphics board, and monitor.

Cost: $39.95 for each level; $99.95 for the set
of three.

Publisher's suggested audience: None stated.

Documentation: Brief description on back of
diskette box.

Description

Patterns in Pitch allows the user to create and/or
hear melodic pitch patterns, 5 to 12 notes in
length, within a tonal framework. The programs
are divided into two types, composition and
dictation. The parameters from which the user may
choose include the following: treble or bass
clef, major or natural minor, number of sharps or
flats in the key signature, the number of pitches
in each pattern, and the tempo at which the
pattern is to be performed. None of the patterns
includes rhythm.

In the composition program, the user enters his
pitches by choosing corresponding scale degree
numbers. Once the tempo is entered, the computer
plays back the pitch pattern.

In addition to the parameters listed above, the
dictation program allows the user to set the range
of the pitch pattern by choosing "narrow" (scale
degrees 1-5), "medium" (scale degrees 1-8), or
"wide" (scale degrees 1-8 plus 5-6-7 below 1). At
the beginning of each exercise in the dictation
part of the program, the first five scale degrees
and an arpeggiated tonic triad are played in order
to establish the key. Once the tempo is entered
and the tonal center established, the computer
plays the pattern; by pressing <R> the user can
hear the pitch pattern repeated; by pressing <N>
the user can begin notating the pattern, again by
choosing corresponding scale degree numbers. Once
the user selects <N>, however, (s)he is unable to
hear the pattern any additional times.

Using a split screen, the dictation program enters
the user's perception of the pitch pattern on the
upper half without noting any errors; the program
then notates the computer, or correct, version on
the lower portion of the screen for the user to
compare. The computer also plays both versions
for the user. There is no scoring otherwise, nor
is there any record keeping.

Level I uses the keys C, G, and F with a maximum
of eight notes. Level II adds D, A, B-flat, and
E-flat with a maximum of twelve notes. In Level
III the user may choose any major or minor key and
pitch patterns up to twelve notes in length.

Evaluation

While the documentation for these programs is
skimpy, instructions are included within the
program. They can also be bypassed if not needed.
The prompts are clear and consistent, and the
methods of response are consistent throughout.
However, it is not clear that in order to "enter"
a note in either the composition section or the
dictation section, the user must press the
<RETURN> key. In addition, the program allows the
user to enter scale degree numbers 9 and 0, for
instance, without prompts with information
regarding the inappropriateness of such responses.
Fortunately the program does not try to notate
these pitches.

The graphics, especially of the treble clef sign
in the staff, are one of the weaker aspects of
this program.

The instructions include a short tutorial on the
harmonic implications of melody, pointing out that
often the subdominant, dominant, and tonic triads
are outlined in melodies through arpeggiation.

The use of the natural minor scale for melodic
fragment exercises seems curious. While the
natural minor scale accomodates melodies which
descend from the upper tonic, it does not provide
the raised sixth and seventh degrees so common to
ascending melodies in the minor mode.

***

Patterns in Rhythm: An Aural-Visual Rhythmic
Program by Vincent Oddo, Electronic Courseware
Systems, Inc., 1984.   This program is available
under the same title in three levels of difficulty
with the third level being the most difficult.

Hardware: Commodore 64 or 128, one disk drive,
monitor (color monitor optional).   Also available
for Apple II+ or IIe with at least 48K, or Apple
IIc with at least 128K, one disk drive, and
monitor, or the IBM-PC or IBM-PC JR. with at least
128K, one 360K double-sided disk drive, color
graphics board, and monitor.

Cost: $39.95 for each of three levels; $99.95 for
a set of all three.

Publisher's suggested audience: None stated.

Documentation: Brief description on back of
diskette box; brief pamphlet regarding instructor
management options.

Description

Patterns in Rhythm allows the user to create
and/or hear rhythmic patterns, some two, and some
three measures in length.   The programs are
divided into two types, composition and dictation.
The user may choose composition in simple or
compound meters or dictation in simple or compound
meters.

In both the composition and dictation programs the
user first chooses among three sets of meters.
Each of the three sets has the same lower number
(2, 4 or 8 in the case of simple meters, and 4, 8
or 16 in the case of compound meters).   The user
then chooses a tempo (slow, medium, or fast) and
duple, triple, or quadruple as the upper number of
the meter signature (6, 9, or 12 in the case of
compound meters).

In the composition programs the user then creates
rhythmic patterns by selecting one of eight
different beat patterns displayed on the screen
for each beat of the exercise.   When the user is
finished, the computer performs the pattern,
adding pitch within a tonal framework.   By
pressing <R> the user hears the pattern; by

pressing <E> the user erases the pattern and may create a new one.

In the dictation drills, the program performs a rhythmic pattern after the user has selected the appropriate parameters. The user may ask for repeated hearings by pressing <R>; pressing <N> will enable the user to notate what was heard by selecting among the eight different beat patterns displayed on the screen for each beat of the exercise. Once <N> is selected, however, the user cannot request additional hearings of the pattern.

After "notating" the answer, the correct version is displayed beneath the user's version for comparison. The program then plays the correct version with an arrow pointing to each beat as it is played. After each "round" (each pattern) the percentage of right answers is displayed on the screen. The program also provides record keeping for the instructor.

Level I provides rhythm patterns in 2/4, 3/4, and 4/4. The compound meter, 6/8, is added to Level II, while Level III employs all the meters listed above.

Evaluation

The documentation for these programs is skimpy, and there are no instructions within the program. While the method of response is consistent throughout, the prompts, such as they are, are not clear. A scoring format provides some motivation; however, there is no personalization except for entering the user's name for record keeping purposes. After the user has typed a name and pressed the <RETURN> key, the program asks the user to press the <RETURN> again. This additional key press seems unnecessary.

The graphics of musical notation are not spectacular. Dotted notes are very difficult to distinguish from undotted ones. In both the composition and dictation programs, 8/8 is listed as a compound meter.

Not being able to hear the rhythmic pattern again once the user has begun to "notate" the answer is a serious problem with the program. Some of the patterns are quite long; the program would be improved if the user could hear the pattern repeated as he notates it.

The most glaring shortcoming of the program is its inability to play the rhythmic patterns accurately. In the "play" mode in both the composition and dictation sections, there is a slight gap between the rhythmic pattern of one beat and that of the next, making the dictation of the patterns extremely difficult.

★★★

Pick the Pitch by Brian Moore (part of the Moore Music Series), Micro Music Software Library, published by Temporal Acuity Products, Inc., 1983, version 1.1.

Hardware: Apple II, II+, IIe computer with at least 48K memory, 3.3 Disk II drive with controller, video monitor; MMI DAC music card and headphones optional; however, the program can be used without sound.

Cost: $50

Publisher's suggested audience: Third grade to adult.

Documentation: A user's guide includes teaching objectives, prerequisite skills and knowledge, as well as details about the program.

Description

Presented in "tutor" or game format, this program drills students on note identification in the context of a staff, clef, and key signature. Given certain parameters selected by the user, the program displays and sounds a note on the screen; the user then responds by entering the letter name of the note and special letter names representing flats and sharps. When the user enters the answer, the program also sounds his choice.

The user may choose among five different clefs in which to work: treble, bass, grand staff, alto,

or tenor. (S)he may choose notes with no
accidentals, notes with single sharps and flats,
notes with double sharps and flats, notes with all
of the above and natural signs, or notes in the
context of key signatures with the possibility of
adding accidentals. The user may also choose to
work with no ledger lines, a mixture of staff and
ledger line notes, or only with ledger line notes.

In the tutor mode, the program displays the pitch
and the directions for entering a response, and
allows the user as much time as needed to make a
response. After making two mistakes on the same
note, the user is permitted to ask the program for
the correct response. In the game mode, the
pitches are presented in the same way but with
time constraints. Ten note values are displayed
at the bottom of the screen. The number of points
represented by these notes depends on their time
value. Larger value notes are worth more points.
As the user makes mistakes, or if the user takes
too much time between note identifications, these
notes go up in puffs of smoke, lowering the user's
score. At the end of each session a score card is
displayed showing the number of rounds, number of
examples, number of points, number of bonus
points, and the total number of points.

Evaluation

This program provides clear and consistent
prompts, the screens are neat and uncluttered, and
the method of response is consistent throughout.
Repeated tries are allowed in the tutor mode. The
scoring and "puffs of smoke" provide motivation,
although there is no personalization or record
keeping available.

The sound and graphics are good. The instructions
are within the program and can be bypassed by
those users who are already familiar with them.
The program uses a limited number of keys, so the
typing skills required seem appropriate for young
users and non-typists.

***

<u>Pitch Drills With Accidentals</u> by George P. Makas,
Micro Music Software Library, 1981, published by
Temporal Acuity Products, Inc., 1982, Version 1.1.

Hardware: Apple II series computer with at least
48K memory, 3.2 or 3.3 Disk II drive with
controller, video monitor; MMI DAC music card and
headphones required.

Cost: $50

Publisher's suggested audience: Beginning and
intermediate students from elementary to adult
levels.

Documentation: A user's guide includes teaching
objectives, prerequisite skills and knowledge, as
well as details about the program.

Description

This program drills note names with accidentals in
treble, bass, and grand staff, depending on the
user's choice. In the program a note appears on a
musical staff with appropriate clef; the user
identifies the note by typing its letter name and
<S> for sharp, <F> for flat, or <N> for natural.
See <u>Pitch Drills Without Accidentals</u> for further
description.

Evaluation

See <u>Pitch Drills Without Accidentals</u> for further
evaluation. Having to type an <N> when the note
has no accidental slows the user's responses and
should not be necessary.

***

<u>Pitch Drills Without Accidentals</u> by George P.
Makas, Micro Music Software Library, 1981,
published by Temporal Acuity Products, Inc., 1982,
Version 1.1.

Hardware: Apple II series computer with a minimum
of 48K memory, 3.2 or 3.3 Disk II drive with
controller, video monitor; MMI DAC music card and
headphones required.

Cost: $50

Publisher's suggested audience: Beginning and
intermediate students from elementary to adult
levels.

Documentation: A user's guide includes teaching
objectives, prerequisite skills and knowledge, as
well as details about the program.

Description

The program drills note names in treble, bass, and
grand staff, depending on the user's choice. The
program also provides drill in transposition; the
user is asked to provide the concert pitch of the
note displayed. The user can choose B-flat, E-
flat, F or A transposing instruments. The user
may also choose the number of exercises to be
tried.

In the program, a note appears on a musical staff
with appropriate clef, and the user identifies the
note by typing its letter name. In the
transposition exercises, the written note is
displayed, and the user must supply the concert
pitch. Transposition drills are all done in the
treble clef. The exercises are not timed. A
pitch identification game is included which is
timed and does not deal with transposition. The
user can choose the speed of the game by choosing
"Amateur," "Semi-professional," or "Professional."
The speed of the items in the game is
automatically adjusted according to the user's
responses. Wrong answers cause both the right and
wrong answers to be displayed on the screen.
There are no second chances or hints given. In
both the drills and the game a score is displayed
on the screen. The final score and the percentage
of right answers are calculated and displayed at
the end of each session.

Evaluation

The documentation is good, with a few exceptions.
The user is supposed to be able to type <R> to
hear the note again, but it does not work. In
each drill the user is asked to choose between
visual drill and practice identifying pitch names
and associating the notation with the sound of

the pitch. Either choice results in a pitch appearing on the staff and the sound of that note; there is no difference. The main thrust of the program is to identify notes visually; the sound of the pitches seems superfluous.

It is unfortunate that both the documentation and the instructions within the program neglect to inform the Apple IIe user that the <CAPS LOCK> key must be depressed throughout the program in order for the user to make any responses.

The prompts on the screen during the drill and game programs make additional instructions unnecessary; they are quite helpful, although the screen becomes a little cluttered. The user may quit at any time. Pressing <ESC>ape takes the user back to the original menu in case he wishes to try another clef or a different transposition level. There are no instructions telling the user what to do in the event that a typing mistake is made when entering the answer.

***

Polywriter, by Phil Ferrand, John Borowicz, David Kusek, and John Melcher, Passport Designs, Inc., 1984.

Hardware: Apple II, II+, or IIe computer with a minimum of 64K, 3.3 DOS, single disk drive with controller (two single unit disk drives recommended), monitor, Soundchaser system or MIDI synthesizer with Passport Designs MIDI interface card, graphics-capable dot-matrix printer with graphics interface card, amplifier, and speakers or headphones. Version 1.0 is written for the four-octave Soundchaser, version 1.1 for the five-octave system, and version 2.1 for MIDI instrument with the Passport Designs MIDI inter-face card.

Cost: $299

Publisher's suggested audience: None stated.

Documentation: Includes a detailed user's manual.

Description

This software allows the user to enter music into
the computer by performing it, edit the
transcription of the music notated on the screen,
and then print it.

In "Create" mode, the user enters the music
directly from the Soundchaser or MIDI-compatible
keyboard. The user may choose among eight printed
output formats: 1) single treble clef staff, 2)
single bass clef staff, 3) piano or grand staff,
4) four-part choral on two staves, 5) treble staff
with piano, 6) bass staff with piano, 7) four-part
choral on two staves with piano, and 8) orchestral
score. For the orchestral score format, the parts
are entered (played) one line at a time and may be
edited four lines at a time. The user may enter
chords with up to sixteen voices on a single
staff.

Following the selection of a print format, the
user designates the key, meter, and tempo in which
the music will be played or entered, chooses how
close together the notes will be printed on the
page (affecting the number of measures possible on
a page), and also sets the "resolution," a
control which compensates for less than absolute
rhythmic precision on the part of the performer.
When the user is ready to start the transcribing
process, (s)he presses the <SPACE BAR>, the
tempo is given by a visual and aural metronome,
and the user begins to play. The user can hear
what (s)he is playing with the metronome in the
background.

At the end of the transcribing session, the user
may reenter the piece if mistakes were made
and/or, have the music transposed, if desired.
The transcription is then saved on a data disk.

In the "Edit" section, the transcription is loaded
from the disk and displayed on the screen.
Moving a cursor around the screen by means of a
series of keyboard codes, the user may change,
add, or delete pitches, durations, the position of
notes, stem direction, and enharmonic spellings.
Only four staves can be displayed on the screen at
any one time. Once editing is completed, the
notation is again saved on a disk and may be sent

to a printer for printing. Orchestral scores are
printed in concert pitch and in standard
orchestral score order. Individual performance
parts are printed in the correct transposition.
Text can also be added to the notation.

Evaluation

Playing the keyboard in the "Create" mode with
enough rhythmic precision and accuracy to create a
decent transcription is difficult, frustrating,
and requires practice. When a reasonable
transcription is finally produced, it almost
always requires editing of some sort. The editing
process is rather tedious, especially placing the
screen cursor at exactly the right place in the
notation. Although the cursor can be moved quite
quickly to various zones on the screen, movement
within each zone is very slow.

The screen prompts are not sufficient for the user
to edit the notation without heavy reliance on the
written documentation, especially if the user has
not spent a lot of time with the program. On the
display where the user chooses to <C>hange, <A>dd,
or <D>elete notation symbols, the user's response
is not displayed on the screen; the user does not
know whether the program received the response.

While the graphics of the notation both on the
screen and on the printer are not remarkable, they
do include beams when appropriate, as well as
automatic stemming in the correct direction. Even
after transposition, the stems are automatically
placed in the proper direction.

Sometimes the results of transposition cause
additional editing to be required. If a piece is
entered in the key of C Major, for example, and
then is transposed to D-flat Major, the new key
signature takes up a large amount of space in the
first measure covering up some of the notes. The
user must reposition the notes at the beginning of
the measure.

Entering an orchestral score is done by playing
one part at a time. However, when the user enters
each additional part, no audio playback of
previously recorded parts is available. The user

must rely solely upon the metronome to assure that
the parts are kept together.

***

Practical Music Theory Computer Series by Sandy
Feldstein, published by Alfred Publishing Company,
Inc., 1982, 1984. Also available from Electronic
Courseware Systems, Inc. and Wenger Corporation.

Hardware: Commodore 64 or 128, one disk drive,
color monitor (optional). Also available for
Apple II+, IIe, or IIc, one disk drive, and
monitor. A small amplifier and headphones may be
desirable.

Cost: Volume I, book and two diskettes, $79.95
         Volume II, book and two diskettes, $79.95
         Volume III, book and two diskettes, $79.95
         Three-volume set/six diskettes, $199.95

Description

This set of programs contains twenty-one units (84
lessons) on six diskettes developed to accompany
Feldstein's Practical Music Theory, a three-volume
text and workbook on the fundamentals of music
theory.

Most of the drills on these disks duplicate the
drills found in Music Made Easy by the same
author. Most of the drills employed in each section
require that the user get 10 correct answers in a
row before the drilling stops. None of the drills
has any time constraints. During each drill, the
number tried, the number correct, and the number
to go are displayed on the screen. After
completing a drill the user is told how many he
tried in order to complete 10 items in succession
without a mistake. There is no record keeping
utility included on the disk

The contents of Volume I, disks 1 and 2, include
the musical staff, pitch names, treble and bass
clefs, whole, half, and quarter notes, bar lines,
measures and time signatures, grand staff, ledger

lines, simple meters, dotted half note, ties and
slurs, repeat signs, first and second endings,
eighth notes and rests, dotted quarter notes,
flats, sharps, and naturals.

The contents of Volume II, disks 1 and 2, include
the octave, whole and half steps, chromatic
scales, major scales, key signatures,
relationships by fifths, common musical terms and
symbols, sixteenth notes and rests, dotted eighth
notes, intervals, syncopation, and compound meter.

The contents of Volume III, disks 1 and 2, include
major triads, major chords within a key, chord
progressions, chord inversions, dominant seventh
chords, transpositions, minor, augmented and
diminished chords, progressions with minor chords,
relative minor keys, natural, harmonic, and
melodic minor scales, passing and neighbor tones,
and composing and harmonizing melodies in major
and minor keys.

Evaluation

There are no instructions within any of these
programs, although the prompts on the screen are
usually pretty clear with some exceptions. Unit
14 displays a time signature and asks the user how
many beats are in the measure and what type of
note receives a beat. The prompts do not indicate
whether the user is supposed to type a number or
type the name of the number in response to the
first question. Trial and error reveals that the
user may enter either.

The methods of response are inconsistent. For
example, in some drills the user must type the
word "eighth" in order to respond to a question
about what kind of note gets a beat in a
particular meter; in other drills the user
responds by selecting a note type from a multiple
choice list. In some, but not all of the drills,
user errors lead to hints and/or second tries.

The graphics of music notation, especially the
clef signs, are rather poor. However, the
graphics do provide beaming for eighth and
sixteenth notes.

While the opening of each section informs the user
that one can leave a section by typing any of the
function keys, attempts to do this fail. There is
absolutely no way to leave a section in order to
choose another one, until the section is
completed.

***

Rhythm Drills by George Makas, Micro Music
Software Library, 1981, published by Temporal
Acuity Products, Inc., 1982, version 1.1.

Hardware: Apple II, II+, IIe computer with a
minimum of 48K memory, 3.2 or 3.3 Disk II drive
with controller, video monitor; MMI DAC music card
and headphones required.

Cost: $75

Publisher's suggested audience: Beginning and
intermediate students from elementary to adult
levels.

Documentation: A user's guide includes teaching
objectives, prerequisite skills and knowledge, as
well as details about the program.

Description

This program provides drill and practice in
aurally identifying rhythmic patterns through the
dictation of rhythms using sixteenth note to whole
note values plus dotted quarters and dotted
halves. The user hears a single-line rhythmic
pattern in a melodic context of eight notes and
notates that pattern by typing a letter name
representing each of the note values. A tempo is
provided by a five-beat pulse given before each
exercise.

The menu from which the user selects a drill
program provides complete information regarding
what note values are included at each level. The
first program uses quarter notes and half notes,
the second adds whole notes, the third and fourth
add eighth and sixteenth notes respectively, and
the fifth employs all the note values of the first

four drills. The last two programs employ only
dotted half notes and quarters and dotted quarter
notes and eighths respectively.

The user chooses among seven different drill
programs, and then chooses the speed of each
exercise. For each exercise, a musical staff with
bass clef and common time meter signature is
displayed. The rhythmic pattern is performed
once, and the user then enters the note values.
The note values to be included in the exercise are
displayed on the screen along with the letters
used to represent them. Examples of the letters
which must be typed for each note value include
<S> for sixteenth note, <Q> for quarter note, and
<.Q> for dotted quarter note. The user may hear
the pattern again by pressing the <R> key, quit
the exercise and go back to the menu by pressing
the <ESC>ape key, or change the tempo by pressing
the <N> key. If the letters typed in are correct
the program displays "correct," notates the
pattern, with pitches, on the staff, and performs
the pattern. If the user's response is wrong, the
program displays "wrong," displays the correct
letters, notates the correct pattern and plays it.

The program keeps track of the user's performance
and maintains a cumulative percentage score. The
score is displayed on the screen during each
exercise. When a session ends, the percentage
score and the number of exercises completed is
displayed.

Evaluation

This program is logically organized and factually
correct. With the exception of the meter
signature being out of proportion with the staff
on which it is placed, the graphics of musical
notation and the sound are good. Instructions are
clear, within the program, and can be bypassed by
those already familiar with them. With one
exception the prompts are especially clear and
consistent, so that the user does not need to
refer to instructions during the program. The
program fails, however, to instruct the user about
how to erase an answer when (s)he changes his or
her mind. Experimentation reveals that the left
arrow key will work.

Although the user types his or her name at the beginning of the program, and the name is always displayed at the top of the screen, it is not used for personalization or for record keeping purposes. The program is not really set up as a game, but the scoring does provide some motivation. The methods of response are consistent throughout, and the user may leave the program at any time by pressing the <ESC>ape key.

The numbers employed in the program for tempo indications are not logical from a musician's viewpoint. The range of numbers is from 50 to 150, with the lower numbers representing faster tempos, the reverse of the meaning of metronome markings.

When the user requests additional hearings of a pattern, the program does not precede the performance of the pattern with beats establishing the tempo as it does on the first playing. Without the tempo being established, additional hearings may not be very helpful.

It is unfortunate that both the documentation and the instructions within the program neglect to warn the Apple IIe user that the <CAPS LOCK> key must be depressed throughout the program in order for the program to accept user responses.

***

The Rhythm Machine by David J. Otterson, Micro Music Software Library published by Temporal Acuity Products, Inc., 1985, 1986, version 1.41.

Hardware: Apple II, II+, IIe computer with minimum 48K memory, 3.3 DOS, Disk II drive with controller, video monitor; MMI DAC music card and headphones required.

Cost: $60

Publisher's suggested audience: Fifth grade to university.

Documentation: A user's guide includes teaching
objectives, prerequisite skills and knowledge, as
well as details about the program, operating
instructions, and instructions for student record
keeping.

Description

In game format, this program provides practice in
recognizing rhythmic patterns aurally. The
program plays a melodic line, using a combination
of notes and rests, followed by a display of four
different rhythmic patterns. The user must choose
the correct pattern from the four; the faster the
pattern is chosen, the more points the user earns.
A cursor points to the various choices, moving by
itself from one choice to the next. The user
presses the <SPACE BAR> when the arrow points to
the pattern he has chosen. When the rhythmic
pattern is played, the four choices are not
visible, and when the choices are visible, the
user cannot hear the pattern.

The user may choose among four levels of
difficulty: beginner, elementary, intermediate,
and advanced. The beginner level includes
quarter, half, dotted half, and whole notes. The
elementary level adds eighth notes and quarter
rests, while the intermediate level adds dotted
quarters, sixteenth notes, and dotted eighth and
sixteenth combinations. The advanced level
includes all variations of four sixteenth note
patterns and syncopation. All patterns are three
measures of common time (no meter signature is
included), the last measure always being a whole
note. The user may also choose to have the
program automatically adjust the level on the
basis of the responses entered, or to stay at the
same level. Sound effects played after each
response are also optional.

The program has a set of utilities which allows
the teacher to maintain a student records log
stored on the disk. Each time a student plays the
game, a record of the performance is added to the
log. There is room for 400 entries.

At the end of each session the program displays a
student score which tells the number of tries,

total points accumulated, how much time elapsed,
and the overall percentage correct.

Evaluation

The prompts in this program are clear and
consistent, as are the methods of response. The
graphics of the notes are fair, but there is no
beaming of eighth notes or sixteenth notes when it
would be appropriate. Errors lead to second tries
and even third tries, but there are no hints.
After the third wrong answer, the program provides
the correct response. The program requests that
the user enter his or her name at the beginning of
the program. Not only is the name used in the
record keeping part of the program, but it is also
used to personalize the drill by referring to the
user by name following both correct and wrong
answers.

The program is factually correct and logically
organized. It has replay value because the
rhythmic patterns are composed at random. The
instructions are clear, within the program, and
can be bypassed by users already familiar with
them. The user may not quit at any time, but must
complete a game first. Once completed, the user
is shown his or her rank among others using the
program and is given the choice of quitting,
continuing play at the same level, or choosing
another level.

The documentation states that the time elapsed for
each exercise is being calculated in seconds. In
actuality the elapsed time seems to increase by
one unit each time the automatic arrow moves
through the four possible choices and must start
over again.

As smaller note values are added in the later
levels of the program, the accuracy of the
program's rhythmic performance of the patterns
diminishes.

***

Rhythmic Dictator by Phyllis G. Parr, David L.
Schrader and David B. Williams, Micro Music
Software Library, 1980, published by Temporal
Acuity Products, Inc., 1982, version 2.2.

Hardware: Apple II, II+, or IIe computer with
minimum 48K memory, 3.2 or 3.3 DOS, Disk II drive
with controller, video monitor; MMI DAC music card
and headphones required.

Cost: $125

Publisher's suggested audience: Fourth grade
through adult.

Documentation: A user's guide includes teaching
objectives, prerequisite skills and knowledge, as
well as details about the program.

Description

In game format, this program provides drill and
practice in hearing basic rhythmic patterns and
"notating" them on a one-line staff, i.e.,
rhythmic dictation. In this program a rhythmic
pattern is a measure's worth of notes. All the
exercises have meter signatures of 4 over an
eighth note, quarter note, or sixteenth note.
Each exercise contains only notes and rests of the
same value. The beat is established prior to each
exercise by pulsing a note which represents a full
measure. All exercises are played on a reiterated
pitch.

The user chooses a beginning pattern level, <A>
through <K>, to determine a starting level, and
then the number of patterns (2, 4, or 6 measures)
per exercise. The levels differ in the number of
patterns among which the user may choose when
"notating" the exercise. The first level offers
the user only two pattern choices, while the last
level provides ten different possible patterns.
The program automatically adjusts to the
individual's skill level. The user is moved ahead
when the score is above 70%; otherwise the user is
moved back to an earlier stage. This adjustment
includes not only moving backward or forward a
level and using longer or shorter exercises, but
also changing the tempo of the exercises to slow,
medium, or fast.

User response requires the use of three keys. The
left and right arrow keys are used to move an
arrow to select a rhythmic pattern among several
patterns displayed on the screen. The <SPACE BAR>
is used to enter the response. The user may
rehear the exercise anytime by pressing the <R>
key, although points are deducted from the score
for each repeated hearing.

A summary of the user's progress is provided at
the end of each practice session. This includes
the date, starting and ending patterns levels,
starting and ending tempos, the number of correct
patterns, and a percentage score for overall
competency. There is no record keeping.

Evaluation

The program is factually correct, and the sound
and graphics are good. However, there is no
beaming of the eighth or sixteenth notes; each
note is given an individual flag. The
instructions are clear, within the program, and
may be bypassed by those already familiar with
them. The screens are neat and uncluttered, the
prompts are clear and consistent, and the method
of response is consistent throughout. The program
allows repeated tries, but no hints.

While the Apple IIe has up and down arrow keys on
its keyboard, the program requires that the user
press the right and left arrow keys when selecting
the rhythmic patterns enumerated vertically on the
screen. To many users this feature may be
bothersome. Employing a beat or pulse which
represents an entire measure rather than a
particular note value may also be bothersome to
some users.

It is unfortunate that both the documentation and
the instructions within the program neglect to
warn the Apple IIe user that the <CAPS LOCK> key
must be depressed in order for any of the user's
responses to be recognized by the program. In
addition, when the user wants to stop working at
one level and try another, (s)he must reboot the
disk.

***

<u>Sebastian</u> by Brian Moore, Micro Music Software
Library, published by Temporal Acuity Products,
Inc., 1983, version 1.2.

Hardware: Apple II, II+, or IIe computer with
minimum of 48K memory, 3.3 DOS, Disk II drive with
controller, video monitor; MMI DAC music card and
headphones required.

Cost: $125

Publisher's suggested audience: Fourth grade to
twelfth grade, college undergraduate ear training.

Documentation: A user's guide includes the
learning objectives of the program, a summary,
prerequisite skills and knowledge, and operating
instructions. The documentation also includes
detailed instructions regarding the creation of
additional files of melodies.

<h2 align="center">Description</h2>

<u>Sebastian</u> is a melodic error detection program
which drills aural and visual discrimination. In
each exercise a melody is notated in the treble,
bass, or grand staff (with key signature) and
displayed on the screen. The user may study the
melody as long as (s)he wishes and then press <P>
to have it played. For each melody the user is
asked whether a rhythmic, pitch, or tempo error
was made in the performance, or whether no errors
at all were made. The number keys are used to
select the type of error or no error. If the
error is one of rhythm or pitch, the user will be
asked to identify exactly which note was played
incorrectly. The arrow keys are used to move the
cursor to the measure in which the mistake was
detected. The program then plays that measure,
and the user must press the <SPACE BAR> during the
playing of the note that is wrong. The user then
has the option of seeing in notation what was
actually played. Each melody is one line long and
contains only one error. The user may also
request additional hearings by pressing <P>.

After each melody is completed, the user receives
a "Report Card" of his current progress, which
displays the level worked on, the total number of

times played (there is a penalty for rehearing a
melody), total errors, and percentage correct.
This information is also stored by the record
keeping utility on the disk.

The package includes a master disk and a student
disk. While the student disk has no melodies, the
master disk contains five files of ten melodies
each. The files are labeled "Simple Sebastian"
(well-known tunes with obvious errors), "Easy
Treble Clef" (simple melodies in treble clef),
"Easy Bass Clef" (simple melodies in bass clef),
"Super Sebastian" (more difficult melodies with
irregular meters), and "Classical Sebastian"
(well-known melodies taken from symphonic
literature). The master disk provides the means
for copying melodies from the master to the
student disk, as well as the procedures for
creating melodies to be placed in files on the
student disk. There is space on the master disk
for five additional files of melodies created by
the instructor. Each file may contain up to ten
melodies, and the creator may designate as many as
nine errors in each melody. When the melodies are
played for the user, the program randomly chooses
one of these errors to be used in the performance.

The utility for creating new melodies provides the
instructor with the means to notate clef (treble,
bass, or grand staff), key signature (up to four
flats and five sharps), meter signature, tempo
marking, accidentals, notes and rests of varying
values, (including notes with stems up or down),
and the means to choose a tempo and to designate
various pitch, rhythm, and tempo errors. The ten
melodies per file do not all have to be entered at
one sitting; the file can be established and added
to at a later time.

Evaluation

The graphics of musical notation and the sound in
this program are quite good, although no beams are
used. The program is logically organized and
factually correct. The instructions are within
the program and can be bypassed by users already
familiar with them. However, they are very brief
and uninformative. This is not really a drawback
because the prompts within the program are
consistent and very clear.

The program provides hints and second tries when users make mistakes. After two consecutive errors, the program offers to play the whole exercise with the wrong note, to play one measure at a time, or to play the correct version of the melody. The program asks the user to type his or her name at the beginning of the program, and then uses the name in comments to the user during the exercises. In addition to personalized comments, sound effects are also used for both right and wrong answers.

When creating additional melody files, the instructor must refer to the written documentation for every detail. The utility program provides prompts but not the codes needed to enter the notation. One must know the melody prior to notating it, because the program requires that the number of measures in the melody and the number of notes and/or rests in each measure must be entered in advance of the actual notation. One must enter an accidental for any note requiring it, even if the note is sharped or flatted by the key signature. Entering the tempo for each melody is accomplished by providing a number from 1 to 255. Entering a higher number means that the tempo will be slower than entering a lower number. This may bother some users because the numbers have nothing to do with traditional metronome markings.

Another bothersome feature of the creating utility is the fact that the melodies can be only one line in length. This space limitation makes the constructing of the melodies a trial and error process. Because some measures may contain more notes than others, it is very difficult to predict how many measures will fit on one line. One frequently is not permitted to enter the last note or two of a planned melody because it is too long. The composer must then redesign the melody.

While the original Sebastian melody files cannot be erased, individual melodies within each file can be switched on or off by the instructor to suit the needs of individual students. However, the melodies are never displayed in notation within the utility program. Instead, the instructor is shown the melodies in a file by number only, making it rather difficult to decide which to switch on or off.

***

Sebastian II by Brian Moore, Micro Music Software
Library, published by Temporal Acuity Products,
Inc., 1985, version 1.1.

Hardware: Apple II, II+, or IIe computer with
minimum of 48K memory, 3.3 DOS, Disk II drive with
controller, video monitor; MMI DAC music card and
headphones required.

Cost: $125

Publisher's suggested audience: Fourth grade to
twelfth grade, college undergraduate and graduate
ear training.

Documentation: A user's guide includes the
learning objectives of the program, a summary,
prerequisite skills and knowledge, and operating
instructions. The documentation also includes
detailed instructions regarding the creation of
additional files of melodies.

Description

See Sebastian for description and evaluation of
this program. Sebastian II adds intonation to the
list of possible errors that the user must detect.
A pitch error may be either a wrong note or a note
that is slightly out-of-tune. In addition, the
melodic lines may be notated in treble, alto,
tenor, or bass clef, or grand staff.

The Sebastian II master disk contains five files
of ten melodic lines each. These files represent
the following five levels: Level 1 includes
simple scales in treble clef; Level 2 includes
simple melodic patterns with wrong note and
rhythmic errors; Level 3 contains melodies with
key and time signatures, treble and bass clef and
grand staff; Level 4 has more complex melodies in
all clefs with out-of-tune errors; and Level 5
includes non-tonal melodies in mixed meter with
double sharps and double flats.

The "Report Card" in Sebastian II includes the
total number of melodies completed and an overall
percentage score.

Evaluation

Sebastian II has several weak points. In Level 1,
in which no tempo markings are given, "tempo" is
listed among the possible errors in the exercises.
Also in Level 1, the user is asked in which
measure the mistake was made. However, this
particular level has no bar lines; the whole
exercise is one extended measure. The menu from
which the user selects a level only lists the
number of each level. The user must refer to the
written documentation where each level is
described in order to make an intelligent
selection.

* * *

Seventh Chords by Vincent Oddo, Electronic
Courseware Systems, Inc., 1984.

See Aural Skills Trainer.

* * *

Sir William Wrong Note by J. Timothy Kolosick,
Micro Music Software Library, 1982, published by
Temporal Acuity Products, Inc., 1983, version 2.1.

Hardware: Apple II, II+ or IIe computer with a
minimum of 48K memory, 3.2 or 3.3 Disk II drive
with controller, video monitor; MMI DAC music card
and headphones required.

Cost: $150

Publisher's suggested audience: College level
ear training.

Documentation: A user's guide includes teaching
objectives, prerequisite skills and knowledge, as
well as details about the program and information
about teacher options and record keeping.

Description

This program drills the user in the identification of wrong notes (error detection) in four-voice chords. The user may choose any combination of ten chord types on which to be drilled: major, minor, diminished and augmented triads, major seventh chords, dominant seventh chords, minor seventh chords, half-diminished and fully-diminished seventh chords and augmented sixth chords. The program displays a chord in correct notation on the grand staff and then plays the chord with a wrong note in one of the voices. The user first selects the voice (soprano, alto, tenor, or bass) with the wrong note. After the proper voice is selected the user chooses the note actually played from among four possible wrong notes displayed on the staff next to the voice that is wrong. The user may hear the correct chord (by pressing <R>) or the wrong chord (by pressing <W>) played at any time. The program allows three chances to identify the incorrect voice and two chances to identify the note actually played. After the maximum number of errors have been made, the program provides the correct answer. There are no time constraints in the program.

At the end of each exercise, the user has some control over the next chord to be played. The options include hearing the same chord with a different wrong note, hearing a new chord of a different type and a new error, or selecting a chord from a new category.

The user can receive, if requested, a report card of current progress showing the number of chords attempted, the number of different chords, the types of chords drilled, and the number of extra hearings requested. No grading or percentages are displayed; the user's guide states that the purpose of the program is to provide drill and enjoyment. Long-term record keeping of the information on the report card is available.

Evaluation

The sound and the graphics of musical notation are very good in this program. The instructions are clear, within the program, and can be bypassed by

users already familiar with them. The prompts are
clear and consistent, as are the methods of
response. The program allows repeated tries, but
offers no hints when errors are made.

Feedback is provided for every response. Correct
responses are given positive remarks and the chord
is played as in a fanfare, while wrong answers
receive the comment, "Sorry, that was incorrect.
Try again." The visual feedback has one slight
problem. When the user chooses the correct wrong
voice, "excellent" or "good show" are displayed on
the top of the screen. Unfortunately, this
positive reinforcement on the top of the screen
remains displayed while the user goes on to the
next part. If the user then selects an incorrect
"wrong" pitch, a second message is displayed in
the middle of the screen, informing the user that
his response was incorrect. These two conflicting
remarks displayed on the screen at the same time
can be confusing at first.

Neither the documentation nor the instructions
within the program warn the Apple IIe user that
the <CAPS LOCK> key must be depressed throughout
the program in order to make any responses.

***

Songwriter by Samuel Wantman and Art Bardige,
Learning Ways, Inc., published by Scarborough
Systems, Inc., 1983.

Hardware: Commodore 64 or 128, one disk drive,
monitor (color optional); joystick (optional).
Also available for the Apple II series of
computers, the Atari, and the IBM-PC.

Cost: $20

Publisher's suggested audience: Age five to
adult.

Documentation: Includes a user's manual. Each
chapter describes commands, musical ideas, and
provides step-by-step instructions. A glossary of
musical terms is included.

Description

Songwriter provides the user with the means to compose melodies. The program does not make use of standard musical notation. Instead, a piano keyboard of two octaves and a fifth is displayed on the screen. The user moves a cursor on the keyboard choosing each of the notes in the melody. As each note is entered, it is sounded and displayed as a vertical dash on the screen above the key chosen on the keyboard. The dashes vary in length depending upon the rhythmic duration chosen for the note. Higher notes appear on the right side of the screen, while the lower ones appear on the left, in keeping with the location of high and low notes on the piano keyboard. As each note is added, the dashes representing the notes scroll to the top of the screen and eventually disappear. The documentation compares this graphic notation of the music to a "piano roll" used on player pianos.

After completing a melody, the user may play it back or store it on a data disk. Over twenty-five songs are included on the **Songwriter** disk. Some of the pieces included on the disk are "Simple Gifts," "Flight of the Bumble Bee," five pieces by Telemann, excerpts from the "William Tell Overture," and "Jingle Bells." These "songs" can be loaded and played. As they are played, their graphic notation scrolls from the bottom of the screen to the top and then disappears.

When composing his or her own melodies, the user may listen, erase, change, or record. In addition to controlling the pitch and duration of each note of the melody, the user can add rests, set the length of each measure, set and/or change the tempo, create, edit and store musical ideas, and change the sound quality. Three sounds are preset within the program, and others can be obtained through experimentation.

Evaluation

Instructions are not included within the program. The user must refer to the written documentation in order to figure out what the various prompts displayed on the screen mean.

The graphic representation of the piano keyboard does not look like a keyboard. With a color monitor, the "black" keys are still black, but the "white" keys are colored blue or orange. In addition, the "black" keys are the same length as the "white" keys.

The rhythmic representation employed in the program is unlike that in traditional music notation. Durations of notes are selected by changing a fraction displayed in the lower left corner of the screen. The possibilities for the upper number include 1, 2, 3, 4, 5, 6, 7, or 8, and 1, 2, 3, 4, 6, 8, 12, 16, 24, or 48 for the denominator, or lower number. While a half note or an eighth note are typical in traditional rhythmic notation, many users may find the use of a "third" note, a "twelfth" note, or a "twenty-fourth" note a bit unusual.

***

Standard Instrument Names by David Williams, Al Blackford and Julie Schulze, Micro Music Software Library, published by Temporal Acuity Products, Inc., 1981.

Hardware: Apple II series computer with a minimum of 48K memory, 3.2 or 3.3 Disk II drive with controller, video monitor; (MMI DAC music card and headphones required only if sound effects are desired).

Cost: $50

Publisher's suggested audience: Fourth grade to adult.

Documentation: A user's guide includes the objectives of the program, a summary, prerequisite skills and knowledge, operating instructions, and instructions for changing any options.

Description

In game format, this program provides drill and practice in identifying musical instruments from their descriptions, spelling the names of the

instruments, and recalling them when given their
descriptions. The user may select among three
methods of drill, three speed levels, and between
two sets of musical instruments.

In "Select-a-Name," a description of a musical
instrument is displayed on the screen, and the
user must select the appropriate name among the
multiple choice answers provided. In "Spell-a-
Name," the name of a musical instrument appears
briefly on the screen and then disappears; the
user must type the name with absolutely correct
spelling. In "Recall-a-Name," a description of an
instrument is again displayed, and the user must
type the name with absolute precision without
benefit of multiple choice answers or seeing the
name displayed even briefly.

While the user may select a response time (slow,
medium, or fast), the program automatically
increases or decreases the speed based upon the
user's performance during the drill.

The user may choose between two sets of musical
instruments: the first set contains the names of
more commonly used instruments; the instruments in
the second set are more rare.

When the user "quits," a "Report Card" is
displayed providing level attained, speed, number
of tries, number correct, and the percentage of
correct responses. There is no long-term record
keeping.

Evaluation

The sound effects (although optional) in this
program are good; their only purpose is to
provide motivation when the user's response is
correct (fragments from musical literature in
major keys, fanfares) and to admonish when the
response is incorrect (fragments from musical
literature in minor keys). The program uses a
personalized approach by providing comments to the
user followed by his or her name.

The program is factually correct. Instructions
are clear, within the program, and can be bypassed
by users already familiar with them. However,
instructions cannot be recalled during the program

should the user require some review. The program
presents clear and consistent prompts, and the
screen is neat and uncluttered. The program
allows second tries if an answer is incorrect,
although it does not provide any hints. After the
second wrong answer, the program provides the
correct one.

The typing skills required in order to enter
responses, especially in timed drills such as
these, go beyond not only the skills of fourth
grade children, but also beyond the typing
abilities of most adults. Since running out of
time counts as an error, many novice typists, no
matter how thorough their musical knowledge, might
find the program very frustrating.

In order to respond to certain prompts at the
beginning of the program and in order to type the
spelling of instrument names in the spell and
recall sections of the program, the <CAPS LOCK>
key on the Apple IIe must be depressed. Neither
the written documentation nor the prompts and
instructions within the program inform the user
about this necessity.

***

Super Challenger: An Aural-Visual Game by Stephen
Walker, Electronic Courseware Systems, Inc., 1984.

Hardware: Commodore 64 or 128, one disk drive,
monitor (color monitor important to this program).
Also available for Apple II+ or IIe with at least
48K, or Apple IIc with at least 128K, one disk
drive, and monitor, or the IBM-PC or IBM-PC JR.
with at least 128K, one 360K double-sided disk
drive, color graphics board, and monitor. This
program is also available in a MIDI version for
the Commodore 64 or 128 and Apple II+ or IIe with
Passport Design MIDI interface card; or for the
Commodore 64 or 128, Apple II+ or IIe, or IBM-PC
with Roland MIDI interface card and a MIDI-
compatible music keyboard or synthesizer.

Cost: $39.95

Publisher's suggested audience: None stated.

Documentation: Brief description on back of
diskette box.

Description

This program is an aural-visual game designed to
increase the user's tonal memory of a series of
pitches that are played by the computer. The user
may choose among games based on pitches in the 12-
note chromatic scale, pitches in the 8-note Major
scale, or pitches in the 8-note harmonic minor
scale. The user may also choose among seven
difficulty levels: 5, 10, 15, 20, 25, 30, or 35
notes! Each pitch is reinforced by a key on a
displayed keyboard lighting up. On color monitors
these keys are different colors. The program
plays a note and displays the color bar. As each
pitch of the series is added, the program plays
the whole series starting from the beginning, and
the user must play back the entire series from the
very first note. A counter at the bottom of the
screen keeps the user informed about which pitch
in the series has just been added.

In order to enter answers the user presses the
number keys <1> through <8> on the computer
keyboard for the major and harmonic minor games.
The chromatic scale game employs the top row of
keys on the keyboard from <1> through <0> and the
next two keys to the right (the <+> and <-> keys
on the Commodore 64, for example). <H>elp, with
instruction on which keys to use, is available for
each one of these games.

When the user is successful, a series of sirens go
off and (s)he is congratulated. When an error is
made the program informs the user which note in
the series was missed. The score, which is shown
to the user after the session, may qualify the
user for the "Hall of Fame."

Evaluation

The instructions for this program are clear and
within the program and the method of response is
consistent throughout. Errors do not lead to
hints or second tries. Once the instructions are
read and understood, there is no need for prompts.

The program is accurate and factually correct. It can also be addicting!

***

Theory Fundamentals by John E. Hatmaker, Wenger Corporation, 1985.

See Music Drills: Ear Training Series Part I: Theory Fundamentals.

***

Theory Sampler by Dennis Bowers and David B. Williams, Micro Music Inc., published by Temporal Acuity Products, Inc., 1986, Version 1.2.

Hardware: Apple II, II+, IIe with minimum of 48K RAM, one disk drive DOS 3.3, and monochrome monitor. DAC board optional but important to this program. On Apple II or IIe the <A> and <Z> keys replace the up and down arrow keys.

Cost: $125

Publisher's suggested audience: Junior high through university level.

Documentation: Includes a detailed user's guide, with instructions for each program on the disk.

Description

The program involves the spelling and aural recognition of modes, scales, triads, and seventh chords. The modes include dorian, phrygian, lydian, mixolydian, aeolian, locrian, and ionian, as well as harmonic minor and melodic minor scales.

In "Mode Construction" the user is shown a series of pitches on the treble staff and asked to alter certain pitches (by pressing <F> for flat or <S> for sharp) to create the mode or scale requested. <E> erases an accidental if the user has made a mistake. By pressing <K> after completing the

mode the program provides a key signature. The
necessary accidentals for the various forms of the
minor scales remain displayed. The user may
choose the following levels: 1) major scales to 3
sharps or flats; 2) Level 1 plus all minor scales;
3) Level 2 plus church modes; 4) all levels to 5
flats or sharps.

In "Mode Recognition" the user hears a mode or
scale and is given a list of choices from which
the user highlights a choice by pressing the up or
down arrow keys. The levels chosen by the user
include the following: 1) major, melodic or
harmonic minor; 2) Level 1 plus natural minor and
dorian mode; 3) Level 2 plus lydian and mixolydian
modes; 4) Level 3 plus phrygian and locrian.

In "Triad Construction" the user is asked to
construct triads of specific type and specific
inversion in ascending close position. Given
three neutral pitches on D below the treble staff,
the user raises or lowers these three pitches
through the use of arrow keys, so that the
resulting triads appear in arpeggiated form. The
user chooses whether to spell triads according to
their quality or according to their function. The
user also chooses root, first or second inversion,
major, minor, diminished, augmented, or all types.

In "Seventh Chord Construction" the user is asked
to build a specific seventh chord in a specific
inversion, similar to the way triads are
constructed above. The choices are root, first,
second or third inversion, MM, Mm, mM, half
diminished, or fully diminished.

In "Chord Recognition" the user chooses whether to
hear triads or seventh chords and whether the
chords will be arpeggiated or played as block
chords or both. After the chord is played the
user identifies it by using the arrow keys to
select the triad from multiple choice answers.
The user may choose to hear major, minor,
diminished, or augmented triads. The levels of
seventh chords are 1) MM, Mm, mm in root position;
2) Level 1 plus half and fully diminished
sevenths; 3) Level 2 plus first inversion; 4)
Level 3 plus second inversion; 5) Level 4 plus
third inversion.

Evaluation

The disk includes instructions for each program
which can be bypassed if the user is already
familiar with them. The user may get instructions
at any time during the drill and may quit at any
time. All the programs have good prompts
reminding the user what to do. At the end of each
session a "Report Card" lists how many items were
attempted, how many were correct responses, how
many were incorrect, a percentage score, starting
level and ending level. There is no record
keeping for the teacher.

Each time the user is successful on an item he is
congratulated and a "fanfare" is played. Users
are given second chances when they make mistakes,
but there are no hints to help them make
corrections. After two wrong answers, the correct
answer is provided. In all the programs users can
hear the correct item, whether it be a scale or a
chord, by pressing <P>, or hear the item they
constructed by pressing <R>. In all programs the
user may also choose to lock into a particular
level or to have the level be self-adjusting based
on performance during the drill. Users can hear
items as often as they wish without penalty, and
there are no time constraints.

***

Toney Listens to Music by David B. Williams, Micro
Music Software Library, published by Temporal
Acuity Products, Inc., 1983, version 2.1.

Hardware: Apple II series computer with 48K
memory, or 3.3 Disk II drive with controller,
video monitor, MMI DAC music card and headphones.

Cost: $90

Publisher's suggested audience: Ages three to
eight.

Documentation: A user's guide includes teaching
objectives, prerequisite skills and knowledge, as
well as details about the program and instructions
on how to use teacher options.

Description

This program focuses on music discrimination
skills and drills the user's aural ability to
distinguish between the same and contrasting
musical materials. It includes 10 levels of 25
items each with fragments of familiar tunes (Old
McDonald, etc.), included in level 1. An animated
"Toney" appears in the middle of the screen, with
two boxes numbered 1 and 2 below. The program
uses a non-verbal format and employs visual
symbols to help students press the correct keys.
The <T> key (to hear Toney's material), the <1>
key (to hear or select the material in Box 1), the
<2> key (to hear or select the tune in Box 2), and
the <SPACE BAR> (to raise a hand and give the
answer) are the only keys employed. In the
familiar tunes section Toney plays the first
phrase of a familiar tune and the student's task
is to decide whether the phrase heard in Box 1 or
in Box 2 is the same as the one Toney played.
When an answer is correct Toney's headset wiggles,
his eyes move, his nose wiggles, or his feet move
in approval. When the answer is wrong, Toney's
mouth changes from a smile to a frown.

The remaining levels involve the following: 2)
and 3) comparing interval direction with intervals
a major third or larger; 4) comparing four-beat
rhythm patterns using half, quarter, dotted
quarter and eighth notes; 5) comparing four to
eight beat melodic patterns using stepwise and
triadic motion; 6) comparing interval direction
using intervals a minor third or smaller; 7)
comparing tempos or timbres of phrases of familiar
children's songs; 8) and 9) comparing first
phrases of familiar children's songs with one or
two notes changed in pitch; and 10) comparing
four-beat rhythm patterns using half, quarter,
dotted quarter, eighth, dotted eighth, and
sixteenth notes and rests.

Evaluation

While the prompts and methods of response used in
this program are consistent, its non-verbal format
makes the prompts unclear at first. Instructions
are included within the program, but require the
ability to read. The animated graphics are very
good and there is no musical notation. Errors

lead to repeated tries, but there are no hints given.

Teacher options include maintaining student records, changing the tempo of items, changing the order of materials from a preset sequence to a random order, establishing performance criteria, and altering the levels as well as the number of items per level.

One negative aspect of this program is the need to go into the teacher options section of the program in order to indicate to the program the location of the DAC music sound card (slot 2 or slot 4).

***

Trombone Positions by David G. Schwaegler, Wenger Corporation, 1984. Part of the Wind Instrument Fingerings Series which includes five woodwind programs (flute, oboe, clarinet, bassoon, and saxophone) and five brass programs (trumpet, French horn, trombone, baritone horn, and tuba).

Hardware: Apple II, II+, IIe, or IIc, one disk drive, video monitor. Also available for the Commodore 64 or 128, one disk drive, and monitor.

Cost: $29 for each program, or $99 for a set of five.

Publisher's suggested audience: Beginning, intermediate and advanced levels are available on the disk.

Documentation: Brief descriptive pamphlet.

Description

This program provides drill and practice in matching appropriate trombone positions with notes displayed on the musical staff with bass clef. A note is displayed on the staff (or on ledger lines), and the user enters the correct position by marking a trombone position chart, i.e., by pressing certain computer keyboard keys which represent the positions on the trombone. The range of the notes drilled in the program includes

all notes, and enharmonic spellings as well, from
C two octaves below middle C to B-flat above
middle C.

A diagram of the trombone slide, with F attachment
valve, is displayed vertically on the left side of
the screen with numbers ("Z" for the F attachment)
from the computer keyboard printed at each
position. On the right side of the screen a
diagram of the left and right hands is displayed,
indicating which finger of each hand controls the
positions represented on the chart on the left.
Each key acts as a toggle; when it is pressed it
is displayed in reverse video, indicating that the
position has been entered by the user. When it is
pressed again, it goes back to normal.

The user may choose among three programs on the
disk. "Position Drill", with three levels
(beginning, intermediate, and advanced) has no
time constraints and allows the user to get help
with correct positions. The "Game," with the same
three levels, times the user with a clock; the
user may choose from three speeds. (The Commodore
version uses a mallet and a gong instead of the
clock.) In "Note Names Drill", a note appears on
the staff and the user must type in its letter
name (no second tries).

The disk also has a "toolkit", accessed by a
password, which allows the teacher to create a
student records file (for up to twelve students),
preset drill levels, preset the speed of the game,
and edit the preset positions by allowing
selection of primary and alternative positions for
the notes.

Evaluation

The graphics in this program are good, and the
prompts are consistent throughout, as are the
methods of response. The instructions are
included in the program and can be bypassed by
users who are already familiar with them. Part of
the instructions are displayed on the screen
during the drill and game, which, in addition to
the musical staff, clef, note, and the diagram of
the instrument keys, makes the screen quite
cluttered.

The range of the notes drilled in this program
does not include notes below the C two octaves
below middle C. None of the pedal notes is
included. The program does not provide a separate
diagram for the numbers of the positions when the
F attachment needs to be employed. This would be
helpful since when the F attachment is engaged
there are actually only six positions available
instead of seven.

***

Trumpet Fingerings by David G. Schwaegler, Wenger
Corporation, 1984. Part of the Wind Instrument
Fingerings Series which includes five woodwind
programs (flute, oboe, clarinet, bassoon, and
saxophone) and five brass programs (trumpet,
French horn, trombone, baritone horn, and tuba).

Hardware: Apple II, II+, IIe, or IIc, one disk
drive, video monitor. Also available for the
Commodore 64 or 128, one disk drive, and monitor.

Cost: $29 for each program, or $99 for a set of
five.

Publisher's suggested audience: Beginning,
intermediate and advanced levels are available on
the disk.

Documentation: Brief descriptive pamphlet.

Description

This program provides drill and practice in
matching appropriate trumpet fingerings with notes
displayed on the musical staff with bass clef. A
note is displayed on the staff (or on ledger
lines), and the user enters the correct fingering
by marking a trumpet fingering chart, i.e., by
pressing certain computer keyboard keys which
represent the valves on the trumpet. The range of
the notes drilled in the program includes all
notes, and enharmonic spellings as well, from G
below middle C to C two octaves above middle C.

A diagram of the three trumpet valves is displayed
on the left side of the screen with various

letters and characters from the computer keyboard
printed on each valve. On the right side of the
screen a diagram of the right hand is displayed,
indicating which finger of the hand controls which
keys represented on the chart on the left. Each
key acts as a toggle; when it is pressed it is
displayed in reverse video, indicating that the
key is part of the fingering entered by the user.
When it is pressed again, it goes back to normal,
or open.

The user may choose among three programs on the
disk. "Fingering Drill", with three levels
(beginning, intermediate, and advanced) has no
time constraints and allows the user to get help
with correct finger placement. The "Game," with
the same three levels, times the user with a
clock; the user may choose from three speeds.
(The Commodore version uses a mallet and a gong
instead of the clock.) In "Note Names Drill", a
note appears on the staff and the user must type
in its letter name (no second tries).

The disk also has a "toolkit", accessed by a
password, which allows the teacher to create a
student records file (for up to twelve students),
preset drill levels, preset the speed of the game,
and edit the preset fingerings by allowing
selection of primary and alternative fingerings
for the notes.

Evaluation

The graphics in this program are good, and the
prompts are consistent throughout, as are the
methods of response. The instructions are
included in the program and can be bypassed by
users who are already familiar with them. Part of
the instructions are displayed on the screen
during the drill and game, which, in addition to
the musical staff, clef, note, and the diagram of
the instrument keys, makes the screen quite
cluttered.

In an attempt to emulate the actual hand positions
on the instrument, the program instructs the user
to place his or her hands on the computer keyboard
with each finger on a certain key. This is rather
awkward and seems unnecessary at first, because
the program only allows the fingering to be

entered one key at a time anyway. Once the user
starts the "Game," however, it becomes apparent
that in order to keep up with the clock, one's
hands must be kept over the appropriate keys.

***

Tuba Fingerings by David G. Schwaegler, Wenger
Corporation, 1984. Part of the Wind Instrument
Fingerings Series which includes five woodwind
programs (flute, oboe, clarinet, bassoon, and
saxophone) and five brass programs (trumpet,
French horn, trombone, baritone horn, and tuba).

Hardware: Apple II, II+, IIe, or IIc, one disk
drive, video monitor. Also available for the
Commodore 64 or 128, one disk drive, and monitor.

Cost: $29 for each program, or $99 for a set of
five.

Publisher's suggested audience: Beginning,
intermediate and advanced levels are available on
the disk.

Documentation: Brief descriptive pamphlet.

Description

This program provides drill and practice in
matching appropriate tuba fingerings with notes
displayed on the musical staff with bass clef. A
note is displayed on the staff (or on ledger
lines), and the user enters the correct fingering
by marking a tuba fingering chart, i.e., by
pressing certain computer keyboard keys which
represent the valves on the tuba. The range of
the notes drilled in the program includes all
notes, and enharmonic spellings as well, from C
three octaves below middle C to B-flat below
middle C.

A diagram of the four tuba valves is displayed on
the left side of the screen with various letters
and characters from the computer keyboard printed
on each valve. On the right side of the screen a
diagram of the right hand is displayed, indicating
which finger of the hand controls which keys

represented on the chart on the left. Each key
acts as a toggle; when it is pressed it is
displayed in reverse video, indicating that the
key is part of the fingering entered by the user.
When it is pressed again, it goes back to normal,
or open.

The user may choose among three programs on the
disk. "Fingering Drill", with three levels
(beginning, intermediate, and advanced) has no
time constraints and allows the user to get help
with correct finger placement. The "Game," with
the same three levels, times the user with a
clock; the user may choose from three speeds.
(The Commodore version uses a mallet and a gong
instead of the clock.) In "Note Names Drill", a
note appears on the staff and the user must type
in its letter name (no second tries).

The disk also has a "toolkit", accessed by a
password, which allows the teacher to create a
student records file (for up to twelve students),
preset drill levels, preset the speed of the game,
and edit the preset fingerings by allowing
selection of primary and alternative fingerings
for the notes.

Evaluation

The graphics in this program are good, and the
prompts are consistent throughout, as are the
methods of response. The instructions are
included in the program and can be bypassed by
users who are already familiar with them. Part of
the instructions are displayed on the screen
during the drill and game, which, in addition to
the musical staff, clef, note, and the diagram of
the instrument keys, makes the screen quite
cluttered.

In an attempt to emulate the actual hand positions
on the instrument, the program instructs the user
to place his or her hands on the computer keyboard
with each finger on a certain key. This is rather
awkward and seems unnecessary at first, because
the program only allows the fingering to be
entered one key at a time anyway. Once the user
starts the "Game," however, it becomes apparent
that in order to keep up with the clock, one's

hands must be over the appropriate keys at all
times.

***

<u>Tune It II</u> by Fred Willman, Electronic Courseware
Systems, Inc., 1984.

Hardware: Commodore 64 or 128, one disk drive,
monitor (color monitor optional). Also available
for Apple II+ or IIe with at least 48K, or Apple
IIc with at least 128K, one disk drive, and
monitor, or the IBM-PC or IBM-PC JR. with at least
128K, one 360K double-sided disk drive, color
graphics board, and monitor.

Cost: $39.95

Publisher's suggested audience: None stated.

Documentation: Brief description on back of
diskette box; brief pamphlet regarding instructor
management options.

Description

In a game format this program provides the user
with practice in matching pitches. The computer
plays two pitches; the user then raises (with the
<H> key) or lowers (with the <L> key) the second
pitch until both pitches sound exactly alike. The
<S> key is used when the user believes the two
pitches are the same.

Four difficulty levels are provided: easy with
visuals, difficult with visuals, easy with sound
only, and difficult with sound only.

The "visual" levels include arrows indicating the
relative positions of the two notes on a graphic
representation of a stringed instrument
fingerboard. The relative position of the first
pitch is indicated by an arrow on the left side of
the fingerboard, and that of the second pitch with
an arrow on the right side of the fingerboard. As
the second note is adjusted, the arrow on the
right side moves. When the two pitches are in
tune, the two arrows are pointing at each other.

The user must play three "games" at a particular
difficulty level in order to choose a different
level. When three "games" are completed, the
score is automatically saved on the disk.

The user's score in total points accumulated is
continuously displayed on the screen. Record
keeping is included as an instructor option.

Evaluation

The instructions are clear, within the program,
and can be bypassed by those familiar with them.
The prompts are clear and consistent, the program
is factually correct, and the use of color and
sound is quite good.

The graphic representation with arrows moving up
and down on a string instrument fingerboard may be
confusing to string players, or to others
familiar with how stringed instruments work,
because the movement of the arrows showing the
positions of the two notes on the fingerboard is
misleading. A lower-sounding note is shown to be
lower on the fingerboard (or closer to the bridge)
than a higher-sounding note! In reality, as one
moves his or her finger down the fingerboard of a
stringed instrument, away from the nut and toward
the bridge, the pitch will get higher, not lower.

***

Tuner by Don Pederson, CONDUIT, 1982.

Hardware: Apple II+, IIe, or IIc with a minimum
of 48K, one disk drive, and monitor. The ALF
three-voice synthesizer card can be used for sound
production in lieu of the Apple speaker.

Cost: $35

Publisher's suggested audience: Secondary school
and college level students.

Documentation: The "User's Notes" are a bit
skimpy; no prerequisites are listed. However,
operating instructions are included.

Description

This program provides drill and practice in the
skill of matching the intonation of two pitches.
The disk includes a brief tutorial or introduction
to tuning. It points out that when two pitches
are out of tune, the pitch which is higher is
considered sharp, while the pitch which is lower
is considered flat.

The object of the drill is for the user to tune a
second pitch to the first pitch played. The two
pitches involved are less than a half-step apart.
The user can raise the second pitch by pressing
<R>, lower it by pressing <L>, press <P> to hear
the two pitches again, and press <I> to indicate
that (s)he believes the pitches are in tune. Each
time an adjustment is made, the program plays the
two notes again. The program provides immediate
feedback by displaying the word "RIGHT" when the
user has indeed matched the pitches, "CLOSE" when
the pitches are not quite in tune, and "ERROR"
when the two pitches are still out-of-tune. When
"CLOSE" or "ERROR" are displayed, the program also
displays in which direction, sharp or flat, the
second pitch is out-of-tune with the first.

When "RIGHT" or "CLOSE" are displayed the program
goes on to the next item. When "ERROR" is
displayed the user must keep responding until a
"RIGHT" or "CLOSE" is attained. Sound effects
accompany each evaluation.

The user may exit the program at any time by
pressing the <ESC>ape key. Upon exiting, the user
is provided a "Summary," or overview of the
session. This includes the number of problems
attempted, how many were correct, how many were
close, and how many were left out-of-tune, how
many times the second pitch was left sharp, how
many times it was left flat, and a percentage of
accuracy. The program also keeps track of the
last score, should the user repeat the program.
The program is then able to remark that the user
improved, got worse, or stayed the same in
subsequent sessions. However, there is no long-
term record keeping on the disk.

Evaluation

The program is logically organized and factually
correct. It has clear and consistent prompts, and
the methods of response are consistent throughout.
There is no personalization, but the scoring
format provides motivation. The instructions and
the tutorial, both of which are included within
the program, can be bypassed by users already
familiar with them. Help can be gotten any time
by pressing <H>.

Some users may find the pace of the drill somewhat
slow. After each adjustment, the user must wait
for the program to play the two pitches. In order
to use the ALF synthesizer card, one has to remove
the right-protect tab from the diskette and answer
some questions about the number of synthesizer
cards in the computer and the lowest number of the
slot in which the cards are located.

***

12 [Twelve]-Bar Tunesmith by Fred Willman,
Electronic Courseware Systems, Inc., 1985.

Hardware: Commodore 64 or 128, one disk drive,
monitor (color monitor optional). Also available
for Apple II+ or IIe with at least 48K, or Apple
IIc with at least 128K, one disk drive, and
monitor, or the IBM-PC or IBM-PC JR. with at least
128K, one 360K double-sided disk drive, color
graphics board, and monitor.

Cost: $39.95

Publisher's suggested audience: None stated.

Documentation: Brief description on back of
diskette box.

Description

This program allows the user to compose and to
hear simple diatonic melodies using the eight
scale degree numbers of the C Major scale and four
different rhythmic durations. In composer mode,
the screen displays the eight scale degree

numbers, four dashes of different lengths, and
several commands on the bottom of the screen. The
user may choose to "add a note," "erase a note" or
"end the tune." The user enters pitches by moving
an arrow (with the cursor keys) to the number of
the scale degree desired, and then gives each
pitch a rhythmic value by moving the cursor to one
of the four dashes. As the user makes choices,
the melody is "notated" graphically on the screen;
pitches are represented by four dashes of
different length (representing duration) and by
their relative highness or lowness on the screen
(representing pitch). The user can hear each tune
as it is being composed and can erase notes if
necessary after reconsideration. Tunes are
automatically saved on the disk upon completion,
and can be loaded and played by choosing the
player option. The disk comes with some tunes
already stored on it. The user can change the
tempo of the tunes under the player option by
moving the cursor arrow to one of a series of dots
between the words "slow" and "fast." Through
instructor options tunes can be deleted from the
disk.

Evaluation

The sound and the graphics in this program are
fair. The instructions are within the program on
the title page. At first glance, these
instructions seem to apply to the title page only,
where the user must make a choice between the
composer and play modes. It would be a great help
to the program if these brief instructions or some
sort of prompts were also included on the screens
where the user is making compositional and tempo
decisions.

It is difficult to ascertain the audience for whom
this program is written. The musical
sophistication needed to write tunes using scale
degree numbers (none of which is explained in the
program) make this program somewhat difficult for
young children. At the same time, the use of
graphic notation is too primitive for those
musically able to cope with the scale degree
numbers.

***

Addresses of Computer Manufacturers

Apple Computer, Inc.
20525 Mariani Avenue
Cupertino, California   95014

Atari, Inc.
P.O. Box 50047
60 E. Plumeria Drive
Sunnyvale, California   94088

Commodore Business Machines, Inc.
487 Devon Park Drive
Wayne, Pennsylvania   19087

Control Data Corporation
8100 34th Avenue, South
Minneapolis, Minnesota   55402

International Business Machines Corporation
1133 Winchester Avenue
White Plains, New York   10601

Addresses of Peripherals Manufacturers

Alf Products (Alf synthesizer cards)
1448 Estes
Denver, Colorado   80215

Apple Computer, Inc. (game paddles, AppleMouse)
20525 Mariani Avenue
Cupertino, California   95014

Koala Technologies Corporation (Koala Pad)
3100 Patrick Henry Drive
Santa Clara, California   95054

Mountain Computer, Inc. (MusicSystem DAC boards)
300 El Pueblo Road
Scotts Valley, California   95066

Office of Instructional Technology (University of
    Delaware Sound Card)
Willard Hall
The University of Delaware
Newark, Delaware   19716

Passport Designs, Inc. (Soundchaser)
116 North Cabrillo Highway
Half Moon Bay, California   94019

Sweet Micro Systems (Mockingboard)
150 Chestnut Street
Providence, Rhode Island   02903

Temporal Acuity Products, Inc. (MMI DAC board,
    Micro-Brass Valve Simulator)
Building 1, Suite 200
300 - 120th Avenue N.E.
Bellevue, Washington   98005

Wico (joystick)
6400 W. Gross Place Road
Niles, Illinois   60648

Addresses of Software Publishers

Alfred Publishing Company
15335 Morrison Street
P.O. Box 5964
Sherman Oaks, California   91413

Commodore Business Machines, Inc.
487 Devon Park Drive
Wayne, Pennsylvania   19087

CONDUIT
The University of Iowa
Oakdale Campus
Iowa City, Iowa   52242

Digital Concept Systems, Inc.
4826 Bucknell
San Antonio, Texas   78249

Electronic Arts, Inc.
2755 Campus Drive
San Mateo, California   94403

Electronic Courseware Systems, Inc.
1210 Lancaster Drive
Champaign, Illinois   61821

Indiana University
Audio-Visual Center
Bloomington, Indiana   47405-5901

Minnesota Educational Computing Corporation
Distribution Center
3490 Lexington Avenue North
St. Paul, Minnesota   55126
(612) 481-3500

Office of Instructional Technology
Willard Hall
The University of Delaware
Newark, Delaware   19716

Passport Design, Inc.
116 North Cabrillo Highway
Half Moon Bay, California   94019

Scarborough Systems, Inc.
25 North Broadway
Tarrytown, New York   10591

Springboard Software
7807 Creekridge Circle
Minneapolis, Minnesota   55435

Temporal Acuity Products
Building 1, Suite 200
300 - 120th Avenue N.E.
Bellevue, Washington   98005

The Wenger Corporation
Music Learning Division
1401 E. 79th Street
Bloomington, Minnesota   55420-1590

W. C. Brown Educational and Professional Software
2460 Kerper Boulevard
P.O. Box 539
Dubuque, Iowa   52004-0539

Bibliography

Appleton, Jon, and Perera, Ronald C. The Development and Practice of Electronic Music. Englewood Cliffs, NJ: Prentice-Hall, 1974.

Bateman, Wayne. Introduction to Computer Music. New York: John Wiley and Sons, 1983.

Chamberlin, Hal. Musical Applications of Micro-Processors. Rochelle Park, NJ: Hayden Book Company, 1980.

Crombie, David. The Synthesizer and Electronic Keyboard Handbook. New York: Alfred A. Knopf, 1984.

Dodge, Charles, and Jerse, Thomas A. Computer Music: Synthesis, Composition and Performance. New York: Longman, Inc., 1984.

Eddins, John, and Peters, David G. A Planning Guide To Successful Computer Instruction. Champaign, IL: Electronic Courseware Systems, Inc., 1981.

Gilkes, Lolita W. Commodore 64/128 Music Software Guide. Drexel Hill, PA: Unsinn Publications, 1985.

Hammond, Ray. The Musician and the Micro. Dorset, England: Blanford Press, 1983.

Higgins, Wiliam. Teaching Music With the Apple II Microcomputer. Grantham, PA: Messiah College, 1984.

Hofstetter, Fred T. Making Music on Micros. Drexel Hill, PA: Unsinn Publications, Inc., 1986.

Horn, Delton T. Electronic Music Synthesizers. Blue Ridge Summit, PA: Tab, 1980.

Howe, Hubert S. Electronic Music Synthesis. New York: W. W. Norton and Company, Inc., 1975.

Jenkins, John, and Smith, Jon. Electronic Music: A Practical Manual. Bloomington, IN: Indiana University Press, 1974.

234 Appendix D

Marshal, Pamela, and Wallcarff, Dean. Computer Music Catalog. Boston: Digital Music Systems, 1983.

Moreen, Denis C. Directory of Computer-Assisted Instruction Materials In the Field of Music. Belmont, CA: College of Notre Dame, 1983.

Morgan, Christopher, ed. The Byte Book of Computer Music. Peterborough, NH: Byte Books, 1981.

Nuamann, Joel, and Wagoner, James D. Analog Electronic Music Techniques In Tape, Electronic, and Voltage-Controlled Synthesizers. New York: Longman, Inc., 1984.

Pelligrino, Ronald. The Electronic Arts of Sound and Light. New York: Van Nostrand Reinhold, 1983.

Pierce, John. The Science of Musical Sound. New York: W. H. Freeman and Co., 1984.

Roads, Curtis, and Strawn, John, eds. Foundations of Computer Music. Cambridge, MA: MIT Press, 1985.

Rudolph, Thomas E. Music and the Apple II. Drexel Hill, PA: Unsinn Publications, Inc., 1984.

Schrader, Barry. Introduction to Electro-Acoustic Music. Englewood Cliffs, NJ: Prentice-Hall, 1982.

Strange, Allen. Electronic Music: Systems, Techniques, and Controls. Dubuque, IA: William C. Brown, 1982.

Wittlick, Gary; Schaffer, John; and Babb, Larry. Microcomputers and Music. Englewood Cliffs, NJ: Prentice-Hall, 1986.

Publishers' Suggested Audience Index

Advanced

Beginner

College and Adult

None Designated

Secondary

Software Indexed by Computer

Apple

Subject Index

Mode Identification and/or Construction

Music Symbols

Music Terms

Non-harmonic Tones

Note Names and Clefs

Note Values

Part-writing

Printing Music

Rhythmic Dictation

Dictation I, 33
GUIDO, 54
Hear Today...Play Tomorrow, 63
Melodic/Rhythmic Dictation, 90
Mr. Metro Gnome I, 105
Mr. Metro Gnome II, 107
Mr. Metro Gnome III, 107
Mr. Metro Gnome IV, 108
The Music Class: Ear Training, 114
The Music Class: Rhythm, 115
Music Drills: Ear Training Series, Part III:
    Dictation I, 129
Music II: Rhythm and Pitch, 139
Music: Rhythm, 153
Patterns in Rhythm, 184
Rhythm Drills, 195
Rhythm Machine, 197
Rhythmic Dictator, 200
Toney Listens to Music, 216

Rhythmic Notation

Mr. Metro Gnome I, 105
Mr. Metro Gnome II, 107
Mr. Metro Gnome III, 107
Mr. Metro Gnome IV, 108
The Music Class: Rhythm, 115
Music in Theory and Practice Tutor, 141
Music Made Easy, 147
Music II: Rhythm and Pitch, 139
Music: Rhythm, 153
Music Theory, 163
Practical Music Theory Computer Series, 193

Rhythmic Performance

Mr. Metro Gnome I, 105
Mr. Metro Gnome II, 107
Mr. Metro Gnome III, 107
Mr. Metro Gnome IV, 108
The Music Class: Rhythm, 115
Music II: Rhythm and Pitch, 139
Music: Rhythm, 153
Music Theory, 163